EMERGING TECHNOLOGIES / LIFE AT THE EDGE OF THE FUTURE

Emerging Technologies / Life at the Edge of the Future invites us to think forward from our present moment of planetary, public and everyday crisis, through the prism of emerging technologies.

It calls for a new ethical, responsible and equitable path towards possible futures, curated through in-depth engagement with and across experiential, environmental and technological possibilities. It tackles three of the most significant challenges for contemporary society by asking: how emerging technologies are implicated in the sites of everyday lives; what place emerging technologies have in an evolving world in crisis; and how we might better imagine and shape ethical, equitable and responsible futures. The book interweaves three narratives, each of which advances three sets of concerns for our societal futures: 'Emergence', which addresses futures, trust and hope; 'Worlds', which addresses data, air and energy; and 'Technologies', which addresses the future of mobilities, homes and work.

Not simply a critical study of emerging technologies, this book is also an approach to thinking and practice in times of global crisis that plays out a mode of future-focused scholarship and action for the first half of the twenty-first century.

Sarah Pink is a design anthropologist, documentary filmmaker and methods innovator. She is a professor and Director of the Emerging Technologies Research Lab at Monash University, and an investigator in the ARC Centre of Excellence for Automated Decision-Making and Society.

EMERGING TECHNOLOGIES / LIFE AT THE EDGE OF THE FUTURE

Sarah Pink

Routledge
Taylor & Francis Group

LONDON AND NEW YORK

Cover image: © Getty Images

First published 2023
by Routledge
4 Park Square, Milton Park, Abingdon, Oxon OX14 4RN

and by Routledge
605 Third Avenue, New York, NY 10158

Routledge is an imprint of the Taylor & Francis Group, an informa business

© 2023 Sarah Pink

British Library Cataloguing-in-Publication Data
A catalogue record for this book is available from the British Library

Library of Congress Cataloging-in-Publication Data
Names: Pink, Sarah, author.
Title: Emerging technologies : life at the edge of the future / Sarah Pink.
Description: Abingdon, Oxon : Routledge, 2023. |
Includes bibliographical references and index.
Identifiers: LCCN 2022011053 (print) | LCCN 2022011054 (ebook) |
ISBN 9781032022420 (hardback) | ISBN 9781032022413 (paperback) |
ISBN 9781003182528 (ebook)
Subjects: LCSH: Technological innovations--Moral and ethical aspects. |
Technological innovations--Social aspects. | Technological forecasting.
Classification: LCC T173.8 .P535 2023 (print) | LCC T173.8 (ebook) |
DDC 600--dc23/eng/20220706
LC record available at https://lccn.loc.gov/2022011053
LC ebook record available at https://lccn.loc.gov/2022011054

ISBN: 978-1-032-02242-0 (hbk)
ISBN: 978-1-032-02241-3 (pbk)
ISBN: 978-1-003-18252-8 (ebk)

DOI: 10.4324/9781003182528

Typeset in Bembo
by Taylor & Francis Books

CONTENTS

ACKNOWLEDGEMENTS

In any work that draws on ethnographic research, my first thanks go to the many people who have generously shared their time and experiences in research with me. Without them it would have been impossible to bring their important stories rooted in everyday experiences, imaginaries and possibilities to this work. Second, I thank my many academic colleagues and collaborators in research and research partners from organisations we have collaborated with. Rather than naming everyone here, I do so where I discuss work through which we have been connected or cite the projects we have worked on together. The arguments and views I put forward in this book are my own, as are any errors or omissions. However, without colleagues and friends neither the research that has informed some of these ideas, nor the motivation to generate them may ever have come about. I hope that my own contributions to the same projects will be of equal use in enabling colleagues to develop their own independent writing. Third, much of my work is partnered with industry or other sectors. I am grateful to the organisations and individuals whose own applied research ambitions, critiques and commentaries have given impetus to my own research agenda and helped me to understand what the issues beyond academia are. Fourth, I thank all the organisations and individuals who publish and share information, arguments, analyses, interviews and podcasts online; they offer an amazing array of knowledge, which has become an expanded ethnographic fieldsite for me.

In this book, I discuss diverse research projects, spanning the last 20 years of my career. I thank the following organisations who have generously funded my research. The vision, development, online reviews and theoretical development of this book, and specifically research into future automated mobilities, futures, trust and hope, are part of my work as a Chief Investigator in the Australia Research Council funded Centre of Excellence for Automated Decision Making and Society (CE200100005) (2020–2027). Other research discussed in this book was supported by: an ESRC (UK) PhD scholarship (1991–1994) which funded research into bullfighting cultures in Spain; the 'Slow Food and Cittàslow UK: changing local lives?' funded by the Nuffield Foundation (2005–2007); 'Communication skills of non/low English speaking construction workers and English speaking site managers' funded by Constructionskills UK (2008–2009);'Management of OSH in Networked Systems of Production or Service Delivery: Comparisons between Healthcare, Construction and Logistics', funded by IOSH, UK (2011–2014); 'Co-creating, visualising and sharing knowledge: using digital and mobile technology to improve construction health and safety', RMIT University (2014–2015); 'Acoustic design innovations for managing motorway traffic noise by cancellation and transformation', funded by Transurban (2016–2017); 'Locating the mobile: intergenerational locative media practices in Tokyo, Melbourne and Shanghai' (ARC Linkage Project LP130100848) with Intel (2014–2017); 'Prácticas de futuro, espacios de creación digital e innovación social en la cultura digital (D-FUTURE)' Convocatoria 2014 – Proyectos I+D – Programa Estatal de Fomento de la Investigación Científica y Técnica de Excelencia Subprograma Estatal de Generación de Conocimiento (2015–2017); the Data Ethnographies Lab was part of the Digital Ethnography Research Centre (DERC), and supported by RMIT University; 'NUX – Natural User Experience' in collaboration with SAMSUNG Research Institute Brazil and Federal University of Pernambuco, Brazil (2017–2018); 'Human Expectations and Experiences of Autonomous Driving' HEAD, in collaboration with Halmstad University and Volvo Cars, Sweden. Vinnova, Sweden (2016–2018); 'Sensing, shaping, sharing: measuring and imagining the body in a mediatized world' RJ Foundation, Sweden (2015–2018); 'Visual Sensing Language', City of Melbourne partnership (2020); 'City Data Futures Prototype', City of Melbourne partnership (2021); Intelligent Home Solutions for Independent Living, McLean Care Deakin partnership grant with Department of Health; 'Social work and social distancing: Learning from the impact of the COVID-19 pandemic on child protection, service users and the capacity to keep children safe', ESRC, UK; 'Lower effort energy demand reduction' part of the EPSRC Transforming Energy Demand through Digital Innovation Programme (2010–2014); 'Digital energy futures: forecasting changing residential electricity demand' (ARC Linkage LP180100203); Workers in transition through automation, digitalization and robotization of work (AUTOWORK), Norwegian Research Council. I also thank the many co-researchers, research partners, research participants and colleagues to whom I have sent extracts from this book as I write it: Yolande Strengers, Rex Martin, Melisa Duque, Kari Dahlgren, Sue Thomson, Alicia Eugene, Ben Horan, Michael Mortimer, Hannah Korsmeyer, Harry Ferguson, Laura Kelly, Mark Pivak, Tegan Kopp, Bianca Vallentine, Robert Lundgren, Debora Lanzeni, Shanti Sumartojo, Ilya Fridman, Benjamin Sovacool, Dylan Furszyfer Del Rio.

Finally, I thank Monash University, Australia, for supporting me to found and pursue the vision of the Emerging Technologies Research Lab, from which the argument of this book is inextricable.

EMERGING TECHNOLOGIES

Emerging Technologies / Life at the Edge of the Future is for anyone who considers themself a stakeholder in our future and is interested in, hopeful for, or concerned about, emerging technologies. This includes researchers, scholars and students, professionals, or people who are curious about what engaged scholarship brings to the central and crucial question of our futures. Because emerging technologies are on the cusp of what may happen next, they also create the perfect prism through which to explore what life at the edge of the future – life in anticipation – is like. Rather than simply asking the unknowable question of *what* will happen next, we must learn to understand *how* our futures will unfold and *how* we may live well with emerging technologies. How might we best become participants in constituting ethical, equitable and responsible futures? What roles should emerging technologies – artificial intelligence (AI), automated decision-making (ADM), data, platforms, and automated and connected devices like autonomous flying cars, workplace robots or home automation systems – play in our futures?

I write this book from (but not exclusively about) Australia, whose unforgettable fireworks over Sydney Harbour represent the country's Southern hemisphere move into the Gregorian Calendar's new year, before much of the rest of the world. There is a further, more ominous, way that Australia might represent snippets of possible global futures before they happen elsewhere, beyond its new year's fireworks being released a few hours sooner. It has recently been suggested that in a decade parts of Sydney might be so hot that they will be uninhabitable (Purtil 2021, January 24). In Melbourne, there is increasing risk from rising sea levels to the beachside blocks of city neighbourhoods (Malo 2019, December 15), and in the summer months bushfires have consumed the environment across the country, killing wildlife and filling the air with smoke. The environmental crisis has continued unfolding in everyday life as I have researched and written this book. In 2020 I travelled through New South Wales, surrounded by the effects of drought,

DOI: 10.4324/9781003182528-1

bushfires and increasingly high temperature weather events, in 2021 the same sites were flooded, and at the beginning of 2022 the state's COVID-19 infection rate was greater than ever before.

Staying with the Australian example, while enormous challenges are evident, there are simultaneously powerful claims regarding the future. Australia's Commonwealth Scientific and Industrial Research Organisation (CSIRO) claims to 'shape the future … by using science to solve real issues to unlock a better future for our community, our economy, our planet' (CSIRO n.d.). Science and technology do of course participate in how futures play out. But do they actually 'shape' the future? For social scientists the question is different, I instead consider how technologies are entangled in the processes through which futures emerge. It is increasingly clear that if we are to confront our futures with emerging technologies, we need to account for the complexity of how futures come about beyond simple problem-solution narratives. The science and technology studies scholar Sheila Jasanoff urges us to contest such 'linear storytelling' as we face 'mounting problems of inequality, diminishing resources, and a looming climate calamity' (2021: 17). But how can this be achieved in an engaged and generative way?

The sense that we are in a current crisis is a recurring contemporary theme, which I take up in chapter *hope*. But to move away from linear and causal sequences, also means abandoning the conventional notion of crisis. The anthropologist Janet Roitman tells us the idea of crisis is used as a punctuation point in history, 'often serving as a transcendental placeholder in ostensible solutions to that problem' (Roitman 2013: 13). If we see ourselves as in a current crisis, in need of a solution, the present is then converted into a powerful launching pad for emerging technologies poised and promised to deliver solutions to society. Yet when we unpick this apparently straight line, it becomes clear that emerging technologies are rather differently entangled in the climate and public health crises. Their status as solutions becomes complicated when we look at the complexities of their relationship to the problems. It is, for instance, ironic and emblematic of the nature of capitalism that, for example, technologies, which draw on the resource extractive industries associated with climate change, are subsequently used to combat wildfires (Cowan 2021, July 15), or that the public health crisis, air quality and the pandemic can be seen as part of the same trajectories (chapter *air*). Jasanoff proposed that we should 'imagine the future along as-yet-untraveled pathways of change' (2021: 17). The next step, now, entails exploring *life at the edge of the future*.

However, we also require new social science approaches capable of engaging with and intervening in possible futures (Pink, Raats et al. 2022). Rather than simply going up against the logics of capitalism head on, modes of engagement that undercut their assumptions, reveal the flaws in their conceptual apparatus, and show why they are inadequate for the current circumstances, are highly effective in illuminating new ways forward (Pink & Lewis 2014). This necessitates a new interdisciplinary futures oriented social science that exceeds existing critique. It must rethink expertise, our own situatedness and our interventional capabilities. *Emerging Technologies/ Life at the Edge of the Future* argues that we must play this out.

In this chapter, I introduce emerging technologies and discuss the characteristics and situatedness of some of the stakeholders in their futures. I also argue for an undisciplined anthropology and explain the structure of this book.

Emerging technologies

Emerging technologies and the (possible) futures associated with them are continually reported in mainstream and technology news media and across business and consultancy communities. I am concerned with two layers of emerging technologies. The first includes artificial intelligence (AI) and automated decision-making (ADM) systems. These technologies are notoriously difficult to define, yet their definitions are crucial because they enable and mobilise particular understandings of how they are situated in power dynamics, their capacities and future possibilities. The academic journal *AI & Society* began publishing in 1987, and AI has long since been in our vocabularies, as a centrepiece in the fascination of science-fiction and in a more mundane sense in the early work of computer scientists. Recently, AI has become increasingly central to future-focused practices and visions of industry, government and not-for-profit sectors. Academics (often in partnership with industry) are concerned to work towards ethical and accountable AI. Emerging technologies have also rapidly taken centre stage in research across the social sciences, humanities and design, as well as in science and technology disciplines, and priority areas for research funding: 'Promises and hypes of new technologies have been shown to mobilize researchers, industry actors and policy makers to move and invest into emerging technology fields' (Konrad & Böhle 2019: 102). A prominent example is the interdisciplinary AI Now Institute at New York University in the United States (https://ainowinstitute.org/), but there are many more.

In contrast to AI, in the social sciences the term ADM is a much newer concept. It is less glamorous than AI, and interviews I carried out in 2021 suggest it is not used by all business leaders in technology companies or by all data scientists. However, in academic and advocacy circles the concept of ADM has grown in importance, since it directs attention away from the controversial issue of if machines can be 'intelligent' and directs us to consider the possibilities and consequences of automation. The non-profit research and advocacy organisation AlgorithmWatch (https://algorithmwatch.org/en/) includes AI under the umbrella of ADM. The Australian Automated Decision-Making and Society (ADM+S) Centre (www.admscentre.org.au/) and the Scandinavian Rehumanising Automated Decision-Making network (I am a member of both) centre ADM. AlgorithmWatch sees ADM systems as 'ways in which a certain technology – which may be far less sophisticated or "intelligent" than deep learning algorithms – is inserted within a decision-making process' (AlgorithmWatch 2020). This shift directs us away from AI and ADM technologies themselves, towards the pressing questions of their social and political situatedness: how, by whom and under what conditions are machines engineered, designed and permitted and used to make decisions? And what are the societal, ethical and regulatory implications?

According to AlgorithmWatch, ADM systems involve 'a socio-technological framework that encompasses a decision-making model, an algorithm that translates this model into computable code, the data this code uses as an input … and the entire political and economic environment surrounding its use' (AlgorithmWatch 2019). Rather than being politically, ethically or socially neutral, AI and ADM are always contingent on and part of complex configurations of circumstances. Such definitions are significant, not only intellectually, but practically. As the legal scholar Rashida Richardson points out, AI and ADM systems 'can construct social reality by reflecting and preserving power relations and social conditions'. Therefore if their legal definitions are embodied with awareness of these political and social conditions they 'can serve as an important public policy intervention' (Richardson 2021: 9). The social and political realities of AI and ADM should moreover be not only configured by western social, institutional and legal systems, but as Indigenous Australian scholarship insists, people's relationships to memory, history, land and non-human species (Harle et al. 2018; Abdilla 2018). A requirement to define emerging technologies as part of the diverse and continually emergent, contingent circumstances of life and society, underpins the agenda advanced in this book.

Developments in AI, ADM and algorithmic capabilities such as predictive data analytics and machine learning (ML) associated with them are important to attend to for two reasons. First, they are the infrastructures that make possible new software and hardware developments in automated and connected emerging technologies intended for everyday applications. Examples include autonomous driving (AD) and flying cars, otherwise known as electric vertical take-off and landing (eVTOL) vehicles, digital voice assistants that can empathise with human emotions, climbing robots designed to work in places that are dangerous and difficult for construction workers to reach, as well as new applications of smartphones. Second, they are what I call anticipatory infrastructures (Pink, Dahlgren et al. 2022) in that they fuel the socio-technical imaginaries that underpin how experienced futures are envisioned. For example, the existence of ADM or AI, makes it possible to imagine some of the technologies, services and promised benefits that I discuss in other chapters, such as: an autonomous flying car providing urban commuting benefits to business travellers (chapter *mobilities*); a digital voice assistant comforting a senior person living alone (chapter *home*); or a robot using machine vision to scale walls and undertake dangerous (for humans) work at height on a construction site (chapter *work*).

The 'top' emerging technologies

The emerging technologies news is a dizzying field where the newest, leading, most recent, fastest and first technologies and technology trends are thrust into momentary limelight, or sustained hype. The excitement is hard to resist when so many lifesaving, wellbeing enhancing and above all capital generating new technologies are apparently poised to change the world for the better across almost every imaginable sphere of life. Or at least that's what you might sense if, like me, for the last five or so years you've been reading the technology news, media, reports and academic papers. A snapshot demonstrates both the diversity and some of the issues. In 2021 the *New York Times* asked if 'Femtech' was the 'Next Big Thing' (Nayeri 2021, April 7). The article discusses a neglected market for women's health technologies in the masculine-dominated, gendered tech space, which is nevertheless expected to grow. In the mobilities field, the market for (obviously problematically gendered) 'unmanned' flying cars is expected to grow; in 2021 EuroNews asked 'Will we be hailing taxis from the sky by 2025?', citing one company which expected to be carrying passengers by then (Shone & Humairah, 2021, December 9). In 2021 *Digital Trends* ('the largest independent premium technology publisher in the world' (Digital Trends, n.d.)) reported that 'Some of the brightest engineers in the world are racing to make science fiction-esque flying taxis a reality … the more optimistic companies say they're getting very close' (Glon 2021, March 20).

Of course, the temporalities of emerging technologies, and how they are gendered, can vary in many ways, and it is not yet clear for how long femtech or un*manned* flying cars will be represented in the media as being poised to become the next life- and society-changing technology. The electric vehicle has been emerging since the last century and has been predicted to flood out into ubiquity both now and many times in the past. AD cars have been hyped since the middle of the second decade of this century, when they were expected to be on our roads by 2020. In chapter *mobilities*, I discuss why we may still be waiting. Moreover, as existing ethnographies with engineers and designers have shown there is nothing predetermined about technology design and development, and there is in fact a lot of waiting: with Debora Lanzeni I have analysed the ongoing stories of the work of drone designers and blockchain developers (Lanzeni & Pink 2021; Pink & Lanzeni 2018); when I interviewed the inventor of an ingestible sensing capsule in 2018 it had been in the making for seven years (Pink 2021b); and in chapter *work* the example of a robotic bricklayer similarly reveals that successful technologies can be in development for many years.

In 2021, the global consultancy McKinsey & Co (whose insights, along with those of other leading consultancies, I reflect on as a barometer of industry analysis) identified a set of new 'top trends in tech': applied AI; next-generation computing; trust architecture; distributed infrastructure; future of connectivity; future of programming; next-level process automation and virtualization; bio revolution; future of clean technologies; and nanomaterials (McKinsey & Co n.d. a). These technologies cluster mainly across the category of infrastructure technologies, and with a focus on tech which may underpin future changes: McKinsey notes that while not the 'coolest trends' or 'most bleeding-edge technologies', these generate investment and patents. *MIT Technology Review*'s top ten 2021 'breakthrough technologies' (The Editors 2021, February 24) list is similar in their clustering around technologies that could infrastructure future possibilities: new vaccines; GPT-3 (large natural-language computer models); data trusts (legal entities which collect and manage people's personal data for them); new prototype battery technologies; the possibility of better digital contact tracing for future pandemics; more accurate positioning technologies than GPS; advances in remote services; AI with better sensory and communication skills; recommendation algorithms; and green hydrogen. *Scientific American*'s list of 'Top 10 Emerging Technologies for 2021' took a focus on 'Innovations to help tackle societal challenges—especially climate change', identifying: new technologies to address decarbonisation; self-fertilising agriculture for sustainable food production; human breath sensors for disease detection; on-demand drug manufacturing; advances in wireless energy and charging; new gene therapies; green hydrogen; advances in biomarker monitoring; zero-waste house-building; and maximisation of Internet of Things (IoT) capacity, including space IoT.

We are seeing an evolution of the debate away from specific technologies like AD cars (which were in *Scientific American*'s top ten in 2015), towards the systems that will support future developments. This doesn't mean that AD cars have stopped emerging, but that we might view them through the new prism of the connected car, wireless EV charging and clean energy, as a new tranche of emerging technologies is pitched to solve societal problems that AD cars are also implicated in. There are in fact many versions of the top tech trends spanning 2021 and 2022, including, for example *Forbes*, which breaks these down into consumer (Marr 2021, December 7) and venture capital (Smith 2021, December 13) trends. For academics, an emerging technology which proposes using AI to predict the future scientific impact of research papers (Ham, 2021, May 17) might be one to look out for. These recent and ongoing technology trends are also conditioned by the reported changes, future uncertainties and new predictions brought about by the climate crisis, and the COVID-19 pandemic.

While these narratives project an exciting and novel world of technological solutions on the way, in everyday life, climate change and the pandemic are still going ahead. This book investigates this in-between space, where emerging technologies hover, but rarely land as whole things and where 'crisis' is often cited as a motivation for their development. I explore ethnographically what happens when features or elements of, for instance, AD vehicles, smart home technologies or workplace robots enter everyday life. What new stories can be told about how they emerge in everyday worlds, with people, become meaningful, and be shaped by the lives and environments they participate in? How can these trajectories dialogue productively with the assumption that each year one could identify ten new emerging technologies that will impact society?

The emerging technologies space

Emerging technologies occupy an anticipatory space, where they and the imaginaries associated with them move and mingle in and through present, near and far futures. This is the space where social scientists also need to create a strong foothold; we need to play in the space where emerging technologies come about, in critical, collaborative and interventional modes. But who are the players and sta-keholders who are already active in the emerging technology space? In that emer-ging technologies potentially permeate most spheres of personal, professional and organisational life, we are all stakeholders, even those who are not actively engaged with or interested in new technologies. However, some voices or narratives get heard over others, and everyday experiences and imagined futures of emerging technologies often remain obscured or unrealised.

My reviews identify a series of key actors, which together create an ecology of political, industry, activist academic and advisory capabilities in the field of emer-ging technologies. They configure to collectively create a dynamic field of hope, fear, critique and action, as they advocate through the full range of optimistic, promissory, dystopian and revelatory future-focused narrative. Yet of course this is not a neutral field of discussion and debate, but rather a politically and economic-ally laden and weighted field. To enter into this field thus involves asking: Who decides what is important? Who are their audiences? Who is complicit with whom?

Consultancies are active stakeholders in the emerging technologies field and produce a significant number of online reports on the topic. This provides a resource for business and industry, as well as a site for academic analysis (in 2020, the Emerging Technologies Lab team analysed 64 energy and technology industry reports (Dahlgren et al. 2020; Strengers et al. 2022) to unpick their claims about future home technologies). Anthropologists Chris Shore and Susan Wright (2018) have traced the rise of the consultancies, originally accountancy firms, which have increasingly expanded their scope, into advisory roles. Accountancy, Shore and Wright outline, is a mode of audit which quantifies and makes visible. However, in recent years with the rise of neoliberalism, they argue, rather than being a neutral profession, it has evolved, in the case of the 'Big 4' consultancies (for details, see Consulting.com n.d.) to be part of a new 'audit culture' complicit with capitalism. Audit culture, they write, 'involves systems of control that create new assemblages and auditable subjects with the aim of enhancing organisational legibility and accountability' (Shore & Wright 2018: 305). However, 'audit cultures' (Shore & Wright 2015, 2018; Strathern 2000) are not only concerned with what has already happened, in fact they also seek to regulate, control, create accountabilities and mitigate risks in the future. A qualitative or soft example of such an 'anticipatory audit' could be a checklist for ensuring that strategies are implemented correctly in the future, so that they can be 'accountable'. For instance, the top consultancy PwC has on its website a 'Responsible AI Toolkit' (PwC 2021) to support the development of Responsible AI. These kinds of technologies are future-facing, in their focus on what *will* need to be put in place in order to mitigate future risks, and thus provide reassuring frameworks with which to move forward into the unknown. The quantification of the future, which has been made possible by predictive uses of big data analytics (discussed in chapter *data*) offers another mode of anticipatory audit. Such frameworks and predictive data offer organisations ways in which to imagine, plan for and participate in futures where emerging technologies can be monetized, while simultaneously influencing some of the modes of participation that may evolve. As advising organisations, the consultancies are at the core of the way emerging technologies could come about within their sphere of influence.

National governments are significant stakeholders in the future of emerging technologies, often presenting them as beneficial to their nations in multiple ways. To take two of the countries I discuss examples from in this book: the UK government has an Office for Artificial Intelligence with a 'National AI Strategy' (UK Government 2021, September 22) that 'builds on the UK's strengths but also represents the start of a step-change for AI in the UK, recognising the power of AI to increase resilience, productivity, growth and innovation across the private and public sectors'; and the Australian government has an AI Action Plan, which 'sets out a vision for Australia to be a global leader in developing and adopting trusted, secure and responsible AI' (Australian Government 2021, June). In neoliberal societies, there is a relationship between governments and the consultancies, and this is no less so in the emerging technologies space. In 2021, the UK government contracted McKinsey & Co to 'provide consultancy on the digitisation of services and automation' (Consultancy.uk 2021, August 23). According to the *Guardian* newspaper in 2021, in a critical article by academics, Rosie Collington and Mariana Mazzucato, the UK, after the US, was the greatest market for consultancy services, whereby the 'UK state's spending on consultancy has ballooned, notably in the past five years' so that between '2017 and 2020, approximately £450m was spent on consulting fees related to Brexit by government departments, with the receipts for Covid-19 contracts coming in at over £600m' (Collington & Mazzucato 2021, September 20). The Australian Financial Review has reported on controversies in the relationship between government and the consultancies, including a 2021 article which reports that the Australian federal government was criticised by the opposition for contracting out '$6 million worth of work on its net zero economic modelling' (Wooton 2021, November 16) to a consultancy. Another 2021 article reports on the case of a, now former, consultancy partner who became caught up in a dispute between two departments within state government (Burton 2021, November 8). Both consultancy and government spokespersons defended their positions. Nevertheless, these controversies reveal the tricky space, which Shore and Wright (2018) and Collington and Mazzucato (2021, September 20) have highlighted. With this context in mind, I take consultancy reporting as integral to the circumstances in which emerging technologies come about.

There are also stakeholders in state, regional and local governments, working more closely on the ground with emerging technologies, and seeking ethical and responsible ways to integrate them. In some cases, these involve collaboration with academics in shared projects. The Emerging Technologies Lab's collaboration with the City of Melbourne is a good example. In our shared projects, discussed in chapter *data*, we have focused on ethical, responsible and equitable ways to engage emerging technologies to align with the values of local people and the City. Humanitarian organisations, not-for-profits and many others, including Small and Medium Enterprises (SMEs), can also be seen as stakeholders in emerging technologies. As discussed in chapter *work*, not all organisations are fully engaged with (or need) the possibilities these technologies offer or promise. Other diverse stakeholders in the field of emerging technologies are discussed through the chapters of this book. This includes both the big engineering firms and the many technology start-ups, all of whom are working on the development and design of AI, ADM and ML as well as making specific technologies and services. There are too many to introduce here, but I discuss a selection of these organisations in the following chapters as we encounter their projects, products and services. There are also many government-funded innovation initiatives, dedicated to specific realms of emerging technologies in society. I invoke various such entities as they appear in relation to the examples discussed in later chapters.

It is also significant to note that national commitments to emerging technologies and investment in their futures, also have their effects through research funding schemes, which themselves have also recently become increasingly politicised. This, as well as industry involvement in research funding means that we need to be aware of the relations through which emerging technologies are researched and developed. Abeba Birhane and colleagues analysed a set of influential papers in Machine Learning (ML) and found that rather than being 'value neutral' they 'are operationalized in ways that disfavor societal needs, usually without discussion or acknowledgment' as well as 'an overwhelming and increasing presence of big tech and elite universities in highly cited papers'. They conclude that the discipline is 'socially and politically loaded, frequently neglecting societal needs and harms, while prioritizing and promoting the concentration of power in the hands of already powerful actors' (Birhane et al. n.d.: 10).

As researchers, we are also stakeholders in emerging technologies, and we must understand how our work is implicated in and entangled in this evolving set of power relations.

Contesting the emerging technologies space

Design researcher Laura Forlano argues that 'technology companies should stop selling the linear narrative of the future of human progress enabled by smartness, thereby shielding technologies in a veil of promise and perfection' since, she continues, 'a wide range of studies in the social sciences and humanities have shown across many contexts including cities, homes, and bodies, the promise of smart technologies are often aspirational at best and abusive, criminalizing, and dehumanizing at their worst' (Forlano 2021). There is plenty of evidence that emerging technologies, once they start to participate in everyday life, have caused significant harm (e.g. AlgorithmWatch 2019, 2020; Eubanks 2018; Sadowski 2020). Madeleine Clare Elish and danah boyd point to the implications of 'the ability to manufacture legitimacy' which they sum up, not only boosts innovation and economies but 'provides cover for nascent technologies to potentially create fundamentally unsound truth claims about the world, which has troubling implications for established forms of accountability' (Elish & boyd 2017: 58).

Approaches rooted in indigenous and decolonising perspectives are exemplary precisely because they call us to attend to everyday ways of knowing, rooted in non-representational and historical relations between people and the environment. As Josh Harle, Angie Abdilla and Andrew Newman rightly point out in the introduction to their book *Decolonising the Digital*, advancing emerging technologies as engineering innovations, seeking ubiquity in 'markets', both specifically a characteristic of colonising approaches and unsustainable. They highlight that neither technology development nor the sources that fund it are 'neutral or benign' but driven by the generation of capital, and the need to find a 'market'. Technology development by Australian Aboriginal peoples is quite different: it has

> shown their utility to sustainably nurture, nourish, and cultivate the driest inhabited continent on earth for millenia, not only demonstrating the successful stewardship of the environment, but the flourishing of a cultural practice of technology embodying the responsibility to care for Country.
>
> *(Harle, Abdilla & Newman 2018: 12)*

Birhane (2021) also challenges existing rationalist approaches to automated technologies from the perspective of relational ethics drawing on approaches including Black feminist (Afro- feminist) epistemologies, and *ubuntu* (the sub-Saharan African philosophy). She similarly argues that 'automated and standardized solutions to complex and contingent social issues often contribute more harm than good – they often fail to grasp complex problems and provide a false sense of solution and safety'. Birhane insists that 'Complex social issues require historical, political, and moral awareness and structural change' (2021: 1). As Forlano (2021) points out we need 'a deeper consideration of the existential harms of the logics of technological systems for the purpose of more liberatory and just futures'. New approaches require a commitment to a different temporality, to a continuously emerging world rather than in search of a market and as Harle and colleagues (2018) stress, to be embedded in the historical relations of place.

Other critical gestures that seek to re-think the role of technology in society include those who advocate for 'Post-automation', which explores 'sociotechnical alternatives' to the assumptions behind an automated society and 'constitute a proposition that challenges portrayals of automation as an inevitable technological force in society' (Smith et al. 2020: 4). Scholars in this field are concerned with 'what are the contours of post-automation societies, in which citizens play a more constructive rather than adaptive role in the development of its technology?' (Smith et al. 2020: 5). They focus on ideas exploring pluralities of possible sociotechnical futures and overturning the paradigm whereby society should adapt to automation and cite the many sites where alternative approaches are already evident, including in makerspaces, fablabs, hackers and democratic and citizen-led projects.

These recent calls to an ethics of care and attention to diversity, contingency and complexity of life in technology design, affirm the possibility and need for a different way forward. If emerging technologies can get caught up in the values of capitalism, neoliberalism and the monetization, monitoring and predictive analytics of so much of society – not to mention academic research and scholarship – the better news is that they can also become bound up with agendas that work differently.

Undisciplined anthropology

A new way forward also requires a revised, engaged and interventional form of scholarship, a shift away from traditional social science (Pink, Dahlgren et al. 2022). There is already an exciting movement towards change in anthropology: 'There is no doubt that anthropology needs rewriting' states feminist anthropologist Lilith Mahmud (2021: 354) in the *Annual Review of Anthropology*, urging scholars to 'turn anthropology into an antiracist, anticapitalist, antifascist, decolonial, and abolitionist feminist project that we would want to be part of'(2021: 354). Or, as anthropologist Hannah Knox, calling for a new openness to other knowledges, warns: 'anthropology risks becoming an anachronism, an authorially powerful study of discrete cultures, an extractivist project that aims to stabilize world-views and align them as so many parts of a global human ecumene' (Knox 2021b: 124). To move forward, I argue, we must disrupt the traditional mainstream of the social sciences – anthropology included. We must become players in the same futures-focused space as other stakeholders in the future of emerging technologies, create new collaborations and bring different, diverse and everyday stories to the centre. I pursue this through a design anthropology of emerging technologies, which, I propose, involves creating a new interdisciplinary and undisciplined anthropology.

This book is experimental in its non-linear narrative and its approach to critique. It is a response to the enduring technological solutionism paradigm that dominates society, as well as to the heroic narratives of scholars who unwittingly endorse this vision when seeking to show up its ills (Pink, Berg et al. 2022). It is inspired by a futures anthropology (Salazar et al. 2017) approach and builds on the opportunities that opened up its route forward, rather than looking back to existing bodies of work that would shape it. In my practice, an ethnographic approach to anthropology involves following the leads, building on what we find and being accountable for our stories. I have drawn inspiration from the work of several scholars, encountered on my way, whose writing coheres with and further invigorates my thinking. I also critically define the limits of some existing scholarship. However, there is an important difference between my approach and that of working *in* anthropology as a reviewer who takes related past anthropological work as the lifespring of one's own. *Emerging Technologies/ Life at the Edge of the Future* is entangled with and relational to anthropology, but it is intentionally undisciplined in that it improvises and experiments; it is not a direct outcome of the debates, discourses and practices of the discipline and while it might inadvertently contribute to some of them, my intention is different: I wish to do anthropology differently, rather than speaking directly to what is already there.

I write from the position of being *in research* and not from that of having finished a 'project'. The project, as far as I am concerned, never finishes, it is constituted through a trajectory of many 'projects' which are intensities of collaboration, thinking, ethnographic and interventional practice, open to each other rather than discrete units. They are also for a university academic like me, datafied and monetised entities, metrics in funding and publication outcomes, the logics and dominant narratives of which I return to often in the following chapters. Undisciplined anthropology also breeds innovative methodologies which I have developed and discussed with research collaborators across the world: futures anthropology (Pink & Salazar 2017), blended practice (Pink 2021a; Pink, Akama & Fergusson 2017), and interventional design ethnography (Pink, Fors et al. 2022). For me this means engaging with the existing scholarship that inspires me, thinking conceptually, participating in interdisciplinary research and experiments, scanning and reviewing online reports from consultancies, government, industry organisations, following the technology news, doing fieldwork, making ethnographic documentaries, drawing on auto-ethnographic insights and collaborating with research partners from across different sectors including in industry, policy, government and not-for-profit organisations.

Finally, my writing has come about from my situatedness as migrant, often a guest, living, working and collaborating across parts of the world, in person or online, making the site and temporality of my work dispersed, held together by the thread of my inquiry rather than by a singular project timeline or physical place.

How to read this book

The first and last chapters of this book, representing the two parts of its title, respectively *Emerging technologies* (this chapter) and *Life at the edge* (the final chapter), begin and end this book. They could be read as an introduction and conclusion, in the sequence in which they are printed, but could also be read otherwise. The middle nine chapters are presented in the contents page as a grid, so as not to suggest that one set or order needs to come first or last. Rather than being numbered, they each have a one-word title, to cross reference between them. They connect with, but require no prior knowledge of, each other. Counter-structures to the linear book open up new ways to read and engage. In this design, I have taken inspiration from existing works where variations have been successfully engaged, such as: Paul Stoller's (1997) technique of moving between the 'intelligible' and the 'sensible' in his *Sensuous Scholarship*; Doreen Massey's (2005) *For Space* composed of a series of essays of different kinds, in different fonts, that address questions on different registers; and Karen Waltorp's (2020) *Why Muslim Women and Smart Phones* (2020) which interweaves two different registers of chapter with visual essays. In this book, I tell nine different connected design anthropological stories about emerging technologies and life at the edge of the future, structured through three threads:

Emergence engages with the anticipatory and experiential concepts of *futures, trust* and *hope*. I investigate how worlds, things and processes emerge and configure at the cusp of the future, and how we feel as we slip over unnoticed into what comes next. These concepts have been shaped and deployed by academic and other sector stakeholders in the emerging technologies field but with diverse meanings and agendas. How might we reconstitute them as shared concepts and practices for new modes of collaboration and engagement?

Environment interrogates three invisible, inevitable and entangled elements of our everyday worlds, *data, air* and *energy*. I examine our circumstances where data is everywhere, air is increasingly quantified for its quality, and filtered and purified for fear of airborne diseases, and the decarbonisation of energy needs to be integrated into our everyday worlds. In this situation emerging technologies have become part of the environment, rather than things that act on it. How can they become better integrated into relationships of care?

Technologies focuses on three domains of future *mobilities, home* and *work*. I explore how emerging technologies have been imagined to impact in each of these fields, the problems they have been invoked to solve, and the future visions associated with them. Yet, stories of other possible futures are revealed by ethnographic research as people imagine and create their own futures with AD cars, smart home devices and workplace technologies. How can we better align and conjoin human, planetary and technology futures?

FUTURES

Emerging technologies are, by definition, on the cusp of the future. They are centred in narratives that predict societal change, utopia and dystopia. They are frequently part of the enduring and inevitable question of what will happen next, in near and far futures. Yet futures are uncertain and unknowable. Attempts to steer or predict them frequently fail. In reality, emerging technologies are poised at the edge of the unknown, the unquantifiable and the possible. The predictive capacities of emerging technologies themselves – big data analytics, artificial intelligence and machine learning applications – augment this future orientation, by offering dynamic quantified modes of visioning futures. The public health and climate crises that characterise our times are inextricably bound up with how emerging technologies become implicated in the imaginaries of energy transition and the futures of home, mobility and work. Uncertainty is an inevitable characteristic of the future, and many resources are put into seeking to mitigate, control or reduce it. This fuels a thriving futures industry, an institutional need to know, plan and prepare, and a growing academic urge to confront and question futures theoretically and empirically.

This chapter is about how emerging technologies are framed in relation to futures; how they become implicated in future predictions, claims, hype and ambition. I discuss how academics have interpreted such future visions and the technologically deterministic, solutionist and gendered narratives they advance. However, these approaches to futures pay little attention to the people who might use, appropriate and make emerging technologies part of their everyday lives. In response, I advocate and demonstrate an interdisciplinary approach based in futures anthropology (Pink & Salazar et al. 2017) and design anthropology (Akama et al. 2018; Smith & Otto 2016). This perspective acknowledges the everyday as continuously emergent, the contingency and uncertainty of futures, and the improvisatory modes through which possible futures are constituted in everyday practice

DOI: 10.4324/9781003182528-2

and experience, and thus connects with the exploration of anticipatory concepts in chapters *trust* and *hope*. I argue that theorising futures as uncertain, ongoing, emergent and never reached, and engaging critical renderings of anticipatory concepts, better equips us to bring together everyday futures and the field of emerging technologies.

The futures industry

There is growing concern with the future, and an impulse to understand the uncertainties implied by the rise in AI and ADM, and the COVID-19 and climate crises. The business anthropologist Grant McCracken (2020) thinks that 'well into the 21st century, the future looks faster, nearer, meaner' as well as being 'both more dangerous and less optional'. He believes that subsequently 'We have to start mapping the future'. McCracken's points are sensationalist, resonating with this moment where there appears to be a different urgency to understand and intervene in futures.

Within this context, the role of professional futurists has grown. In 2020 *Forbes* reported futurists were increasingly 'being hired by businesses to present visions of what the future could look like' (Morgan 2020, March 5). There are also gender questions relating to the futurist profession, *Forbes* notes that 'Roughly one-third of members of the Association of Professional Futurists [APF – see https://www.apf.org/] are women', directing readers to the top 50 women futurists list on the website of the leading futurist Ross Dawson (see https://rossdawson.com/). A third is worrying, suggesting the future field is predominantly composed of men. There is diversity between the expertise and specialism of futurists, but in common, according to the APF:

> A professional futurist is a person who studies the future in order to help people understand, anticipate, prepare for and gain advantage from coming changes. It is not the goal of a futurist to predict what will happen in the future. The futurist uses foresight to describe what *could* happen in the future and, in some cases, what *should* happen in the future.
>
> *(Association of Professional Futurists, n.d.)*

Reinforcing this point, in a 2021 interview with the consultancy McKinsey & Co, the futurist Kevin Sneader quipped 'I want to begin with the caveat that business forecasting exists to make astrology look good', telling readers that 'Forecasts are always difficult, particularly at a time like this when a high level of uncertainty remains'. But with that said, Sneader went ahead to, in his words put his 'stake in the ground' to identify what the McKinsey & Co article and podcast refers to as 'the eight trends that will shape the post-COVID-19 economy' (Huber & Sneader, 2021, June 21). As the language shifts from uncertainty to that of something that will happen, the relationship between possibility and prediction feels blurred.

While many future 'claims' being made in the business world appear predictive, the rhetoric is underpinned by an acute awareness of uncertainty. In 2021 I avidly followed the hype around flying cars, as the possibility that the first urban air taxi or such like would be launched. I was fascinated by a section about 'forward looking statements' which followed a press release about a new business relationship between two companies and the possibilities this created for the future of aerial ride sharing and taxi services. Highlighting the conditional nature of the terminology used, 'the words "believe," "project," "expect," "anticipate," "estimate," "intend," "strategy," "future," "opportunity," "plan," "may," "should," "will," "would," "will be," "will continue," "will likely result,"' and so on. Acknowledging the 'risks and uncertainties' entailed, it states that '[m]any factors could cause actual future events to differ materially from the forward-looking statements in this Press Release' (Joby Aviation 2021, June 2).

As such statements acknowledge, there is a tension between announcing what will happen as a future in which emerging technologies are implicated plays out, and the inevitable uncertainties and shifting temporalities around the possible moments in which these technologies will generate markets. But hype is one of the ways that emerging technologies and futures come into view, and it is important for companies to perform hype as they try to attract investors to their emerging technologies and to imagine their future markets.

As academics (Elliot 2020; Stilgoe 2019) and technology writers (Milne 2020) alert us, the hype and grand claims that accompany technology design and development in the computing and engineering sciences are often unhelpful, and we must be wary of them. According to Madeleine Clare Elish and danah boyd, the hype of the business community participated in creating a vision of the possibilities of AI and data that exceeded their capabilities (2018: 58). And as Science and Technology Studies scholar Jack Stiloe neatly puts it 'As an optimistic technological promise meets the material world, it slows down and morphs into something more realistic' (Stilgoe 2019: 202). For Stilgoe '[in] an uncertain world, technological hype is a way to make claims about the future that seem rooted in scientific rigour'. He suggests '[t]echnological hype is not just exaggeration, nor is it idle speculation; it is an act of persuasion. We should therefore pay close attention to who is predicting what and why' (Stilgoe 2020: 40). Hype that suggests emerging technologies can solve societal problems is not only over-ambitious, but as examples discussed in *mobilties, home* and *work* chapters show, is often empirically and conceptually incorrect. Yet, notably hype doesn't necessarily deceive everyone, and when people know what to do with hype, it can be seen as not simply a strategy to persuade, but a resource that is used in practical ways. For example, Michael Hockenhull and Marisa Leavitt Cohn have studied the performance of hype at Danish tech events. They suggest seeing hype as 'hot air' which is evaluated by participants in the events, and subsequently taken on board selectively in terms of its local relevance. This means that hype is 'translated' as part of a process involving 'the recuperation of critique' where hype or 'hot air' is made 'mundane and compromised' (Hockenhull & Cohn 2021: 317).

In a world of emerging technologies, however, not only do futurists, the consultancies and technology companies themselves make qualified claims that sound predictive. But technologies themselves are hyped for their predictive qualities and capabilities. In the context of the COVID-19 pandemic, it has been claimed that AI can predict and identify asymptomatic carriers of the virus and track down superspreaders (Waltz 2021, February 2). A Deloitte article, about digital twins, invites readers to imagine having 'a perfect digital copy of the physical world'. The digital twin, it suggests would: 'enable you to collaborate virtually, intake sensor data and simulate conditions quickly, understand what-if scenarios clearly, predict results more accurately, and output instructions to manipulate the physical world' (Parrot et al. 2020, January 15). A recent *Nature Computational Science* article moreover reports on new advances in predictive digital twins through the example of unmanned aerial vehicle (UAV), whereby the digital twin of the UAV goes beyond being an asset monitoring device and has predictive capabilities (Kapteyn et al. 2021). AI is not only set to deliver the future promise of the problematically gendered UAV, but to predict the near futures of these technologies as they traverse our skies. Ironically, it becomes represented as holding the additional promise of reducing the very uncertainty that makes it difficult to predict the future of AI itself.

The layering of future visions, predictive claims, hype, get-out clauses and scepticism that shapes the representational world of emerging technologies is one of the spheres in which the inevitable uncertainties of futures are tamed in industry and engineering-led agendas. It is an essential characteristic of the ways in which future technologies are brought to life, where they inhabit futures which are based on the premise and 'what-if' of technological advancement, elaborated in chapter *emerging technologies*, themselves become the anticipatory infrastructures upon which subsequent future visions are built. In the social sciences these future visions have been understood as 'sociotechnical imaginaries' – a concept introduced by science and technology studies scholar Sheila Jasanoff (2015a). Jasanoff's sociotechnical imaginaries framework has two strands. The first involves examining, as she puts it, 'the origin of new scientific ideas and technologies and the social arrangements or rearrangements they help sustain' (2015b: 322). It is useful precisely for interrogating how the social and technical become entangled in the futures imagined by the consultancies, industry and government. Such studies often reveal the 'technological solutionism' (Morozov 2013) of such imaginaries, whereby it is assumed that technological innovations will solve societal problems, and as is also evidenced in the examples discussed in chapters *home, work,* and *mobilities.* Jasanoff's second strand involves examining 'imagination as a social practice' whereby, she proposes 'we follow the embedding of ideas into cultures, institutions, and materialities, whereby the merely imagined is converted into the solidity of identities and the durability of routines and things' (Jasanoff 2015b: 322–323). While, in some cases sociotechnical imaginaries which originate as 'ideas' or discourse may become part of the symbolic and tangible layers of the world as Jasanoff describes it, the sociotechnical imaginaries framework focuses on the representational categories of the social cultural, rather than experiential dimension of life. It subsequently regards human activity as social practice and assumes that social imaginaries are external things to the mundane everyday that are subsequently somehow embedded in identities, routines and things. The implication is that externally derived concrete social imaginaries would thus drive the sensed, felt, and everyday, and the ways that futures can be imagined within it. Of course, discourses about future visions, at all levels and all facets of the representational and symbolic environments in which we live are implicated in everyday experience. But I argue that they are not deterministic of everyday identities, routines or imaginaries, and therefore we need to take the analysis further to the generative sites of everyday life.

Jasanoff's insights belong to a particular trajectory of thought that aligns with culturalist traditions in anthropology, and which attends to how symbolic layers of culture frame the everyday, rather than seeing the everyday as a generative site of imagination. This is where I argue that we need to take a different turn, to attend to the processual worlds of the everyday, where imagination, ethics and trust are constituted indeterminately (Mattingly & Throop 2018, Pink 2022a; Sneath et al. 2009). Sociotechnical imaginaries analysis, as Jasanoff develops it, creates conceptual prisms that demonstrate the logics of discourse and its performativity. However, it does not produce everyday categories, and (as similarly, emerging technologies are not finished products that land in and shape our lives), discursive sociotechnical imaginaries do not shape everyday life. They are often insufficiently aligned with the everyday to find a point of connection. To comprehend how sociotechnical imaginaries participate in the everyday, we should instead explore how and where their points of contact might be, and what kinds of alignments and misalignments can be made visible. I return to this question later. First, I discuss what we can learn through the layer of sociotechnical futures analysis and outline the implications of this for our understanding of emerging technologies and futures.

Much existing academic work that brings together the social and technical elements of futures focuses on the ways that future imaginaries are constituted and mobilised by organisations. For instance, in a special issue of the journal *Futures*, Kornelia Konrad and Knud Böhle discuss how sociotechnical futures are constituted through expert processes, how they 'circulate amongst policy actors and others involved in the governance of innovations', 'shape the governance of innovations and the actual technologies and systems', and subsequently they ask 'how forms of deliberative and reflective future-making can be integrated into policy and innovation processes' (Konrad & Böhle 2019: 101). In media and communication studies, Astrid Mager and Christian Katzenbach's (2021) special issue of *New Media and Society* explores 'the function, power, and performativity of future visions and how they relate to the making and governing of digital technology' (2021: 223). Their point is that sociotechnical imaginaries 'often appear to be multiple, contested, and commodified' and that 'Not only state actors and governments unfold their power to imagine, govern, and program digital innovations and related social practices, but also big technology companies, influential CEOs, corporate communications, technology events, industry consultants, research groups, and grassroot activists' (2021: 226). Emphasising that sociotechnical imaginaries are collective, they keep the concept at the level of the discursive and visible; here, imaginaries are articulated as collective visions and, subsequently, it seems that they cannot be heard when they are not. As regards the everyday, they suggest 'tensions, ambivalences, and ruptures emerge' when 'competing imaginaries, hegemonic narratives, and counter-cultural voices' come up against the visions embedded in technologies (Mager & Katzenbach 2021: 228).

Yet, again, and as is borne out in the ethnographic examples discussed through this book, there is something missing in this rendering of socio-technical imaginaries, since when people encounter emerging technologies in their everyday worlds, the outcome is not always a mode of breakdown but rather involves processes of incremental learning improvisation and the inventive and creative integration of new things into ways forward that work for them. However, these continuously emerging sociotechnical forms are not collective future visions; they are not even imaginaries in the sense of imagining things that are out there in an as yet unfound future. They are not always represented, spoken or lived in ways that are readily visible. Such everyday modes of imagining are indeed not easy for people to articulate. This is partly because they may not have the frames or vocabulary to do so. For example, Annette Markham analyses how in seeking to encourage participants in futures workshops to express ways forward different from those of technological progress, she found that 'alternative imaginaries are limited through embedded or systemic processes of what critical theorists call discursive closure. Markham rightly calls for researchers to 'generate meaningful prompts and models that, in turn, function as more radical scaffolding for people to imagine otherwise' (2021: 384); examples discussed across chapters *data, air, energy, home, work* and *mobilities* suggest how this might occur.

Societal uncertainty

As futures are uncertain and impossible to predict, they subsequently cause concern, not only in everyday life, which I turn to below, but for societal institutions. Uncertainty about futures is frequently dealt with by religions and systems of belief. Examples include early anthropological accounts of how in small scale societies witchcraft accusations and oracles (e.g. Douglas 2004 [1970]) were engaged to create societal truths in situations where they were impossible to determine through other evidence. World religions, such as Islam and Christianity, propose solutions to ontological questions around which there is considerable uncertainty which, as discussed in chapter *trust*, may also have different repercussions for the ways immediate futures are perceived and experienced in everyday life (see Carey 2018; Corsin Jimenez 2011).

Nevertheless, although societies employ these various modes of coping with uncertainty, it is always present, even when the hype and tentative prediction discussed above is foregrounded. There exists a much more cautious anticipatory narrative, through which government, institutions and organisations seek to suppress uncertainty through structures of risk mitigation. The impulse to mitigate risk permeates many moments and actions in the trajectories of emerging technologies, for instance from the research ethics approval processes involved in their design

(Pink 2017), to safety testing (Pink, Osz et al. 2021), to the regulatory frameworks developed to ensure their ethical or safe use, or the ways they are engaged in risk mitigation measures in relation to other undesirable possible futures. However, there are cracks in the logics of anticipatory risk mitigation, which have dual implications. First for the question of how everyday futures come about, and second for how we might redefine anticipatory concepts like that of trust.

The way that risk mitigation plays out has been explained neatly by geographers Peter Adey and Ben Anderson in their work on UK Civil Contingencies, or emergency planning (2011). They describe how for emergency planners the ideal anticipatory system would be one that does not require a decision. Rather it would be one where when an emergency event occurs protocols are mobilised to activate a series of connected responses into action. But, they explain, in reality the contingencies that such events entail mean that decisions continually have to be made concerning the actions required. That is, preemptive planning offers a framework for considering future possibilities and mitigating their effects through predetermined processes. However, the contingent nature of how events (of all orders) play out and the impossibility of predicting what will happen mean that in practice it is impossible to remove risk through such risk mitigation procedures. In my own research, similar patterns have recurred across diverse fields where preemptive frameworks can be found. For academics, the example of university research ethics frameworks will resonate; we are asked to respond to a set of questions that are designed to anticipate and preempt/prevent possible unethical behaviours. By imagining possible scenarios in which researchers might unintentionally follow unethical procedures, the frameworks can introduce a series of steps, both in the application forms and in their requirements of conduct which prevent these from occurring by closing off possibilities and representing certainties about what can or cannot happen in research. By removing uncertainties, the effect is designed to eradicate the need for unanticipated ethical decisions to have to be made in fieldwork. However, because for instance, in the case of ethnographic research it is never actually possible to know what will happen in fieldwork, such frameworks are not necessarily very useful for guaranteeing ethical practice. Rather, in ways that resonate with civil contingencies, ethical decisions need to be made on the spot in contingent circumstances, and in situations that it would be impossible to know and plan for before they happen (Pink 2017).

Finally, preemptive anticipatory frameworks usually tend to be manifested in forms of regulation, and there has been a tendency to respond to the failure of rules with more rules. The philosopher Onora O'Neill (2017) has pointed this out adeptly in her analysis of what has been referred to as the 'crisis of trust' – which I return to in chapter *trust*. O'Neill explains that when quantitative measurements of trust, derived from opinion polls, indicate that trust is in decline, or absent, typical institutional responses are to increase regulation in a quest to increase trust. This, however, can be ineffective for two reasons. First, O'Neill points out that trust surveys do not necessarily provide accurate information about if trust is increasing or decreasing. Second, rules do not necessarily create more trust because they are inevitably 'incomplete and indeterminate' and 'indeterminacy cannot be eliminated by adding further and more detailed rules'. Indeed, she suggests excessive rules might simply bog workers down in compliance tasks or encourage them to deviate from the rules (O'Neill 2017: 402).

These future-focused modes of regulatory preemption also structure issues I focus on in chapters *mobilities, work* and *home*. For example, in projects about worker safety my colleagues and I found that while safety regulations are indisputably important, they often failed to account for the contingent and changing material, social and personal circumstances in which workers perform tasks. Workers in fact improvised in many ways to keep themselves safe, which safety regulations did not account for, and indeed often sought to close off (Pink, Lingard & Harley 2017). Thus, in addition to the overload or deviance that O'Neill associates with them, preemptive regulations are also often simply unrealistic.

Preemptive anticipatory regimes permeate institutions and societies, and their relationship to the hyped futures discussed above is essential to understanding part of the story about how emerging technologies come about. For example, the autonomous driving (AD) car is technologically possible and has been significantly hyped in futures narratives that expound its expected societal benefits. Yet simultaneously it is 'held back' by lack of regulation, or the question of where and by whom responsibility for preemptive decision making to mitigate risks relating to its safety lies. At this intersection we see two powerful futures narratives – the hype and the risk mitigation – meet. We see, moreover, a meeting point between the work of two of the disciplines that have loud and influential voices in this field: Jasanoff's STS approach to sociotechnical imaginaries and O'Neill's philosophy. Yet, as hinted above, neither the narratives they interrogate nor their research frameworks account for people and the everyday worlds in which emerging technologies become part of possible, experienced and imagined worlds. It is to this site we must attend in order to comprehend how these narratives of technological hype and risk mitigation hit the ground, how and the extent to which they impact people's lives and how they are moderated and refigured in the everyday.

Approaching everyday futures

As we face a contemporary world frequently characterised as being in 'crisis', there is a growing focus on futures amongst the ethnographic social sciences. A common finding of scholars who have assessed these developments is that they do not simply represent a new field of study *of the future* but stand to reshape the work of social science disciplines themselves. With Juan F. Salazar (Pink & Salazar 2017), I have argued for a renewed futures approach in anthropology, which is also symptomatic of a desire amongst some members of the discipline to shift anthropological practice towards being more experimental, engaged and interventional. Samuel Gerald Collins also comments how during the decade or so between the first edition of his book *All Tomorrow's Cultures* in 2007 and the second edition in 2021 there was a 'sharp growth in explicit engagement with future temporalities' (2021: ix) which reveals a 'renewed orientation towards future work' (2021: x), albeit across a broad range of themes. This future focus, Collins reinforces, should enable anthropology to actively play a role in the way forward (2021: xv). Indeed, anthropologists are driving new ethical research agendas in 'blended' (Pink 2021a; Pink, Akama & Fergusson 2017) practice, by generating new creative documentary, experimental and design futures research and intervention methods in everyday situations (Pink, Fors et al. 2022). Such approaches produce new conceptual and empirical knowledge, a future-focussed ethics of responsibility and, indeed, contribute to shaping a new research practice and agenda for the social sciences. In a review of futures research in sociology, Jens Beckert and Lisa Suckert have likewise suggested that 'focusing on future perceptions encourages innovative research perspectives within and beyond established sociological paradigms' (2021: 17). They summarise that

> sociology could benefit from more systematically integrating perceptions of the future – as they are reflected in actor expectations, aspirations, and future beliefs – into the discipline's empirical investigations and explanatory models and from integrating the existing knowledge on these issues better.
>
> *(2021: 1)*

The work of sociologists of technology, including Mike Michael's focus on the sociology of expectations and his collaborative research with speculative probes in everyday life (Michael 2016), and Deborah Lupton and Ash Watson's creative workshops are examples of the new speculative and design futures methodologies, designed to produce understandings of how 'little' future imaginaries are produced in everyday life (Lupton & Watson 2022). These moves are significant since they take steps towards refiguring anthropological and sociological theory and practice towards futures, in doing so they activate changes in disciplines that have more conventionally been aligned with history.

As indicated by the collaborative and interdisciplinary nature of these new sociological and anthropological futures approaches, the most effective way to investigate everyday futures is at the intersection of disciplines and with a genuine openness to disrupt their conventions through engagements with new methods and approaches. Futures anthropologists have moreover advocated for a 'dirty' or impure anthropology whose very intention is to radically exceed the constraints of its discipline (Salazar et al. 2017). Interdisciplinary and innovative anthropologists have pursued such an agenda across diverse fieldwork sites. For example, Debora Lanzeni's work with technology developers (Lanzeni 2016; Lanzeni & Pink 2021) brings our attention to futures as moving and indeterminate imaginaries and the speculative ethnographic documentary practice of Juan F. Salazar (Salazar 2017) and 'ethno science fiction' film of Johannes Sjoberg (2017) takes us into possible everyday futures through the speculative experiences of their protagonists. Rather than refocusing outside the discipline and its study *of* things, futures anthropology generates the ability of the interdisciplinary anthropologist to play an interventional role *in* life at the edge of the future. The work of futures anthropology I develop here therefore should not be confused with Rebecca Bryant and Daniel Knight's (2019) *The Anthropology of the Future*. Their work develops the idea that the present is activated and understood by our orientation to the future, focusing on social practice theorist Theodore Schatzki's notion of 'timespace', a 'temporal site' constituted through ends-focused activity (Bryant & Knight 2019: 18) to understand the mundane everyday as a site of anticipation. Bryant and Knight's engagement with Schatzki's work consequently draws the strengths and limits of his approach. Schatzki's social practice theory divides the world into particular sets of analytical units, through which he seeks to explain the dynamic processes of society. His work on timespace sees 'activity as the happening through which practices, society and history exist' (2010: xii). Schatzki's social practice theory has interventional capacities in that it has informed significant arguments against, for instance, neoliberal behaviour change policies (Shove 2009; Strengers 2013), and a useful framework through which to identify and document historical change. However, because social practices are a predetermined analytical category, which pulls together elements of everyday activities to constitute a practice – rather than to challenge the idea of what a practice actually is – they are categories that are used to organise what is found empirically, and as such often pre-determine it. Futures anthropology instead interrogates its categories, in dialogue with ethnographic findings. Just as Jasanoff's (2015) sociotechnical imaginaries discussed above are conceptual units suspended above and not representational of everyday worlds. Social practices are similarly analytical categories, not ethnographic realities. Therefore, like sociotechnical imaginaries they can (and should!) be used as powerful critical tools, they assemble the everyday in ways that help us 'see' it, but in doing so are unavoidably situated outside the everyday.

A futures anthropology instead needs to be *in* (not *of*) the everyday, and to carry the relations this entails with it. It requires concepts that can enable us to encounter and make visible the feelings, emotions, sensations and activities, human and non-human socialities and environments of everyday lives and imaginaries. To understand *life at the edge of the future*, that never-ending state in which we move forward into what happens next, we need concepts that can help us to gather the experiential modes this entails. There is however a second reason why such concepts are needed; because, by enabling us to understand and express how emerging technologies become part of everyday worlds and everyday imaginaries, such concepts can be engaged to contest or collaborate across disciplines. I next explain how and where the anticipatory modes of everyday trust and hope are detectable, in projects prior to my work on emerging technologies, as principles through which possible futures can be considered from such ethnographic sites.

The anticipatory modes of everyday futures

An anticipatory stance permeates the most dramatic and mundane moments of the everyday. In the 1990s I watched Spanish bullfighters performing live with dangerous bulls and studied the photographic cultures that surrounded them. To photograph the bullfight, I was told, one almost needed to be a bullfighter. As I found, without the embodied knowledge to anticipate the moves of the bull and performer it was difficult to know when to photograph (Pink 1997). Nearly a decade later, researching how people cared for their homes in Spain and the United Kingdom, I realised that simply opening a window is an anticipatory action, in which our embodied knowledge senses the immediate future feel of fresh air. The further future-oriented modes through which people experienced their homes led me to the notion of a 'project of home' (Pink 2004). The people who showed me their homes and everyday cleaning explained and envisioned their homes not as they were when I visited, but as they would or could be; telling me what their homes would be like if their partner or children were tidier, when planned (or imaginary) renovations were finished, with support for senior living as they aged, or even once the next cleaning cycle was done, transforming the sensory aesthetic of the surfaces and air. This sparked my interest in the mundane and often invisible anticipatory modes through which the everyday is lived and imagined. As my work on the home developed through studies of everyday energy and digital technology and media use, I began to understand everyday life in the home as structured through anticipatory routines – like bedtime routines – repeated daily but never exactly replicated and always improvised to meet particular contingencies and accomplish particular ends (Pink & Leder Mackley 2016). I also became interested in routines as likely sites for participatory interventions towards sustainable lifestyles, since they were already contingent and dynamic sites in which people had sedimented their own everyday interventions (Pink, Leder Mackley et al. 2017). I spent time with participants, across a series of projects, as we tumbled over the edge of the present into their immediate futures, accompanying them as they used everyday technologies to undertake mundane tasks (like laundry) or reenact everyday routines in their homes I was able to explore with them how it felt to go forwarded in everyday life: what were the feelings that accompanied them as they unloaded laundry? How did they 'know' the machine had made their clothes clean? Why did they have to accomplish a routine that involved putting the television on with a timer so they could comfortably fall asleep at night? (Pink & Leder Mackley 2016). In other words, how did it feel to go forward? what did people need to accrue a sense of 'ontological security'? In the terms I develop below, how did people balance feelings of trust and anxiety as they went forward into an inevitably uncertain everyday future?

In the early 2000s, I started researching with the Slow City Movement (https://www.cittaslow.org/), immersing myself in their committee meetings, events and interviewing people in their projects, seeking to understand the dynamics of their indirect mode of sustainability activism across England, Spain and Australia for about a decade. By following how Slow City groups planned and imagined the futures of their towns through the movement's sustainability framework, I learned to understand the process of becoming a Slow City as an inevitably future-oriented stance. It entailed imagining and hoping for particular sustainable futures, while working on everyday designs and actions – such as offering traditional skills programmes, creating community space projects and constituting new annual ritual events – that would move forward through the principles aligned with such future imaginaries (e.g. Pink 2008a; Pink & Seale 2017). This was a very visceral way of sensing futures from the present, which participants expressed to me performatively and experientially: in one instance, David, the leader of a community garden project, walked the new extension to the path that he envisaged being laid, using his bodily movement forward to express where it would go and holding his arms out to show its breadth and end (Pink 2007); in another a participant stood at the end of a playing field with me, outlining how it would be in the future (Pink 2008b). One Slow City group, for whom future uncertainties were deeply entrenched in their recent experience of the loss of life, homes and environment in what had been one of Australia's most catastrophic bushfires, decided to change the conventions of creating a written application to join the movement. Instead, they sent in a series of videos in which they discussed the criteria required over good wine. They were successful (Pink & Lewis 2014). In these experiences, participants in research invoked the feeling of hope as they enacted and performed the difficult-to-verbalise feelings through which they were able to imagine possible futures in inevitably uncertain worlds.

To share these everyday imaginaries, I needed to be there, with the participants, just as I needed to walk through people's homes with them, to sense how their future homes may feel, I walked through cities and countryside, and shared local foods and celebrations. In each of these projects, I joined people as they both imagined as yet untouchable and invisible futures. The futures imagined in these everyday worlds were mundane – a path, a handrail, a breakfast made from almost exclusively local produce – and sensory, affective and difficult to fully express verbally. They also all highlighted the significance of the interventional (sometimes incremental, sometimes more disruptive) practices of participants in research, in everyday life or as activists, as examples through which to learn how to play an interventional role in life at the edge of the future. That is, they lead us to ask how people participate in and shape near and far everyday futures, in ways that neither the sociotechnical imaginaries and anticipatory logics of risk mitigation, nor the scholars, who make these symbolic or representational layers of culture their objects of analysis, account for.

I argue that attention to everyday futures needs to be at the centre of the ways in which we understand futures, and subsequently of our approach to emerging technologies, as well as to our understanding of the narratives of crisis in which we find ourselves.

Anticipatory concepts for the crisis

The concepts of trust and hope enable us to traverse both conscious and sensory, embodied or non-representational modes of anticipation, and the representational narratives of sociotechnical imaginaries. They are variously engaged across multiple academic disciplines and technologically solutionist discourses that narrate futures.

Significantly, phenomenologically they refer to feelings about what might happen next, but, as I show in chapters *trust* and *hope*, they have been appropriated for other purposes. Some academics seek to invent new concepts through which to express the specificity of the thing or process they wish to describe. I propose that by doing the opposite, engaging concepts that have already been associated with meanings that we wish to complicate, a powerful course of action opens up. Rather than to simply use these concepts to develop an anthropological theory for anthropologists (although I hope anthropologists will be interested), I argue that we should mobilise them to create a distinctively anthropological intervention into the domains where I (and colleagues with whom I have collaborated) believe that understandings of anticipation and future visions need to be re-thought. Chapters *trust* and *hope* are dedicated to proposing how this might be achieved.

I suggest that once we have refigured the concepts through which futures are considered, we will be able to better engage with the so-called crisis that is apparently upon us. The anthropologist Janet Roitman has warned us to be critical of the notion of crisis. Like any dominant concept, it needs to be interrogated, in Roitman's words:

> if crisis designates something more than a historical conjuncture, what is the status of that term? How did crisis, once a signifier for a critical, decisive moment, come to be construed as a protracted historical and experiential condition? The very idea of crisis as a condition suggests an ongoing state of affairs. But can one speak of a state of enduring crisis? Is this not an oxymoron?
> *(Roitman 2013: 2)*

Following Roitman, crisis has become both a way of describing the (already there) contingency and uncertainty to be found in the present, and simultaneously is used as a historical marker in problem-solution narratives, where the logical conclusion of a crisis is its resolution. Anti-crisis, as Roitman expresses it, enables us to consider how narratives of contingency play out differently. This throws new light on our current so-called crisis. It questions, then, if we should categorise our situation – of climate degradation, a highly contagious virus, lockdown measures and vaccination programmes, and seemingly run-away technology development in dire need of regulation – as a crisis? Or is this not just the ongoing state of affairs of an uncertain world being revealed in more powerful terms than ever before, supported by more extensive and diverse media platforms and increasingly potent AI, ADM and emerging technologies. What if we instead turn to everyday trust and hope as our starting points, to consider how moving forward in uncertainty already happens? Chapters *trust* and *hope* consider this possibility.

TRUST

In 2020, in introducing a new report on *Trust in Artificial Intelligence* (Lockey et al. 2020), KPMG – one of the Big 4 global consulting firms – asked: 'Are we capable of extending our trust to AI?', proposing that 'Without public confidence that AI is being developed and used in an ethical and trustworthy manner, it will not be trusted and its full potential will not be realised'(KPMG 2020). In 2021, *Forbes* looked ahead to make trust pivotal in their '5 Biggest Technology Trends' for 2022. Identifying 'transparency, governance and accountability' as a new trend, *Forbes* tells us that 'For technology to work, we humans need to be able to trust it' (Marr 2021, September 27). Trust is a pivotal issue for industry, government and humanitarian organisations as emerging technologies become both inevitable and desirable for their work, albeit slightly differently in each sector.

For the technology industry, trust is crucial. For example, the companies CISCO, IBM and Microsoft all have their own Trust Centres. IBM, amongst other things emphasises the importance of transparent and explainable AI for generating public trust (www.ibm.com/trust), CISCO offers 'Insights, stories and guidance on building your future on a foundation of trust and transparency' (www.cisco.com/c/en/us/about/trust-center.html) and Microsoft focuses on customer trust, where 'Microsoft provides strong customer data protection. We are transparent about our practices, and we stand up for our customer's rights' (www.microsoft.com/en-au/trust-center).

Trust in technology is also a pivotal question for governments; a 2020 EU White Paper – 'On Artificial Intelligence – A European approach to excellence and trust' – has the simple premise that 'As digital technology becomes an ever more central part of every aspect of people's lives, people should be able to trust it. Trustworthiness is also a prerequisite for its uptake' (European Commission 2020: 1). An issue is that 'in addition to a lack of investment and skills, lack of trust is a main factor holding back a broader uptake of AI' (2020: 9). In these circumstances, they identify 'Building an ecosystem of trust' as 'a policy objective in itself', suggesting this 'should give citizens

DOI: 10.4324/9781003182528-3

the confidence to take up AI applications and give companies and public organisations the legal certainty to innovate using AI' (2020: 3).

In the not-for-profit humanitarian and advocacy sector, trust is also central. Here, for example, the Australian Humanitech Red Cross Position paper advocates that 'Regulation and design of technology must be guided by the values of humanity, safety, trust, participation and responsibility'. Humanitech argues that humans should be in control of technology, and that 'safeguards and shared values' should be built into technology through human-centred design; suggesting 'we can build trust by involving the broader community in co-design of ethical and regulatory frameworks' (Humanitech 2018: 8). Europe-based AlgorithmWatch calls for national centres of expertise in ADM, involving 'civil society organizations, stakeholder groups, and existing enforcement bodies … and national human rights bodies to benefit all aspects of the ecosystem and build trust, transparency, and cooperation between all actors' (AlgorithmWatch 2020: 13).

Each of these sectors needs trust, but the logics through which they seek it and the ways they place it in relation to everyday life differ. While technology companies are concerned to be transparent and ethical in the hope of gaining customers' trust, governments seek to regulate technology so that the public will trust it. In contrast, for the humanitarian sector, co-designing the ethics and frameworks, with humans, is the way to generate trust.

What I call the 'trust problem' is prevalent across many domains of emerging technology, not least those discussed in chapters *mobilities, home* and *work*. Flying cars or electric vertical takeoff and landing (eVTOLs) aircraft are predicted by some to be a reality as urban air taxis by 2025 or soon after (see chapter *emerging technologies*) and trust is seen as essential; as reported by a leading eVTOL engineering company, for the 'average commuter' the question is '[i]f they don't trust the air taxi, they will endure the stress of driving' (Altran, 2020). In 2020 the smart, home voice assistant Alexa (amongst others) was reported to be 'at the center of a sweeping European Union antitrust inquiry into how Silicon Valley uses data to gain a tight grip on growing markets' (White & Bloomberg 2020, July 17), and in 2021 media reports highlighted the launch of Amazon's sidewalk and the privacy issues it invoked (Fowler 2021, June 8). In the future of work, Autodesk's *Trust Matters* (2020) report explored trust in the construction industry – one of the most dangerous workplaces. How might future intelligent, automated and connected machines, and differently or re-skilled workers participate in and generate shifts in relations of trust? The report suggested 'technology can create trust, by improving transparency, enhancing communication, and providing evidence of success' (Autodesk 2020: 5). I examine these manifestations of the trust problem across *mobilites, home* and *work* in their respective chapters. Here I interrogate trust and its applications.

Trust as a concept

Trust is an anticipatory concept. It refers to something pivotal to how we engage with our immediate, or proximate, possible futures. It is understood by philosophers and sociologists as involving cognitive, emotional and social familiarity and confidence (e. g. Frederickson, 2014; Lewis & Weigert 1985; Luhmann 1979). But trust is notoriously difficult to define, and whenever it is defined a competing definition is not far away. Trust can be an everyday feeling, part of the social and technical discipline's jargon used to describe transactional relationships, and an aspiration and challenge for industry, policy and activist groups. Experientially, trust emerges in the spaces where we can never know for sure what will happen next, and holds us steady as we move forward, wrapping us with a sense of familiarity and confidence. Experiential trust is ephemeral, emergent, contingent and shifting, it may be hard to describe but is manifested in our sensory and emotional engagements with people, things and environments. It cannot be held still, captured, given or taken.

By contrast, quantitatively trust becomes a resource, a commodity, which is measurable. It has quite different characteristics to experiential trust. It is crystallised in survey questions, extracted from respondents, or observed in technology tests or laboratory experiments. Bottled as such, trust levels are frequently used across to define, measure and categorise people's relationships with each other, with organisations and with technologies. I argue that we need to attend more to experiential trust and the diverse everyday circumstances in which it is generated. Without doing so, it is impossible to understand how and why emerging technologies might participate in possible futures.

Trust is central to emerging technology visions, particularly when it comes to the idea that people do not trust technology and the subsequent question of how to engender such trust. Unsurprisingly there are divergent views on how to generate trust, the most relevant of which I discuss below. This means that we need new ways to talk about trust, to create dialogue between quantitative and qualitative interpretations, and the ideologies attached to them. Such a step requires us to dislodge trust from the certainties, causality and predictions that the sciences associate it with.

Thus, we need to see trust beyond simply being a descriptive concept, and rather as a generative metaphor. There is a growing impetus and need to question our metaphors. Sally Wyatt (2021) calls on us to interrogate the meanings and materialities of metaphors that are mobilised in dominant sociotechnical future imaginaries; while Abeda Birhane (2021) draws on relational ethics grounded in Afro-feminism and sub-Saharan African philosophy in her decolonising critique of how western metaphors and philosophies are mobilised in rationalist problem-solution technology narratives. Seeing trust as a concept and a metaphor to be interrogated, makes it both an analytical category and a contested imaginary. It simultaneously makes trust a category that can be re-mobilised analytically and critically as what Henrietta Moore (2004) has referred to as a concept-metaphor.

Trust is a particularly interesting conceptual category because it has consistently been mobilised with other concepts, according to the stakeholder interests and academic disciplines involved: the philosopher Katherine Hawley sees trust as being at the centre of a 'web' of concepts 'reliability, predictability, expectation, cooperation, goodwill, and – on the dark side – distrust, insincerity, conspiracy, betray and incompetence' (2012: 3); the anthropologist Matthew Carey (2018) analyses trust relationally with mistrust; human–computer interaction (HCI) researchers reply on a causal chain of trust, acceptance and adoption of technology (Raats et al. 2020); and the computing and engineering sciences and technology industry and government have turned attention to how to create trustworthy organisations, technologies and systems through concepts such as fairness, accountability, transparency and explainability (Pink 2022a). Each of these renderings of trust and its companion concepts creates a different route through the trust maze.

To understand *emerging technologies*, and how trust figures in *life at the edge of the future*, a first step is to consider how trust is conceptualised and mobilised in dominant narratives and agendas surrounding emerging technologies, and to compare this with everyday trust. Existing dominant definitions of trust frequently reproduce the technological solutionist agendas critiqued in chapters *emerging technologies* and *futures*, whereby technological solutions are thought to solve societal problems. Rather than solving the question of how to generate trust, they sustain and exacerbate a situation in which trust levels are measured as being low, and where trust becomes an increasingly valuable but elusive commodity. I propose and outline an alternative; by conceptualising and mobilising trust as a theoretical, practical and experiential category through which different stakeholders in change processes and academic disciplines can collaborate to consider ethical and responsible futures. Re-thinking trust through a futures anthropology moreover helps dispel problematic portrayals of the 'social sciences' as conceptualising trust 'in terms of rational self-interest' (Hawley 2012: 5). Which is not a vision of or for the social sciences that I would like to see going forward.

I draw on five years of my own and collaborative ethnography and literature research into trust in relation to emerging technologies and data. I have avidly followed how concepts and logics of trust are represented across industry, consultancy and government reports, in computer and engineering science reviews and research and in the social and philosophical sciences. This world of materials and experiences, in which I have immersed myself, followed 'ethnographic hunches' and learned constitutes my international fieldsite. I treat it ethnographically, respectfully contesting the metrics of the systematic review, to dialogue between examples of the logics which I have encountered, and the design and futures anthropology theory outlined in chapters *emerging technologies* and *futures*.

What is the trust problem?

By the second decade of the 2000s, digital, automated and connected technologies and data were a growing, and sometimes mystifying, concern for industry and public sector organisations. My readings of government and industry reports and discussions with diverse research partners turned increasingly to the question of the need for trust in these emerging technologies. Yet there seemed to me to be a gap in what we knew about trust. In a 2017 article, the philosopher Onora O'Neill, citing 'ubiquitous claims that trust has declined, and even that there is a "crisis of trust"' cast doubt on the very mechanisms – opinion polls – by which societal trust was conventionally evaluated (O'Neill 2017). A 'trust problem' was evidently mounting.

The trust problem, based on the perception of a lack of trust, or a trust deficit – has fed into a quest for 'trust solutions'. The quantification of trust – via opinion polls, surveys and testing practices – is a key source of the problems and challenges associated with it in dominant discourses. It might seem obvious to say that reducing an emergent experiential state or a feeling to an intangible resource and subsequently a commodity is a difficult challenge. If, for contemporary digital capitalism, data is the new oil (a metaphor critiqued in chapter *data*), then trust seems like a new genie which simply cannot be captured.

Dominant discourses assert that for society to reap its expected benefits, technology must be trustworthy, and publics (see also chapter *mobilities*) must trust it. As is repeatedly evident across the reports and websites of the consultancies, government, and industry organisations, there is an enduring belief that trust is central and essential to the successful application of emerging technologies in society. While with different emphases and intentions, these narratives follow the same path. Capitalism needs trust and technology companies need people to trust technologies so they can create markets. Governments want people to trust the technological systems they install in order to accrue the societal benefits they propose to bring about and implement effective governance and regulation. Movements towards AI for 'social good' need society to trust AI so it can fulfil the social good they believe technological solutions are capable of driving.

Unsurprisingly, given the level of demand there is for trust, there is correspondingly much contemporary concern about public, consumer or user trust in emerging technologies in general and in AI in particular. This is frequently investigated through large surveys, and the sense of a crisis or deficit in trust is as evident as ever in recent surveys about trust in emerging technologies as it was in O'Neill's (2017) discussion of a 'crisis of trust'. However, trust surveys are not only prominent in their ubiquity but also in the extent to which they influence subsequent policy. For example, the European Consumer Organisation (BEUC) reports, on the basis of a 2019 survey across Europe, that 'While they see benefits, consumers have low trust in AI and its added value, as well as concerns such as the abuse of personal data and the use of AI to manipulate their decisions' (BEUC 2020: 5). In 2020, in the UK, the Chartered Institute for IT reported, following a survey they carried out, that 'The majority of people do not trust computers to make decisions about any aspect of their lives' (BCS 2020, September 8). These surveys were cited as context for the UK Government's 2021 Ethics, Transparency and Accountability Framework for Automated Decision-Making, which consequently notes 'a distinct distrust in the regulation of advanced technology' (UK Government 2021, May 13). Similarly, the Australian Human Rights Commission (2021) *Human Rights and Technology* report asserts that 'Public trust is essential for Australia to harness the opportunities presented by new and emerging technologies'. It goes on to cite a series of national surveys that suggest 'Public trust in some new technologies is low'. The report responds to these statistics through a set of solutions, which commendably put human rights at the centre of their agenda, but which tend to mirror the dominant uses of trust discussed below, whereby they consider that public trust would be contingent on appropriate regulation.

So, what should we make of these surveys and the extent to which they influ-ence well-meaning recommendations and actions in policy and regulatory fields? My anthropological training and experience make me critical of claims to knowl-edge through surveys, because they produce information decontextualised from the flow, emotions, experience and contingencies of life as it is lived. Philosophers also see trust surveys as limited: Katherine Hawley (2012: 42) notes that their questions tend to be 'vague and ambiguous'; and O'Neill sums up that while '[polls] can provide evidence about generic attitudes to types of institution or types of office holder, such as trusting or mistrustful attitudes' in fact 'they offer no evidence about the judgements that people make when they decide to trust or refuse trust to particular individuals or institutions for particular matters, in which they often dif-ferentiate cases with some care' (O'Neill 2017: 405).

However, the implication of trust surveys for those who rely on them is that when trust comes into view as an essential resource which is in deficit, the sub-sequent challenge regards how to increase something as ephemeral, indeterminate and intangible as trust? In dominant narratives, trust has been reduced to a quan-tifiable thing, making it appear less slippery than I have suggested it might be. Nevertheless, the difficulties are acknowledged. The global consultancy PwC's website expounds that 'You can't buy trust — you have to earn it', under this heading it continues that

> Trust has never been more important. It's the link that connects your organi-sation, your people, your customers, your stakeholders and the world. We know that trust isn't something you can buy off the shelf. It's something you earn through every interaction, every experience, every relationship and every outcome delivered.
>
> *(PwC n.d. a)*

Trust in AI, and associated future technological visions, such as for automated and connected mobilities or energy systems, is an enduring concern for governments around the world. And here again the onus is often put on the design of technol-ogy to earn trust. For instance, the European Union's 2019–2024 focus on 'Excellence and trust in artificial intelligence' proposes that 'Artificial intelligence (AI) can help find solutions to many of society's problems. This can only be achieved if the technology is of high quality, and developed and used in ways that earns peoples' trust' (European Commission n.d.). Equally, in the context of algo-rithmic failure in the UK, when highschool leavers' exams were incorrectly graded, the Ada Lovelace Institute recommended that 'more transparent, accountable and inclusive process in the deployment of algorithms, addressing the issues highlighted above, could help to earn back that trust' (Jones & Safak 2020, August 8). In these narratives, therefore, trust is constituted as a resource, which must be 'earned' through the design of technologies and systems that people will trust. In research this is sometimes articulated in the question of what it is about technologies that people trust – for example, in the question of whether people are more likely to trust an anthropomorphic or mechanoid robot after it makes mistakes and seeks to repair them (Esterwood & Robert 2021).

I argue that such an approach is extractive by nature. Trust itself becomes an object, an intangible resource, commodity and asset which can be earned or won from people categorised as publics, consumers or users and held on to. Trust, objectified and fixed as a response to a survey or a datafied purchase action is measured in the moment it is checked on a list or a purchase is made. Following this logic, gaining, and keeping discrete and measurable units of trust could sustain markets, power structures and so-called societal benefits. Here, trust cannot necessarily be bought but it can be monetized.

There are moreover further worrying elements of the trust problem. Due to the impulse to gain, measure and keep trust, it becomes a concern that catalyses further economic activity, which itself is seen to reap other 'benefits'. Trust is not only a commodity that may generate markets for emerging technologies (not to mention the environmental damage that stems from the resource extraction and e-waste attached to those goods), but it is also an earner for a series of other industries. The impulse to generate and keep trust generates fees for consultancies and finances research projects and positions in industry and academia. For example, the UKRI (UK Research and Innovation) Trust in Autonomous Systems Programme was funded with £33m GBP as 'a UK focal point for active engagement with the autonomous systems agenda, facilitating conversations across academia, government, regulators, businesses and the public' (UKRI 2020, November 4). There is also a tradition of research in the human–computer-interaction (HCI) field that investigates how to generate trust in technology. In brief, as Kaspar Raats' extensive review of this field explains, this research area has approached trust as being part of a causal chain of concepts and associated events, embodied in the Technology Acceptance Model (TAM) whereby trust in technology would lead to people (in the form of rational actors) accepting the technology and consequently adopting it (Raats et al. 2020). The TAM model is mirrored in approaches taken by the consultancies, and in their influence on industry and government more widely. By way of example, a 2021 five-country survey-based report on Trust in AI produced in collaboration between the consultancy KPMG and the University of Queensland in Australia, saw the relationship between trust and acceptance as equally pivotal, whereby 'trust strongly influences AI acceptance, and hence is important for the societal uptake of AI and realising its benefits' (Gillespie et al. 2021).

The so-called crises, deficits and challenges of trust that have characterised the first two decades of the twenty-first century thus constitute a 'trust problem', which has proved impossible to solve despite the many resources different stakeholders have invested in it. Is it not then time to reconstitute the problem? I return to this question later. But trust is not the only 'problem'.

The trustworthiness solution

In parallel to discussions of trust, recently attention has turned to the argument that trust can be gained by making systems and technologies trustworthy. This logic, like the TAM model outlined above, is a technologically deterministic model which assumes that technological innovation – towards trustworthy machines – will lead to human trust. It suggests a 'solution' to the 'trust problem' in that it sidetracks the problem of how to generate trust in technologies and systems that already exist and where surveys have suggested a trust deficit. Instead, it poses the new challenge of creating trustworthy technologies and systems, which will draw in trust. It has thus created a 'trustworthiness solution', which like the 'trust problem' comes in different forms.

David Spiegelhalter, a statistician, outlines the trustworthiness agenda in a nutshell:

> In this age of misinformation and loud, competing voices, we all want to be trusted. But as O'Neill has said (O'Neill, 2013), organizations should not try to be trusted; rather they should aim to demonstrate *trustworthiness*, which requires honesty, competence, and reliability.
>
> *(Spiegelhalter 2020)*

In Australia, in a similar vein, the Human Rights Commission's 2021 *Human Rights and Technology* report proposes that 'Robust human rights protections are considered essential for that public trust' and notes the Australian Academy of Science's point that 'building public trust should be about building trustworthy systems' (2021: 28). The US National Artificial Intelligence Initiative (www.ai.gov/) has 'advancing trustworthy AI' as one of its strategic pillars and details many projects through which this is pursued (United States Government n.d.). Following this logic, the new challenge for these organisations emerges as entailing how to create trustworthy technologies, systems and organisations.

Another facet of the trustworthiness solution lies in the question of how to create trustworthiness, and this is particularly evident in the case of emerging technologies such as AI and ADM. This is a global concern, taken up at 'high levels', for instance, in 2019 Luciano Floridi (a member of the High-Level Expert Group (HLEG), who developed them) commented on the EU's 'Seven essentials for achieving trustworthy AI', and said that they 'have been designed to establish a benchmark for what may or may not qualify, from now on, as trustworthy AI'. For the European Commission, these essentials were: human agency and oversight; robustness and safety; privacy and data governance; transparency; diversity, non-discrimination and fairness; societal and environmental well-being; and accountability (Floridi 2019). The Big 4 consultancy Deloitte also offers a 'Trustworthy AI Framework' (Saif & Ammanath 2020, March 25) with six paired dimensions: fair/impartial; robust/reliable; privacy; safe/secure; responsible/accountable; and transparent/explainable. Such benchmarks have worthy intentions, but they still leave the question of how such trustworthy AI might be developed and designed by engineers and computer scientists and technology companies. And how and where the everyday might be implicated in their implementation. Elsewhere, I discuss existing approaches in the engineering and computer sciences, to the generation of trust, through trustworthy machines that embody human ethics (Pink 2022a). Examples include a shift in some areas of the computing and engineering sciences, evidenced in the HCI field, suggesting that trustworthy machines must have characteristics of fairness, accountability, transparency and explainability (FATE), which in some work means replacing the TAM with a new FATE model (e.g. Shin 2021).

This agenda implies a spike in the trustworthy AI research industry, poised to seek to 'solve' this new technological challenge endorsed by government agencies and industry. In the journal *AI and Ethics* there has been a call for research funding in the AI field to be contingent on the embedding of trustworthiness:

> that grant funding and public tendering of AI systems should require a Trust-worthy AI Statement within the grant proposal or tendering document. The statement would outline the actions planned by applicants to ensure their project and/or product can be deemed trustworthy and benchmarked against the rigorous standards.
>
> *(Gardner et al. 2021)*

Therefore, the trustworthiness solution already does, and will continue to, under-pin many industry and government reports, sustain the salaries and careers of many consultants, and many researchers and academics in the engineering and computing sciences, lead to interesting new technology and systems designs and inform policy. But given the trajectory of technologically solutionsist approaches and imaginaries, it seems highly likely that rather than solving the trust problem, it will invoke new problems, which will continue to sustain the next generation of players in the innovation game, while global temperatures rise and public health deteriorates. Hence, trustworthiness is not just a solution, but also a problem.

Critiques of the trustworthiness agenda are already emerging, and thus the 'trust-worthiness problem' comes into view. In an editorial in the *Journal of Trust Research*, Peter Ping Li argues for keeping the 'trust-as-choice' model associated with as opposed to 'trust-as-attitude'. The latter, whereby trust would solely depend on expected trustworthiness, and would therefore not guarantee a trust outcome, he points out, would render 'trust redundant as a construct' (Li 2012: 102). Li's point is significant in highlighting the propensity of trustworthiness models to separate trust from the com-plexity of everyday practice and experience. The trustworthiness challenge has also been challenged by legal scholars Johanna Gunawan, David Choffnes, Woodrow Hartzog and Christo Wilson who point out that the problem is that there has been a failure to produce trustworthy technologies. They

> argue that a good way to help close the technology trust gap is through rela-tional duties of loyalty and care, better frameworks regulating the design of

information technologies, and substantive rules limiting data collection and use instead of procedural 'consent and control' regimes.

(Gunawan et al. 2021: 1507)

Such approaches, although led by regulatory frameworks, also begin to situate our relationships with emerging technologies more closely in the everyday through concepts such as care that resonate more closely with everyday regimes. Rather than simply investing trustworthiness in machines, organisations and systems, and depending on causal logics to create trust, we need to turn to the sites where trust is experienced and generated, which means confronting the messiness, complexity, contingency, emotions and sensations of the everyday.

Reconstituting the concept of trust

In the previous sections, we have seen how outside the social sciences, trust is usually treated as a binary or sequential concept. In philosophy, the desirability of being trusted and of trustworthiness are emphasised. Hawley has reflected on the advantages of being trusted and disadvantages of being distrusted (2012), and O'Neill supposes that 'Our aim – everybody's aim – is surely to trust the trustworthy, but not the untrustworthy' (O'Neill 2018: 293). Sequentially, trust in emerging technologies has increasingly been pitched as an outcome of transparency, accountability and explainability being exhibited by trustworthy technologies (for instance, in algorithmic and human decision-making processes). Once it has been gained, trust is seen as leading to the public or consumer acceptance and subsequently the adoption and use of emerging technologies (for instance, the idea that trust in self-driving cars will lead to public acceptance and consequently their promised societal benefits). These discussions of trust predominate in industry and government sectors and in academia in engineering disciplines and as the examples in the previous sections show, form causal sequences through which the trustworthiness solutions are developed to address trust problems. The concept of transparency offers a good example of how sequential concepts are used with trust in industry and policy narratives. For instance, in the consultancy sector, PwC sees building trust as one of 'two interconnected needs that clients face in a world of technological disruption, fractured geopolitics, climate change and the enduring impacts of the COVID-19 pandemic' (the other is 'to deliver sustained outcomes'). Here transparency is also expected to play a pivotal role in leading to trust since they write: 'Our approach to building trust is designed to meet rising expectations of transparency and stakeholder engagement' (PwC n.d. b). The UK government's Centre for Data Ethics and Innovation blog states that 'There is clearly some way to go to build public trust in algorithms, and the obvious starting point for this is to ensure that algorithms are **trustworthy**' [bold in original]. While asserting that 'a transparent approach is vital to building a trustworthy environment' they are cautious to 'not assume that greater transparency from public sector organisations will inevitably lead to greater trust in the public sector' and suggest that the nature of the information and accountability provided is fundamental to ensuring that transparency is effective in this respect (MacDonald & Durkee 2020, December 1). In these causal chains, rather than being generated in everyday situations, trust is seen as constituted through actions driven by institutions, taking attention away from the complexity of everyday life. I argue that binary and causal approaches to trust not only limit what we can know about how trust comes about, but they also distract attention from the ontological, epistemological and empirical questions about trust which will lead to a deeper understanding. Anthropology offers us a way to create a definition of trust based in an ethnographic-theoretical dialogue.

Anthropologists have rarely put trust at the centre of their inquiry (with exceptions discussed below). Yet anthropology has been co-opted into influential discussions of trust, where for instance, the philosopher O'Neill probes the question of how to judge others' trustworthiness. Citing the work of anthropologists Gillian Tett and Douglas Holmes, O'Neill takes a culturalist approach to understanding trust, as something that people evaluate communicatively through discourse with others. For O'Neill, culture provides a solution to the inability of law and regulation to create accountability by 'addressing the indeterminacy of principles and rules that the extension or proliferation of law, regulation and accountability by themselves cannot provide' (2017: 409). The philosopher of trust Morten Frederickson (2014) has proposed a Bourdieusian relational theory of interpersonal trust, to argue that 'Relational analysis does not in any way allow researchers to draw causal conclusions in the sense which has become dominant – relational causality is complex, multi-directional and multi-layered' (2014: 188). More recently Hubert Etienne (2021), draws on anthropology and philosophy to suggest that the production of 'trustworthy AI' does not solve problems because the understanding of trust that underpins it misconstrues trust as rational choice. He suggests, trust is a social phenomenon, and involves a social rationality. While the anthropology he uses to evidence this point entails early anthropologies of small-scale societies undertaken before or around the mid-twentieth century. Etienne is right that we need to further investigate the question of trust, and this is another indicator that we need a new anthropology equipped to critique the casualties and binaries that underpin rational actor understandings of trust. O'Neill is also right to focus on questions of indeterminacy. However, to address the question of what trust is, we need to go beneath the layers of the 'social', beyond the objectifying practices of early anthropology, and past the representational layers of 'culture'.

Recent anthropologies of trust employ the discipline's comparative focus to explore how trust is generated and experienced in non-capitalist societies with non-Christian religions. Alberto Corsin Jimenez (2011) critiques sociological and organisation studies' formulations and mobilisations of trust as interactional and transactional, whereby 'Trust emerges as an epiphenomenon of social knowledge: what people's relationships look like after the fact of cognitive re-appraisals' (Corsin Jimenez 2011: 178). He compares this to Rane Wilerselv's ethnographies which show how trust is differently constituted amongst Yukaghir hunters in north-eastern Siberia. There, Corsin Jimenez (2011: 190) suggests, trust 'emerges as the forever self-eclipsing relationship through which people re-place themselves into new relationships'. Other anthropologists have shifted attention to mistrust (Carey 2018; Mühlfried 2019; Sousa Santos 2021). Matthew Carey compares trust as he saw it manifested in Christian northern Europe, with mistrust as he encountered it in the Moroccan Atlas, where Islam is the dominant religion. Carey suggests that refocusing on mistrust disrupts the enduring and dominant focus across western society on trust as a solution to all manner of things, from issues within personal relationships to societal issues. With people in the Moroccan Atlas, he found that 'Proximity and familiarity do not necessarily equate to knowability or certainty and cannot be used as a basis for generating expectations and predicting future behavior'. He suggests that this challenges dominant assumptions (in western cultures) of an 'umbilical relationship between the holy trinity of proximity, familiarity, and trust' (Carey 2018: 8), thus also disrupting the assumption discussed above, that trust is necessarily part of a causal chain. For Carey, instead, trust and mistrust are co-constitutive rather than opposed or mutually exclusive, in that people realise that others are not always trustworthy (2018: 11).

What follows from this is the potentially more widely applicable idea that trust and mistrust are interdependent in everyday relations. Trust is contingent and shifting, rather than ever existing as a bounded state, as it does in the either/or binaries that constitute the logics of surveys, or occupying fixed positions in the causal chains of models of trustworthiness. As this interpretation confirms, trust is hard to capture, not only because it is not universally a default mode of being, but also because when it is found it is neither fixed nor static in one person, relationship or thing. Ethnographic research about people's experiences of autonomous driving vehicles – discussed in chapter *mobilities* – has also revealed that trust is also situationally and relationally contingent in contemporary western cultures (Lindgren et al. 2020; Pink et al. 2019). While familiarity with a self-driving car and with the situations in which one experiences it means that a driver's confidence and knowledge about the car grows over time, this does not mean that their trust in the machine correspondingly grows in exact parallel and quantity to their knowledge. Rather, trust evolves and changes over time and is situational and relational rather than a fixed way of being and feeling.

A theory of everyday trust

At the beginning of this chapter, I characterised trust as an anticipatory concept. Its near-future focused orientation plays out across its different mobilisations. In the trust problem, trust is required so that near-future visions and the concrete benefits that are attached to them may be realised. In the trustworthiness problem, trustworthiness is thought to bring about the trust needed for the future imaginaries scaffolded onto AI and the emerging technologies it will be embedded in might come about. Yet, when interpreted as being part of the social, cultural and experiential circumstances of life, conversely trust can be neither captured nor deployed to solve these problems. Trust is ephemeral, contingent on multiple other environmental, social and experiential elements; it is part of the ongoing flow of the everyday, where, as an anticipatory state it shapes how we slip over the edge of the present into the future.

A design anthropological theory of trust therefore flips the dominant visions articulated by trust problems and trustworthy solutions, to treat trust as an anticipatory 'feeling, or category of feeling, which describes [a particular kind of] anticipatory sensations' (Pink 2021c). As I have advanced progressively through a series of publications (see Pink 2022a), focused on how everyday trust emerges in relation to emerging technologies and data (e.g. Pink, Lanzeni & Horst 2018; Pink, Osz et al. 2021), to trust entails not a simple evidence-based rational choice, or interactional or transactional relationship with another entity, but is embodied, sensory and non-representational; an 'experience of feeling or disposition towards something' (Pink, Lanzeni & Horst 2018). As such trust is bound up with ways of knowing, incremental processes of learning and is 'a sensation often achieved through the accomplishment of mundane everyday routines' (Pink 2021c). Trust happens in movement, in activity and in the inevitable forward flow of life: 'To trust therefore is not a fixed or finished interaction between two things. Rather it is an always unfinished feeling' (Pink 2022a), just as, from a design anthropological perspective, emerging technologies cannot be understood as finished products (Pink, Fors & Gloss 2018). In this sense trust can be understood as emerging as part of the 'feeling between what we know and what we think we know', and 'a way of imagining-in-the-body, or a sensuous mode of anticipation' (Pink 2021c).

This design anthropological approximation, building on the concepts of emergence, contingency and improvisation, enables us to rethink the meaning of trust, as an anticipatory, processual concept, which contests and elaborates definitions of trust and trustworthiness critiqued in the previous sections. It emphasises the shifting nature of trust, and its emergence from the contingent circumstances of the everyday, as opposed to its being a fixed quality of a relationship which can be extracted from its everyday site and commodified. This invokes a new question about the relationship between trust and other concepts. Whereas, as outlined above, in techno-solutionist narratives trust has been set within binary and causal relations to other concepts, a design anthropological approach sets up the relationship between trust and other concepts differently. By asking ethnographically what other feelings emerge relationally to trust in everyday experience we can work from the ground up to create the categories that best serve the anticipatory states that characterise people's (diverse) experiences with technology. One example involves how the ethnographically inspired sister concept, anxiety, has enabled me to contextualise and understand how trust comes about as emerging technologies become part of the everyday, how the feelings associated with trust are sustained in everyday life, and how they shift. This pairing of concepts does not imply a generalised casualty between them but is a practical theoretical methodological and empirical device. I follow this discussion through the ethnographic examples in the chapters *mobilities, home* and *work*.

In my work with Debora Lanzeni (Pink, Lanzeni & Horst 2018), trust and anxiety have been used to stand for moving sets of feelings rather than static states.

Ethnographic research, undertaken in Barcelona, Spain and Melbourne, Australia, revealed how trust becomes evident as generated through the everyday routines of storing and moving data that tech developers and designers as well as other professionals engaged in as part of their everyday work practice. In our study of data anxieties, things almost never went wrong, so anxiety was hard to see, but trust was evident in the routines. In the studies outlined in chapters *mobilities, home* and *work*, these relationships between trust and anxiety configure differently. For instance, in chapter *mobilities* we see how the concept of anxiety as a barrier to the trust, acceptance and adoption of electric cars becomes a straw person as it is dispersed by the real concerns and priorities of the everyday, as exemplified in the case of electric cars. Just as an interrogation of trust to redefine it as an everyday affair dissolves the 'trust problem', reworking anxiety has a similar effect. In chapter *home*, by way of contrast, we learn about how when seniors started to use smart home technologies, they expressed a series of anxieties which they worked through. And in chapter *work*, in the dramatic changes of circumstances which occurred in the COVID-19 pandemic in the UK, we see how social workers suffered professional anxiety that became relational to how they improvised to make digital technologies and communications part of their routine work practices. The growing feelings of trust that their integration of new technologies into their work practices ultimately engendered, was not because they considered the technologies trustworthy but because they came to trust in their own professional capacities of judgement in a new technological environment.

Collectively, these examples indicate that people do not trust because they feel confident in emerging technologies or systems. Rather, they trust in circumstances and situations. We do not trust things because they are familiar, but because we make things part of routines and relationships that feel familiar. Trust is always conditional, but not simply on an evaluation of the evidence about if a particular technology or system is trustworthy, rather because it shifts and changes with the contingent and messy ways in which life goes forward.

Future trust

When trust is treated as extractable, quantifiable, a commodity, it is also aligned with the capitalist and colonising underpinnings of western science and engineering. This is hardly surprising when we view emerging technologies from a decolonising perspective. Writing from the position of indigenous Australia, Angie Abdilla argues that with their 'imperialist roots, modern technologies are far from culturally neutral' and that western technology design and development is mainly 'predicated upon the logic of extractive colonialism' which depletes the environment of its natural resources in its quest to 'dominate worldwide economic markets' (Abdilla 2018: 75). Extractive approaches to trust follow a similar path.

We need to reclaim trust, and to refigure trust and trustworthiness problems and solutions towards new shared categories. Trust is a common concept and is crucial to the question of what we might see from and how we might step over from the edge of the future. But it is differently mobilised across different disciplines and stakeholders in the emerging technologies field. The shared terminology however offers not only a space for the critique and contestation which this chapter demonstrates and participates in. It also invites us to consider trust and trustworthiness as meeting points, as domains in which we might engage with the ethical questions attached to emerging technologies and futures. The design anthropological definition of trust I have outlined complicates the linear futures narratives associated with existing approaches to trust and trustworthiness in emerging technologies and proposes a realistic and ethical mode of moving forward with trust.

HOPE

Emerging technologies are entangled with hope in multiple ways. Hype or hope rhetoric is splashed across the titles of publications internationally from consultancies, academia, practice fields and popular media, and it encapsulates the uncertainties and doubts associated with the promise of technological solutions involving artificial intelligence, (AI) automated decision-making (ADM) or machine learning (ML). For instance, in the case of AI: *Forbes* has asked: 'AI And ML: Greatest Hype Or Hope?' (Curry 2019, April 2); a *BBC News* piece focuses on 'Artificial intelligence – hype, hope and fear' (Cellan-Jones 2017, October 16); the Humanitarian Practice Network's report is titled 'Humanitarian AI. The hype, the hope and the future' (Spencer 2021, September); and a *Lancet* article asks 'AI-augmented multidisciplinary teams: hype or hope?' (Di Ieva 2019).

The underbelly of the hope invested in AI is the possible harm associated with it. There is much concern about AI hype in the healthcare field, where both hope and harm take on particular dimensions. The many examples include the United States' National Academy of Medicine's publication 'Artificial Intelligence in Health Care: The Hope, the Hype, the Promise, the Peril' (Matheny et al. 2019). In *The Conversation*, Nicholas Davis and Aleksandar Subic write that 'Hope and fear surround emerging technologies'. What role does this hope and fear play in the stories through which emerging technologies become and are imagined as part of our futures? With a focus on Australia, Davis and Subic conclude that 'Governing emerging technologies is as much a moral and political task as a technocratic challenge', they argue that 'all Australians need to be involved in discussing what we want from technology, and helping to design the institutions that can help us avoid costs we're not willing to bear as a society' (Davis & Subic 2018).

Hope in emerging technologies is a complex field. It heralds the benefits such technologies are supposed to have in society, while it augments the perception of risk and harm, and raises societal questions about how to mitigate risk. This is a

DOI: 10.4324/9781003182528-4

familiar pattern of identifying risk and seeking modes of governance, structures, processes or ways forward through which to evade it. Yet, what is exciting about reading this field as it emerges, in pieces such as those cited above, is the degree to which people as diverse as engineers, journalists, the consultancies, health care and humanitarian experts, to name just a few, are not necessarily going along with the hype. And they are moreover reflexively considering alternative ways forward.

There is evidence of a move towards rejecting what I call the 'hope solution', an ironic and critical label which sits alongside the 'trust problem' discussed in chapter *trust*. The 'hope solution' highlights the role of hype and hope built on the anticipatory infrastructures of AI and ADM. In chapters *emerging technologies* and *futures*, I discuss how hype is integral to the ways emerging technologies are represented in news and business media, and how the expectations associated with them go on to fuel research agenda and funding. With this, the hope that emerging technologies will solve societal and environmental problems underpins the visions of futures that accompany the hype. However, I argue, there are limits to the future visions which provide us with technological 'hope solutions', and there is a need for new design anthropological understandings which can contribute constructive complications to the emerging technology futures that are hoped for. If AI and ADM make it possible for certain futures to be imagined (chapter *emerging technologies*) then they also make possible the hope that is associated with those futures. But alongside the hope there is also fear, or at least an awareness that promises or solutions based on hope frequently require some re-thinking. While this does not yet mean that the dissolution of technological solutionism is in progress, it does invite us to ask what the place of hope is in relation to emerging technologies. What is it to hope? And what kind(s) of hope might be grown as alternatives to the 'hope solution'?

One option involves exploring how emerging technologies may be implicated in new hopes for new generations – anthropologist Tim Ingold suggests 'Imagining the world as a plenum, … affords a way of thinking about democracy and citizenship that could give hope to future generations'. Ingold laments such a way of thinking has been marginalised by 'the relentless expansion of big science, aided and abetted by state actors and multinational corporations'. He proposes we start by asking 'how *ought* we to live?' But, he determines, 'Big science is not interested in this question because it believes it can already deliver the answer – or if not already, then in a future within its sights. But it has no answer for what lies beyond its predictive horizons' (Ingold 2021: 336). Thus, writing against prediction, Ingold's work suggests a focus on a different kind of hope to that which is promoted in the promise of what he calls big science – towards instead a mode of hope which stems from what is incrementally learned and knowable through our everyday attention to the ecologies of which we are part.

Switching the way we think about hope in this way invites us to question a world where the future is constituted by targets, predictions and false promises. It suggests accruing hope through the journey rather than investing it in the end point. In doing so it questions the hopes that are presented to us in dominant narratives and invites us to take an approach with full care (not just be careful) about what we hope for. Anthropological discussions of hope thus contribute a sensitivity to the plural, processual and indeterminate character of hope. They are often based in ethnographically rich and detailed stories of how hope emerges, is experienced in the everyday lives of individuals and collectives, supported by a theoretical literature about the concept of hope, its history and its potential.

Anthropologies of hope invite us to study hope in the everyday, to ask how emerging technology futures move forward with hope, as part of everyday anticipation in Rebecca Bryant and Daniel Knight's sense (2019). However, they also inspire consideration of how hope might be mobilised. Hirokazu Miyazaki's proposal of 'hope as method' (2004) has explored how hope could become a site for interplay of 'commonality and difference across academic and nonacademic forms of knowledge' (Miyazaki 2006: 149). Here I also propose we engage hope methodologically, but not only as a technique for investigation, but through a further lens, as an interventional category – or concept-metaphor (Moore 2004) – for engagement. How might a processual, everyday concept of hope be reconditioned as part of an interventional practice for our current times of 'crisis'?

Hope as a concept

The concept of hope has long been discussed in the social sciences – from Ernst Bloch's enduringly influential three-volume work, *The Principle of Hope* (1995 [1954, 1955, 1959]), to include the ensuing work of Vincent Crapanzano (2003), Hirokazu Miyazaki (2004, 2006), Nauja Kleist and Stef Jansen (2016), Rebecca Bryant and Daniel Knight (2019) and Tia DeNora (2021). It is wide ranging, in terms of where it is found, and the effects that are attributed to it. My interest in hope is ultimately related to its potential for understanding and intervention in the field of emerging technologies. This requires not only determining what hope is, but moreover, working out how to attend to its relationality to other analytical concepts, and to other empirical experiences and activities.

The first layer of interest concerns how future hopes are generated through and in relation to the future visions of technological solutionism. Here, narratives of hope are pinned on predictions that technology will impact society in particular ways and built on the promise of the capacity of AI, ADM or ML to be able to deliver such effects through their implementation, for instance, as we see in chapters *home, work* and *mobilities*. These kinds of hopes depend on the mobilisation of other concepts, like uncertainty, trust and ethics as outlined in chapters *trust, futures* and *emerging technologies*. Here, narratives of hope are situated within cycles of hype; they are likely not to fulfil their promises, in part because often these promises were unrealistic to start with, but also because they are detached from their everyday life counterparts. This leads us to consider everyday hope.

One of the tricky aspects of everyday hope – the second layer of hope I am concerned with – is that it needs to function as an analytical category which engages with the indeterminacy of the everyday but can simultaneously show hope as it evolves. For example, sociologists (e.g. DeNora 2021) and sociologically oriented anthropologists (e.g. Bryant & Knight 2019) regard hope as a practice. Embodied as a practice, hope is made visible, we might study how it has been performed and sustained historically, and what its effects are on action and social change. However, in real everyday life hope is rarely isolated as a practice in itself, but rather, emerges relationally to other sentiments, sensations, activities and materialities. Therefore, the definition of hope as a practice performs well academically but is limited as an interventional methodology. Anthropologist Stef Jansen distinguishes analytically between hopefulness and hopes, whereby hopefulness is defined as an affect, and is relational to its negative of hopelessness and hope refers to how 'people who hope for something or hope that something will occur' (Jansen 2016: 499). This is also a useful definition, but, taking it from the abstract into everyday situations, we must also remember that hope and hopes can be mutually contingent. They are also inseparable from other things and processes in the everyday. For example, in the documentary *Laundry Lives* (Pink & Astari 2015), one of the participants, Adi, spoke of his commitments to environmental sustainability and feminism. His home had an area for drying clothes that permitted the family to sun-dry their clothes under a glass ceiling, and he had purposefully taken on traditionally feminine gendered household tasks while he studied and his wife worked. He lived life in a way that might be defined as hopeful in that his everyday activities and sentiments worked towards a particular future in a practical way – a kind of practical intervention, which questioned the gendered activities and commentaries of his neighbours. In terms of his relationship with technology we might understand this as a way of creatively participating in the emergence of the washing machine as a gendered technology, and through and towards gendered equalities, and of creatively making sustainable drying technologies come into being. Yet this was inseparable from his hopes for the future, in relation to which he explained his priorities for a further future, which held hopes for specific achievements. What was striking about Adi's and other participants' discussions of the future is that while our research had focused specifically on technology and sustainability, these became subsidiary to their hopes for the future, which tended to centre on hopes for their children: Adi wished that his daughter would get a PhD. Everyday hope is therefore both performed, constituted and projected as life goes forward.

Analytically everyday hope is also constituted in relation to its sister concepts of uncertainty and trust, as they are similarly part of the everyday. That is, if uncertainty is an ongoing and inevitable state, and trust is the feeling by which we confidently move forward into as yet unknown futures, then hope is the sense through which we anticipate or sense specific possibilities both as they are carried forward by our everyday actions that can open us up to hope for them, and as we contemplate particular possible future goals. This conceptualisation of hope is indeterminate. Hope, like trust, is always emergent from and contingent on the circumstances in which it comes about, upon what we know and sense. A theory of everyday hope informs not just the way I understand how hope operates in everyday life, but also how I propose that hope be mobilised methodologically and through interventions.

To consider hope as an interventional category or concept – the third layer of interest – we must account for how it manifests and moves in the trajectories of life itself, where it is performed in the everyday hopefulness, and embodied in future hopes of the same lives. This layer of hope is likewise indeterminate and ongoingly emergent within the circumstances of the everyday, as for trust, in chapter *trust*.

How can everyday hope become better connected to the worlds where hope and hype are both generated and doubted? Can shared, realistic and ethical modes of hope be generated?

Hope in uncertain worlds

The study of hope offers us a chance to consider how emerging technologies both become the stimulus for stories of hope and get entangled with hopeful narratives that are already in motion. Uncertainty is, I argue in chapter *futures*, a characteristic of life, it is an inevitable companion to the contingency of the circumstances in which life is played out, although often made invisible, or mitigated against through regulation. Although feelings of uncertainty can shift, be temporarily dissolved, muffled or made comfortable through feelings of trust or ontological security constituted through everyday circumstances and activities as outlined in chapter *trust*, uncertainty does not go away. Our response to uncertainty needs to be creative, improvisatory, in situations where we cannot suppress it (or at least not in any permanent way) we need instead to embrace and harness uncertainty as a route towards generating possibility (Akama et al. 2018), and with that, I suggest, hope.

Unsurprisingly, studies of hope tend to usually be undertaken in or emerge from situations where uncertainty is foregrounded, materialised or visible. In their reviews of the anthropology of hope scholars have commonly found an emphasis on the relationship between hope and uncertainty in circumstances involving, political and economic crisis and conflict, or increasing inequalities (Bryant & Knight 2019; Cook 2018; Kleist & Jansen 2016), they have studied hope in the uncertain situations of senior care or proximate death (Cook 2018; DeNora 2021; Sliwinski 2016), and in the uncertain professional trajectory of financial trading (Miyazaki 2006). In fact, Kleist and Jansen propose that 'For the articulation of any hopes for different futures to be possible, there must be a degree of uncertainty, an awareness of it and a willingness to act in it'. They suggest that the relationship between hope and uncertainty is one where, 'hope as a phenomenon is characterized by simultaneous potentiality (in its broadest sense) and uncertainty of the future' (Kleist & Jansen 2016: 379). The action they associate with hope is also represented by Bryant and Knight, who argue that it 'draws the not-yet into the present and motivates activity in the here-and-now'. This hope-inspired action, they outline, might come about in situations as diverse as the promises of politicians to the playing out of football matches. It involves hope for specific outcomes, since it 'is the momentum toward realizing *particular "otherwises"'* (Bryant & Knight 2019: 157, italics added).

Julia Anne Cook's review of recent anthropological and sociological work on hope also sees uncertainty as generative of hope since 'hope does not just take root but, in fact, thrives in the context of uncertainty' (Cook 2018: 387). She also points out that the environment of not-knowing that uncertainty entails leaves hope 'vulnerable to exploitation'. Cook draws from the possibility that experimental medical treatments might be used on patients (even if unintentionally), precisely because they offer them hope. She extends this to 'the need to fully interrogate the present-day and prospective technological developments that often become emblems of hope' (Cook 2018: 387). Technologically solutionist visions and promise of emerging technologies could be seen as representatives of Bryant and Knight's (2019) 'otherwises', in the form of Cook's (2018) 'emblems of hope', hyped by industry and engineers and invested with hope for a 'better', sustainable, optimised, convenient, comfortable futures. This is why emerging technologies and the hope generated in relation to them, need to be interrogated.

Sliwinski (2016: 6–7) draws on Madeleine Reeves' concept of 'infrastructural hope', which has shown how road-building projects in Kyrgyzstan articulate the different aspirations of various stakeholders, to suggest that, likewise, building care facilities in El Salvador can generate 'affective engagement with materiality and [is] replete with promises of better futures.' (Sliwinski 2016: 431). Similarly, emerging technologies, like AI and ADM discussed in chapter *futures* (and see Pink, Dahlgren et al. 2022), themselves become anticipatory infrastructures, inviting imaginaries of further technological possibility, solutions and better lives. But, as also outlined in chapters *emerging technologies* and *futures*, in capitalist economies, emerging technologies often disappoint, fail or simply keep on emerging without satisfying the hopes or even suspending hope indefinitely as they remain poised to hit the ground. As Miyazaki (2006) has also shown, capital accumulation in the trajectory of an individual career can breed hope, after hope, as its promises dissolve. Bryant and Knight emphasise the 'futural momentum' of hope which 'attempts to pull certain potentialities into actuality' but where, 'potential is never actualized in all the ways that are possible' and subsequently breeds new hope (Bryant & Knight 2019: 134).

Examples abound, across the sites where uncertainty, technological promise or possibility and hope co-configure – in the media, in industry and government ambitions, and in everyday imaginaries. In the COVID-19 pandemic, digital solutions to tracking and tracing the pandemic have contributed to quantitatively driven cycles of hope and despair as numbers of infections and deaths grow and then thankfully wane. As air filtration and purification solutions are rolled out in schools, and their uptake in homes increases (chapter *air*) and as automated energy management systems are hyped as solutions to problems of demand and supply (chapter *energy*) and autonomous driving (AD) cars have been promised to solve a host of issues including increasing road safety, reducing carbon emissions and giving time 'back' to the busy (chapter *mobilities*). In reality, the impact of air filtration in schools on the spread of COVID-19 is still unknown, people generally are not keen on having their home energy systems controlled by external agencies, and AD cars did not fulfil their promise to be on the roads by 2020. Yet, these technologies – or rather the possibilities the idea of these technologies invoke – can be said to have generated hope in some cases. The work of Canay Özden-Schilling (2015) (see also chapter *energy*) suggested that the energy engineers amongst whom she did her fieldwork hoped that the automation of the smart grid would lead to a better balance between energy supply and demand. Families may hope schools will be safer in 2022 with air filtration units installed, and research discussed in chapter *air* showed that people hope that air filtration and purification in their homes would keep their families safer. While AD cars are not close to being ubiquitous on our roads, electric vehicles (EVs) have been on the horizon for over 100 years and are currently generating a new waves of hope across industry and in everyday life, amongst those who believe they will create a step change towards an environmentally sustainable future by helping to reduce carbon emissions.

Hope is continually configured and reconfigured. In a world where it bears an unavoidable relationship to our inevitable state of uncertainty, it is fundamental to our being, and to the way we move forward in life and the world. But when, like uncertainty (Samimian-Darash & Rabinow 2015), it is studied as a societal phenomenon, hope raises additional concerns. In a practical sense, the experience of hope is not universal in its quality or quantity, it is unequally distributed: as Cook and Hernán Cuervo emphasise, 'some individuals are afforded greater access to the conditions under which hope can be easily sustained than others, suggesting that sustained forms of hope may constitute a way in which inequalities are manifest' (2020: 1116). In the next section, I take this question further, in the context of an exploration of how hope might instead become a uniting force, sentiment and concept, in such a way that might contribute to greater equality.

Hope as a method

While conventionally, anticipatory concepts or modes of anticipation have formed the subject of study in the social sciences, they are increasingly being engaged methodologically, as modes of research. In a series of workshops and a symposium during 2014–2016, the designer Yoko Akama and I explored uncertainty as methodology, urging researchers and practitioners to take seriously the generative potential of uncertainty as demonstrated through a series of examples in which we brought together design and anthropology to create circumstances of uncertainty as a basis from which to generate new modes of possibility, beyond what would otherwise have been knowable (Akama et al. 2018). Elsewhere, and in chapter *trust*, I argue that trust might be engaged methodologically, as a concept-metaphor that resonates across disciplines, stakeholders, and everyday worlds, and therefore offers a site through which we might complicate, generate and negotiate new meanings, connections and collaborative knowing and understanding (Pink 2022a; Pink et al. 2020), and interventions.

The concept of hope offers similar possibilities, which, combined with my interest in understanding how change in which emerging technologies are implicated happens and is imagined, is why I sequence it with uncertainty and trust in this book. Miyazaki's work provides an ideal starting point. For Miyazaki, hope, as a method, 'unites different forms of knowing' (2004: 4) and is not just a way of bringing together diverse knowledges and experience; it can also perform as 'a method of radical temporal reorientation of knowledge' (2004: 5). In this sense, it has similarities with trust, as a way of sensing and knowing which is concerned with how we move forward in life and the world. In proposing that hope might be a 'methodological problem, and ultimately a method', Miyazaki differentiates hope from being a 'product or strategic moment in a language game or semiotic process' and instead insists that hope is (like uncertainty and trust) a universal characteristic of being. As he puts it, to see 'hope as a common operative in all knowledge formation', in tandem with engaging hope as a method, 'allows us to begin to confront the most fundamental problem – what knowledge is for' (2004: 9).

In Miyazaki's argument, engaging hope as method 'points to an emergent high-risk opportunity for the future of critical hope at the intersections of global capitalism and its critiques and thereby points to an exit from critique as we know it' (2006: 165). It involves a 'feminist willingness to redefine radically and imaginatively the constitution of a critique rather than defend one's own critical practices in a morally empowered manner'. By way of example, he brings together the 'hope in capitalism' revealed by a research participant who attempted to implicate Miyazaki in his own hope by starting a business with him, with the kind of hope that social theorists invest in critiques of capitalism. These points are important, since they remind us of the utility of concepts like hope, trust and uncertainty, for studying the complexities of living and imagining with possibility. Miyazaki leaves us with a cliff-hanger for a future never realised: the practical applications of this approach, or the possibilities it offers remain undiscussed. Had he entered into a business arrangement with the participant, the story might have taken a turn that we will never learn about. But what would happen if anthropologists started to get involved in the practical application of hope as a mode of participation in the world? I reflect further on this question in the following section.

Hope as intervention

Scholars in the social sciences are increasingly enthusiastic about hope as not only a method for understanding how change happens and how futures are constituted, but also as a mode of engagement beyond the academy. Alongside the interventional futures anthropology which Juan F. Salazar and I have proposed elsewhere (Pink & Salazar 2017), there is growing recognition that the 'new, or renewed, interest in hope resonates well with anthropology's recent shift towards the future' (Haug 2020: 74). This new move towards hope in scholarship, is differentiated from the kinds of hope that it has been suggested existed in the past. For instance, in 2006, Miyazaki wrote of 'social theorists' shared sense of the loss of hope in progressive politics and thought' which he considered contextualised as part of a sense that academia, the world and capitalism have changed in such a way that the 'relevance and critical edge' of social theory was also lost (Miyazaki 2006: 149). This does not mean the death of social theory. As I argue throughout this book, social theory is useful, but it does not step out of academia well unaccompanied and unmoderated by real-world engagements with life as it comes about. What this 'loss of hope' rather calls for are new ways of engaging in a world where capitalism, the innovation agenda and the technological solutionism of engineering and science dominate. One of the purposes of a design anthropology of emerging technologies is to create this new space of engagement. Following the mission and manifesto of futures anthropology (Salazar et al. 2017), how might hope become implicated in this agenda, for a radically new anthropology (and by extension a new social science) with an ambition to intervene in the world as we move forward? How might hope be mobilised in the work of an interventional design anthropology of emerging technologies which plays and ultimately collaborates in the spaces where other ways of hoping and versions of hope are mobilised?

Some would argue that hope is indeed up to this task. Anthropologist Michaela Haug seeks to 'envision an anthropology that is more hopeful about the potential it holds to counter often overwhelmingly destructive narratives and to engage in shaping less violent, less unequal and less destructive futures' (Haug 2020: 74). Haug argues that we need to account for hope because it 'can unfold such an enormous transformative potential' (Haug 2020: 87), thus implying a way forward for hope to be harnessed as a participant in engagement and intervention. Sociologist Tia DeNora sees hope as a 'technique of world-making' whereby 'we project our hopes into the world and in ways that alter those worlds and the ways they are perceived' (2021: 128). She understands 'hope as a complex form of situated practice', both visible through the study of how change happens, and which might be harnessed 'to offer resources for people coping in extremis' (DeNora 2021: ix–x). In the case DeNora discusses, this includes those who are in pain or near the end of life.

Where does such hope come from? The anthropologist Ghassan Hage highlights how in the circumstances of 'ecological crisis', human hope has been built on future vision which involves 'continually extracting from nature' (2016: 467). Resonating with Miyazaki's ambition to create modes of hope that are open to others, Hage proposes that 'one has to think about modes of imagining one's own hope with the hope of others and not at their expense' (Hage 2016: 466). He argues for a politics of '[c]o-hoping with the other', whereby the other might be another human or another species (Hage 2016: 467). Ingold similarly suggests that we might 'turn to others for what they have to teach us of knowing-in-the-world as a form of commitment, of being and letting be, and to find the ontological and ethical force of this commitment as a foundation for hope' (2021: 78). I return to these moves towards shared hope later. But first, what might interventional design anthropological hope look like empirically, at the scale of the project?

One way that hope can be brought to its interventional potential is through our engagements with people in the world. Indeed, hope can be detected as part of various of the projects I discuss across this book. For example, in the *Smart Homes for Seniors* documentary (Pink 2021), discussed in chapter *home*, we encounter participants in the later years of their lives, where one's everyday hopes might be articulated as to enjoy life and one's family. Hope was not necessarily for a personal far future, but hope as lived can become relational to emerging technologies. For example, hope was evident where participants emphasised the use of smart lights which can be voice or button activated in advance of getting up in the night, to light the way ahead, and thus reduce the risk of having a fall which could lead to hospitalisation and loss of independence. Here hope is situated, as DeNora suggests, but it is not just a situated practice, in the sociological sense, but a situated feeling and way of being. At different life stages hope shifts, and as such the ways we hope with emerging technologies is likewise re-framed, because hope as a feeling is always not only indeterminate but always, like the imagination (Sneath et al. 2009), emergent from the specific circumstances in which it is found. If we centre hope as a prism through which to understand the meaning of everyday interventions with emerging technologies, we might create shared hopes, or engage hope as an affective mode of empathy. It is through experimenting with people in everyday life that hope might become materialised and experienced in and through emerging technologies, in place of hope being projected from an external source, as the promise of technological solutionism. In chapter *data*, I introduce the City Sensing Data Futures project, where shared values were identified between the city and participants, in order to propose a design for future city data and engagements with it to come about. The anthropologist Alicia Sliwinski suggests that 'when hope signifies anticipation, it is a valuative capacity, because it ascribes worth to something into which one projects one's mental energies; and second, that this capacity can bring values to the world' (2016: 437). If we then bring together what we were able to know about the hopes of participants with the hopes of the city, towards shared values, we can also identify the place of hope in the City Data Sensing project. Hope therefore participates across these layers of everyday and institutional life, as a research practice and as an interventional device.

Therefore, everyday hope can be related to specific experiences, and possibilities, but it is not necessarily fixed on a hoped-for singular static outcome with a fixed end point. Kleist and Jansen ask 'how are they [hopes] generated, distributed, negotiated, sustained and/or transformed—in other words, how do hopes themselves develop over time?' (2016: 388). Everyday hope is processual, it entails an unfolding of hope. In Miyazaki's (2006) story of the successive possibilities in which his participant pinned his professional hopes, hope is not necessarily fixed on one end, but rather hope is a way of being and living which shifts according to what opens up along the way. That is, hope, like trust, is always contingent, and flexible and ongoing. For Ingold this places hope at the centre of how we might design 'for the sustainability of everything' which requires that design is 'driven not by plans and predictions but by *hope*. With plans and predictions we can be optimistic that their realisation is just around the corner. There is light at the end of the tunnel' – as is illustrated well in the cases of EVs and AD cars discussed in chapter *mobilities*. But, Ingold continues,

> hope and optimism are not the same. The difference is that optimism antici-pates final outcomes; hope does not. The verb 'to hope' is not transitive – like 'to make' or 'to build' – but intransitive, like 'to grow' and indeed 'to live' … It denotes a process that does not begin here and end there but carries on through.
>
> *(Ingold 2021: 332)*

Here lies the difference between everyday approaches to living in and hoping to contribute to the mitigation of the climate crisis on the one hand, and on the other the ambition to, for instance, meet net zero carbon emissions by 2030 or 2050. Everyday hope is part of the flow of life, for instance, a person might hope they could make such a contribution by purchasing solar panels, charging their electric car in the morning and reducing their energy demand. But they might simulta-neously be confronted with having a medical condition that meant that to be able to sleep well at night they needed to keep the air conditioning on all night, when there was no renewable energy available. Hoping one will sleep well (a common priority as discussed in chapter *energy*) and hoping to contribute to mitigate climate change (another frequent hope) are everyday modes of hope. They are interwoven with, attributed value and representing values in relation to the material, social and other obligations and priorities of life as it plays out, and in the situation I have described, also potentially contingent on each other. They may both be related to bigger interventional agendas. For instance, the ambition to achieve net zero carbon emissions or to achieve organisational goals at work the next day. While there is a sense of alignment between for example the everyday hope to participate in mitigating climate change and the institutional hope to get to net zero, the reason why it doesn't necessarily play out is precisely because it is a matter of the ground level of processual everyday life, which has no endpoint outcomes, seeking to collaborate with the institutional level endpoint outcome of net zero. The hopes are similar, but they are not shared, because they were not born of a common category.

Hope and (the current) crisis

In her interrogation of 'crisis' as a representational device that casts history into a problem-solution narrative, rather than an empirical fact, the anthropologist Janet Roitman asks: 'what sort of narrative could be produced where meaning is not everywhere a problem?' (Roitman 2013: 95). Roitman (as do many of the scholars of hope cited above) alerts us to the modes of hope entailed in how 'Martin Luther King Jr. pronounced "I Have a Dream," reinscribing his politics in hope for the future'. Roitman's discussion leads us to the conclusion that a dream cannot be witnessed (2013: 96), and similarly hope is an orientation towards futures that is experiential, but non-determinate. It is a mode of sensing futures as open-ended possibilities, rather than as solutions to problems created by history. Thought of as such, hope is an alternative to the techno-solutionist narrative that frames dominant imaginaries about the ways emerging technologies will participate in futures. Hope might thus be seen to play a particular role in the currently defined crisis, both in the sense of breaking down the understanding of crisis as a problem needing a solution, in questioning the ability of emerging technologies to serve as engineering solutions to situations of crisis, and in enabling us to better understand how to move forward through crisis in such ways that enable technologies of hope to emerge.

That is, if the consensus is that we are in crisis, even if following Roitman, a processual theory might be *contra* to the definition of crisis, the implication is that we are in need of a fix, although notably not one that is a solution. As unfolds from the literature I discuss next, there seems to be an academic urge to repair the circumstances in which we find ourselves, and as such, a call to hope. The values that converge around this call likewise point us to hope. Turning to Stephen Jackson's speculative question: 'where might hopes operated through repair intersect with other forms of relationality and attachment that have also attracted the periodic attention of repair and STS scholars: for example, reciprocity, love, and care?' (Jackson 2019: 345). In this section I explore how we might conceptualise hope in times of perceived crisis, what kinds of interventions are being proposed to restore hope and how these might realistically proceed.

In times of crisis, one of which the current moment is frequently seen to be, hope is frequently invoked as something that is needed or has been lost. In 2016, Kleist and Jansen reported a 'hope boom in anthropological studies' which they suggested reflected the convergence of 'a sense of increasing unpredictability and crisis, and a sense of lack of political and ideological direction in this situation' (Kleist & Jansen 2016: 373). By the early years of the 2020s we have entered new realms of 'crisis', and an invigorated experience of everyday and future uncertainty. DeNora, on completing her book *Hope* (2021) in 2020, writes of the intensification of 'Global issues – climate crisis, violence, hostility, pandemics, homelessness, displacement, racism and racial hostility, economic hardship, modern slavery, loneliness, anxiety, mental illness' (2021: ix) which she argues 'underlines a global need for hope and a corresponding need to confront hope – what hope is and what can, and cannot, be achieved by hoping' (2021: ix–x). Drawing on Martin Luther King Jr's notion of 'creative protest' as embodying the action inspired by the dream, she argues that 'Creativity is … a core requirement for effecting change' (2021: x). Ingold, following the thread of his earlier work, argues convincingly that 'at the time of present crisis, with the world on a knife-edge' we need to actively participate in creating the world in such a way that unites 'creator and created in one act' (2021: 28). Since '[o]nly by restoring faith and hope in the perpetuity of beginning – or, in a word, in *creation* – can we open a real future to coming generations' (Ingold 2021: 28). To repair a world in crisis, then, we must start from the inside, creatively, carefully and hopefully weaving our way forward. Ingold's vision would heal the planet and the relations within it.

Another way to think about how hope is invested in other ways forward to those offered by capitalism is to consider how it is implicated in material politics of repair. Repair is aligned with several non-capitalist processes, including revaluing which, in particular, I have worked on with Melisa Duque (Pink, Fors et al. 2022). If we then implicate hope as a central pillar of what repair both invokes and is inspired by, the possibility of harnessing this potential creates a dynamic way forward. To some extent these points respond to the questions posed by STS scholar Jackson in his probing of the relationship between hope and repair. Jackson asks, if

> the material world shape[s] or participate[s] in hope in any way—and if so, which ways? Is there anything inherently hopeful about acts of repair? If forms of hope practiced through repair can be quietist and conservative, can they also be critical and political?
>
> *(Jackson 2019: 345)*

The short answer is 'yes'; these speculative ways forward resonate with the potential of an interventional approach to hope, as a material and political project. Yet, like Miyazaki's encounter with his financial trader participant, repair has a deep entanglement with capitalism, as my work with Juan F. Salazar and Melisa Duque, about the everyday creative, improvisatory, activist and arts practice modes of repairing and modifying banknotes (Pink, Salazar & Duque 2019), has demonstrated. Even if repair resists the notion of the emerging technology that comes out into its market as a complete and finished product ready to impact society as separate from it, empirically, the materialities through which repair and improvisation emerge are often codependent with the very paradigms they contest. This is not to say that we should abandon repair as a mode of interventional hope, but that we need to be aware that it can raise further questions relating to what such a methodology of engagement might constitute. In a time of crisis then, paired with a crisis of loss of hope, can repair – rather than a technological fix – offer a more viable way towards regenerating and invoking new modes of shared and collaborative hope?

The future of hope and emerging technologies

Hope, like trust, is an anticipatory concept, bound up with possibility and uncertainty. It is also a category that moves across fields, that invites debate and subsequently provides a ground for discussing some of the most fundamental issues relating to futures, across disciplines and stakeholders.

Here I argue for a definition of hope that can be used relationally with the other future-focused concepts discussed in this book. For example, hope refers to a further possible future than trust, and as a concept can be mobilised as a prism through which to examine and compare how people imagine far futures in which they would feel comfortable and familiar and the places of emerging technologies in these possible worlds. How can hope best be mobilised towards making ethical and responsible futures?

We need to better bring the hope that emerges from everyday worlds in crisis to the processes through which solutions to crisis are thought. By understanding hope as lived, rather than as an end point, unlikely to be reached in the way it is imagined, we can better surface and engage with the contingencies that make things play out in the way that they do. Everyday hope creates and generates paths forwards, hope in the form of future promises or end points can only be lost. As we, as societies, embark on ambitious programmes to avert the climate crisis and other issues of planetary and public health that are associated with it, we should not hope that technological innovation will provide solutions. Rather, when, for instance, pursuing ambitions like transitions to decarbonisation or to net zero emissions by 2030, 2050 or other target dates, we should immerse ourselves in everyday worlds with the people for whom automated systems and renewable energy technologies and devices need to become meaningful and part of everyday hope (see chapters *air* and *energy*). It is only by bringing together societal and institutional hopes with everyday hope and the values that are connected to it that we can create a shared story, and hopeful trajectory forward, by making hope a common category and experience, uniting and moderating the different scales and temporalities of change that can be hoped for.

DATA

Digital data, sensor technologies, and predictive analytics have rapidly become entangled in everyday worlds and lives, as we individually and societally anticipate our own and environmental futures. In a continuous flow of research, news and everyday experience data have become bound up with our identities, our relations to others and to the environment and with societal relations of power and inequality. It would be impossible to write of emerging technologies without acknowledging the place of data in their conceptualisation, purpose, use and possible futures. This chapter is a call to go beyond the study of data, towards a social science *with* data futures.

In the middle the 2010s, I created the Data Ethnographies Lab, an international group of researchers and scholars who met across Australia and Denmark over a period of about 18 months to present, discuss and debate the relationship between big data and ethnography, and to produce rapid position papers designed to respect and share the collective knowledge each meeting created, short videos, such as Robert Willim's (2016) *Broken data: broken world*, and journal articles (Dourish & Gomez 2018; Pink, Ruckenstein et al. 2018) based on the events. Our work had a unique momentum, as we called for attention to the experiential materialities and sensations of data through ethnographic practice.

As the data hype receded, my focus increasingly incorporated anticipatory technologies such as automated decision-making (ADM), Artificial Intelligence (AI) and Machine learning (ML), for all of which digital data are of course indispensable. This has required a new turn in the study of data, to understand it as embedded in layered realities and future imaginaries of everyday life, citizen scientists (like the air quality data collectors discussed in chapter *air*) and activists and advocacy groups (like AlgorithmWatch, discussed in chapter *emerging technologies*, and the feminist data manifesto discussed below), in the professional lives of data scientists and in the agendas of those powerful institutions who wish to engage

DOI: 10.4324/9781003182528-5

with it for purposes of governance or monetisation, or both. This chapter picks up a similar impulse to that which drove the data ethnographies initiative to bring ethnography to big data: to ensure the everyday is attended to in data futures.

Data futures are notably prominent in recent research endeavours, organisations and approaches, in mainstream corporate and academic initiatives such as Mozilla Foundation's Data Futures Lab (https://foundation.mozilla.org/en/data-futures-lab/), or Monash University's Data Futures Institute (www.monash.edu/data-futures-institute), and in the critical fields of 'Afro Feminist Data Futures' (Iyer et al. 2010) and 'Data Design Futures' (Noortman 2021). Uses of digital data in predictive analytics are as diverse as the organisations, individuals and power relations and inequalities in which they are embedded. In a much-discussed case, the critical work of social scientists, reveals how uses of digital data to profile people and places in 'predictive policing and anticipatory governance' can lead to, and that may 'reinforce or create stigma and harm, particularly when the underlying data or models are poor' (Kitchin 2021: 212). New research globally uses data to understand where risk lies and how we should make decisions for human and planetary futures. For example, in 2021, the technical University of Munich reported on research that collects forest data – the 'Forest Condition Monitor (FCM)' is 'an open-access web-based information tool [which] uses remote sensing data for color-coded visualization of the greenness of European forests' in order to identify areas under stress and alert the owners of forests about 'potential risks' (Technical University of Munich 2021, December 10); while a group at MIT used machine learning to work with limited data sets in order to create a predictive model to help 'physicians select the least risky treatments in urgent situations, such as treating sepsis' (Zewe 2021, December 9). Data are implicated in societies and practices that centre risk mitigation in multiple ways, including to mitigate risks to data itself. A. R.E Taylor's research in a Northern England data centre shows how the materiality of the bunker is used in the marketing and selling of '"future-proof" data security' (Taylor 2021: 77). This anticipatory action mitigates uncertainty through, for instance, 'pre-emptive upgrading' (Taylor 2021: 90). Meanwhile in the business world, the consultancies encourage companies to engage with their data. For instance, for ARUP, 'Whatever the organisational goal, data are increasingly at the centre of the relationship between users, assets, services and investors' (Buscher n.d.); KPMG emphasises 'the value of treating your data as an asset' (Covington 2021, October 11); McKinsey & Co recommends '[t]he future of superior customer-experience performance is moving to data-driven, predictive systems, and competitive advantages are in store for companies that can better understand what their customers want and need' (McKinsey & Co. 2021, February 24). These different strands of environmental, humanitarian, organisational, business and everyday data futures are inevitably interdependent.

Like air and energy, data are also an inevitable part of the infrastructure of the everyday and are implicated in the anticipatory modes through which we move forward to the immediate future, and in our hopes and desires for far futures. Personal data are also implicated in how people move forward through everyday environments (Pink & Fors 2017a), in how we trust and hope, and in the anxieties we experience (Pink, Lanzeni & Horst 2018). The datafication of everyday activities and environments themselves increase, at home, at work, as we plan our travel (see Pink, Berg et al. 2022). Smart home technologies can use data collected in homes in machine learning to predict household needs, Mobility as a Service (MaaS) applications require data for recommender systems to suggest routes to travellers, data-driven workplace recruitment and employee monitoring and recommendation systems have come under much media and academic scrutiny and criticism. People are also starting to take for granted that data are part of everyday life, to understand how it might be useful for them, how they might like it to be used and where they draw the line. For instance, in chapter *air*, I discuss how participants easily imagined that air quality data might become part of the way they make anticipatory data-informed decisions regarding how to keep their families safe from contaminated air. Yet, such knowledge and understanding of access to and the power to control data collection and use is unequally distributed, and this point must always underpin the optimism that possible data futures can hold. We now need to account for how data are lived, engaged and imagined in the everyday, how they participate in the processes through which emerging technologies come about in everyday life and people engage with them in relation to automation. Data, rather than being an independent force which impacts on our lives, are rather situated in a more complex relation to everyday realities and possible futures.

Approaching data as data futures means putting the predictive and anticipatory modes through which data are conceptualised, analysed and experienced at the centre of the analysis. Much significant academic data futures research remains in disciplinary silos, as scholars focus on what data futures mean for their disciplines. The anthropologists Rachel Douglas-Jones, Antonia Walford and Nick Seaver have argued that anthropologists should treat digital data as 'an emergent ethnographic object' to be studied (2021: 9). We need to go further and take the step of bringing together the ways that data are implicated in futures, in the sociotechnical imaginaries and hope of dominant narratives, in the responses and reworkings of critical data scholars, in the work of data scientists and in everyday worlds. We must ask how these futures are connected, where they are and are not aligned, the ways in which they complicate each other and how alternative, collective, data futures might be generated.

Data studies

Data have long since played a key role in society and culture, but as Rob Kitchin expresses it in his *Data Revolution* (2021: 3) 'their production and nature has been transformed through a set of disruptive innovations, including networked digital infrastructures, pervasive and ubiquitous computing, cloud services and open government', leading to a 'profound datafication of the everyday'. Datafication, which involves the quantification of anything into digital data (Cukier & Mayer-Schoenberger 2013) has been extensively studied and has become a mundane and increasingly invisible element across diverse sites of our societal, institutional, everyday and personal experience. Social science and humanities scholars have assembled a vast and often critical literature about how digital data are implicated in everyday experiences, practices, power relations and future visions (see Kitchin 2021). Over these years, scholars in critical data studies (Iliadis & Russo, 2016) established a solid set of principles surrounding definitions, ethics and dominant narratives. Their work emphasises that data are not an objectively existing thing or truth or fact, but always situated and emergent from specific moments and circumstances (see Baym 2013; boyd & Crawford 2012; Markham 2013; Nafus, 2014), and underpins contemporary approaches to data in design and anthropology. As Yanni Alexander Loukissas (2019) has argued, designers would do well to acknowledge that data are 'local'; and an 'anthropology of data provides ethnographic thickness and sited-ness to counter data's ideologies of objectivity' (Douglas-Jones et al. 2021: 20).

The ways in which data are part of life, and their significance in data studies continues to shift. Whereas big data was itself a strong focus just a few years ago, as social scientists and businesses alike sought to understand their possibilities and ethics. Since then they have been increasingly situated in relation to emerging technologies, as part of an evolving ecology of technological promise. For instance, Madeleine Clare Elish and danah boyd trace how surrounded by hype, big data became prominent around 2010 to then be re-situated in relation to emerging technology hype, whereby by 'late 2015' they write, 'technology companies that were once seen as being at the forefront of Big Data began rebranding their efforts as "AI"' (2018: 60). Over the last decade, the growth of big data and dynamic and predictive data analytics, connected with automated decision-making (ADM), artificial intelligence (AI), and machine learning (ML), has kept it at the forefront of the concerns of the consultancies, business and government.

In the first years of the 2020s, predictive uses of digital data are increasingly dominant. Data are bound up with sociotechnical imaginaries of emerging technologies in a number of layers. They are an institutional resource that underpins predictive methods envisioning or modelling futures and imagining how futures might be automated. They are also, moreover, not simply a resource used by emerging technologies such as ADM, AI and ML, but participate in creating the predictive models which anticipate the future worlds in which emerging technologies are designed to generate markets. As I stressed earlier, data futures have become a central interest. But how might we understand such imaginaries? Elish and boyd's work suggests we should be concerned, or at least cautious, since 'part of what makes the phenomena of Big Data and AI so compelling is the hyped imagination of what is possible, not what is realistic' they argue that 'this slippage ... produces an epistemological hazard and that requires concerted attention to the methods of data science and machine learning' (Elish & boyd 2018: 58). What then are the implications of data being engaged as a resource for prediction? What does this mean in everyday worlds? What does a design anthropology of emerging technologies tell us about data? And might interdisciplinary data futures research and interventions be created?

Refiguring data and futures narratives

Data itself is not predictive. Yet emerging technologies are entangled with predictive modes of understanding society and the impact that technology is expected to have on it. Societal structures and processes designed to remove uncertainties from view and mitigate risk, engage data as part of the urge to be able to know, prepare for and preempt the unknowable. When data becomes part of an ever-growing audit culture (discussed in chapters *futures* and *hope*), seeking to account not only for the past and present, but also for future events, activities and even feelings, data analytics is mobilised as a predictive technology, and data in all its incompleteness and unfinishedness becomes the resource that it needs.

How might social scientists best engage with such narratives, which are often converse to a design anthropological understanding of a processual and ongoingly emergent world? In refocusing the temporality of how we engage with data from the social sciences, we need to create an anthropology *with* rather than simply *of* data. As Hannah Knox (2021b) has suggested, modes of hacking inspired by everyday data practices can be effectively engaged to hack a more open mode of understanding in anthropology (see chapter *emerging technologies*). Here, I also wish to modify anthropology – and by implication the social sciences more broadly – but differently, by taking seriously the predictive, futures focused stance that data is frequently associated with and seeking ways to occupy its space.

As Rob Kitchin comments, the predictive, future-focused possibilities associated with digital data stand out: 'A key way in which value is leveraged from data are to use them to try to predict what would happen under different conditions'. He explains,

> a company might want to predict how customers will react to a particular product or campaign, or local government needs to predict how a transport infrastructure might function if a critical element is closed, or a scientist seeks to predict when a landslide might occur and under what conditions.
>
> *(Kitchin 2021: 105)*

The predictive agendas associated with data are clearly outlined and frequently returned to, throughout Kitchin's *The Data Revolution* (2021). This coupled with the anticipatory modes of everyday life within which data becomes implicated, for example in everyday self-tracking (Fors et al. 2019), in the way people store self-tracking data (Pink et al. 2018), and in how they save digital data on hard drives or other devices (Pink, Lanzeni & Horst 2018) or in how the spatial models music recommender systems which developers employ 'are essentially anticipatory for the people who make them, serving as tools for predicting the near future by turning it into the nearby' (Seaver 2021: 45), indicates that we need to take everyday data futures seriously.

Critical media scholars often focus on the dystopian ends that big data analytics and full automation might take us to. For instance, Mark Andrejevic offers a convincing analysis of what could possibly go wrong, when he outlines the logical consequences of data-driven automation when taken to the ends of its technological possibilities to propose: 'automation performs a series of dialectical reversals, transforming processes into their opposite: sociality into hermetic isolation, politics into technics, autonomy into automatism' (2020: 10). The concluding scenes of this logic are definitely worrying. But, they are only possible futures, and to make sense of the real implications of engaging data in automated systems we need to account for the creative and improvisatory ways that people live with data, that is how life actually plays out. Indeed, there are many existing cases of automated uses of data going badly wrong, in particular for instance the frequently discussed case of predictive policing reveals many of the dangers and inequities of predictive data analytics.

Yet, there is an opportunity to tell different stories, to build a new base through which to demonstrate how and where data might respectfully and ethically become implicated in social, organisational and cultural narratives. Such stories are indeed already emerging. In ethnographic work in clinical contexts, we see how data can be engaged in automated systems which support decision making, in ways that are purposefully designed to enable clinicians (Bergquist & Rollandson 2022). Tukka Lehtiniemi and Minna Ruckenstein's (2019) work with data activists in Finland demonstrates the benefits of becoming involved and engaged with data activism, rather than simply taking a critical stance towards the logics of possible data futures they came into contact with. The indigenous Australian consultancy *Old Ways New*'s Tracker Data project is another excellent example. Responding to the collection of physiological data from Australian Football League (AFL) players, the project works with the indigenous player Adam Goodes' AFL tracker data, to 'reveal the hidden dimensions of the cultural inputs though significant Adnyamathanha forms such as Adam's ancestors, the *Wirra* (tree), *Adnja* (rock), *Ngairri* (sky) and *Vari* (river bed)', 'The research and development process for this project will decompress the reductive nature of data capture by bringing to life the cultural relationships and knowledges inherent in Adam's performance as an elite Indigenous athlete and leader' (Old Ways New, n.d.). Such moves present a critical stance which demonstrates a way beyond that of the dystopian ends that critique often arrives at. It inspires a hope-full approach to considering possible data futures. We need to engage the often-unheard futures alongside, collaboratively, and resiliently with those who analyse, and command the planetary relations data have with people, other species and environment. Douglas-Jones and colleagues suggest an anthropology of data should focus on the capacity of data to make relations and to subsequently 'mould and reshape hoped-for futures' (Douglas-Jones et al. 2021: 20). Re-thinking our data metaphors is one way to do this.

Data-futures-concept-metaphors

An element of the hype of data are rooted in the terminologies used to speak and write of it. In a discussion of the use of metaphor in dominant futures narratives about the internet and data, Sally Wyatt describes how metaphors of 'clouds and water, mining and oil' have been used to refer to data, noting the mapping tendencies of cloud computing and the materialities associated with it, and the extractivist narratives that see data as a resource that can be mined (Wyatt 2021: 410) and reminds 'all of us interested in "big data" and other aspects of digitalisation not only to analyse and critique but also to consider our own words and the work they may do to imagine and create different futures' (Wyatt 2021: 411). Wyatt suggests that moving forward, we might make new uses of metaphors, since 'Metaphors, science fiction, speculation and imaginaries can reveal new thoughts or feelings to ourselves and to others and may open up new lines of theoretical enquiry, empirical investigation, technological design and political action' (2021: 413). In earlier work, anthropologist Tom Boellstorff (2012) proposed theorizing big data as 'rotted', to emphasise its complexity, contingency and sociologist Deborah Lupton (2016) coined the idea that data could be 'lively', but also become sick or die. With Minna Ruckenstein, Robert Willim and Melisa Duque (Pink et al. 2018), we suggested that data might further be seen as 'broken', emphasising a further element of its processual and incomplete character, as well as its similarities with other 'things'. These latter approaches seek to bring our definitions of data much closer to the materialities, sensations and experiences of an ongoingly emergent world.

A new interdisciplinary approach to data futures would demand attention to both the relationship of data to place noted earlier, and to the temporality of data metaphors. Beyond extractive metaphors, which by implication refer to something that can be 'captured' and traded as a resource, we might turn to processual metaphors. What happens when we see predictive data analytics as part of processes of becoming, rather than as processes of predetermining an end point? Alongside shifting the temporality of data metaphors to the future, we need to create metaphors that go beyond our own disciplinary reference points. Ultimately, what metaphors might work as interdisciplinary and inter-stakeholder concepts? Rather than using metaphors to stake our claims or to critique others' claims or uses of data, what if there were shared metaphors, like Henrietta Moore's (2004) concept metaphors, through which the meanings, uses and interventions of data could be made transparent, debated, constituted and collaborated in?

In the next two sections, I discuss examples of two possible data futures metaphors – values and improvisation – which bring together different arrangements and layers of stakeholders and ways of knowing. Each metaphor constitutes an experiment in understanding how data-futures-concept-metaphors might work as practical devices for collaboration and how they might specifically refer to futures. Each has been selected on two counts. First, it can be engaged as a data *futures* metaphor on the basis of theoretical understanding of it as a processual and interdeterminiate concept, and, second, because it has become apparent as a practical framing concept in existing projects. Therefore, rather than elaborating on metaphors through a discussion of a series of ethnographic sites, I instead draw together different, usually collaborative projects, to show a trajectory through which each data-futures-concept metaphor (concept for short) came about. The concepts presented here are examples, rather than being a priority or exhaustive list. Indeed, the concepts that are most relevant will always be situated and emerge in relation to specific sites.

Data improvisation

As a future-focused concept, improvisation concerns how we move forward, between the present moment and what might happen next. It offers us a way to comprehend how life at the edge of the future is constituted and experienced. It is related to the concept of trust (chapter *trust*) and is discussed with reference to trust in chapter *work*, as I describe how social workers were able to move forward through improvisatory practices with smart phones as they shifted to digital work during the COVID-19 pandemic. The anthropologist Tim Ingold writes of the 'improvisation of making-in-doing' as the 'wellspring of renewal rather than the brandmark of novelty' (Ingold 2021: 224). Ingold is discussing the transformation of materials, but the same point can be applied to the ways that people improvise with data. It involves what Ingold sees as a kind of ecological thinking, which happens 'not inside-the-head but in-the-world' (2021: 225). The concept of data improvisation is specifically intended to refer to data as improvisation as much as it means improvising with data, in that I am concerned with how data are part of improvisatory modes of living and being, rather than being the object of an improvisatory action. It is interesting to think of data in this way, because it is precisely in the everyday world that personal data becomes connected to what it is around it, rather than being extracted from the sites at which it was created. As such, our data improvisation not only plays a part in how we move forward in life, but it also generates meaning, and value (discussed next). Uses of personal data can correspondingly be implicated in the practices of hope, discussed in chapter *hope*, whereby our engagements with personal data animate the ways we move forward in life, as we go. It is a feeling and a way of being through which values surface.

In chapters *air* and *energy* respectively, I discuss the datafication of air and energy – two of the essential elements of our everyday environments, and in the agendas of innovation paradigms, two resources that are indispensable for sustaining a paradigm of technological solutionism, as well as the STEM research endeavours that support it. In these examples, data have become closely bound up with fundamental elements of our existence, air, energy and even our self-identities become visible through data. My discussions of energy and air data focus on the environment of the home, and below I focus on city data and public space. In each of these contexts people often consider their data to be 'personal' – for instance, people may consider city data about them to be 'theirs' even though they are not the legal owners of it, and in the project discussed in chapter *air* a participant felt that data about the air and possible presence of airborne viruses in their home was too personal to share. Significantly, when people consider data to be 'theirs' they also have ideas about how to use data, and, when they have access to it, they do so in improvisatory ways that make data meaningful and useful to them as they go about their lives and in relation to their priorities.

The example of personal data generated through the use of self-tracking and body monitoring technologies shows very well how data are entangled with the improvisatory modes of everyday living. There is a massive field of social science scholarship around personal data (see Lupton 2016), discussed elsewhere (Fors et al. 2019), and here I focus very specifically on what a design anthropological approach to understanding personal data as entangled in the anticipatory and improvisatory modes of the everyday suggests regarding data futures. Vaike Fors, Martin Berg, Tom O'Dell and I discuss improvisation around personal data in our book *Imagining Personal Data* (Fors et al. 2019). We were concerned (amongst other things) 'with the contingencies of everyday life, the individual modes of improvisation that give meaning to our uses of technology and the feelings that are part of these configurations' (2019: 23), drawn from our ethnographies of the ways that self-tracking came about in everyday life, as well as in the trajectories of technology design and engineering. As a critical response to the 'self improvement narrative' which was identified as part of the dominant visions of the societal benefits to be accrued from the collection and use of personal self-tracking data, we explored instead everyday self trackers, as well as the inventors of self-tracking systems or devices. We did fieldwork in everyday life situations with people who use self-tracking devices, undertook our own autoethnographies with the devices and engaged with members of the quantified self movement. I interviewed Chris Dancy (whose smart home technology project is discussed in chapter *home*) and Kourosh Kalantar–Zadeh, an engineer who invented a gas-sensing ingestible capsule which produces data from inside the gut, and is likely to gain a large global market, and my colleagues Vaike Fors and Martin Berg did research with self-tracking technology developers as well as biohackers.

What became clear from this research is that the self-improvement narrative did not always play out in the everyday life situations where we encountered self-trackers, but rather people frequently improvised to create and use personal data in ways that were meaningful to them, on an everyday basis. We found improvisation and repair everywhere. Participants used the devices in novel ways to produce data that they were not designed to collect. Often their priority was not to collect objective data about their bodies, but to create data that participated in their everyday narratives. For instance, David, one participant whom I interviewed, put his wristband in his pocket rather than wearing it on his wrist when he was cycling. This meant that he would be able to generate 'steps' data when cycling, so that he could accrue steps for his exercise, in circumstances where his cycling data would not be added to his step count. It didn't matter that the steps counted were not steps. It also didn't matter if he 'trusted' the data in a transactional sense. What was important was the meaning, the everyday hope – the sense through which we anticipate specific possibilities which lie further ahead (discussed in chapter *hope*) – that was associated with the practice of creating and collecting data and the ways of knowing about his exercise and body it offered.

Although the gas-sensing capsule mentioned above was intended for medical and diagnostic applications, in my interview with Kourosh, the engineer (Fors et al. 2019: 135–136), he described its everyday future as much more open, as a gateway to knowing about our bodies: 'It's like googling yourself all the time, you are addicted for instance all the time to googling … Just imagine if it's about you and your body'. That is, the meanings and uses of data do not have to have any end point as they might in predictive stances. Rather they can be open to come about, and in emerging in this way, bringing new ways of knowing, and as such modes of hope and inspiration. In other research, Minna Ruckenstein has shown how data scientists work with data, how they are 'repaired' where they are incomplete and damaged (Pink et al. 2018) so that they can be used in data analytics. Again, we can see these data practices as practices of hope; work with data with the end of producing meaning with it in mind.

Across these contexts we can see how data emerge and become meaningful through improvisatory processes. Technologies that were designed to collect data in one way are used in another. A technology that has been developed and was intended to be marketed with a particular use in mind is thought of by its inventor as being open to other uses, which might come about as people discover its potential in relation to their own interests. Improvisation is also at the core of designing in uncertainty (Akama et al. 2018: 35). Data improvisation as a concept helps us both understand how data are co-implicated in the way that people move through the inevitable uncertainty of everyday life (see chapter *futures*). Living with data, working with data, and designing devices or services that data are part of is always uncertain and this means that data improvisation is the way that we move forward in life with data.

Data-values

The concept of value has resonated through my collaborative research about emerging technologies and futures. My work with Debora Lanzeni and Melisa Duque (Lanzeni & Pink 2021; Pink, Fors et al. 2022; Pink & Lanzeni 2018; Pink, Salazar & Duque 2019) in particular has directed me towards the concepts of value and values. Here I propose the concept metaphor of data-values as a way to encounter value of and values as part of the anticipatory modes through which data becomes part of life, in its predictive capacities and in the constitution of imaginaries of the future everyday.

The anthropologist David Graebner's consideration of value and values is a perfect starting point. Graebner sought the connections between these concepts, while noting that the former tends to refer to the commodity or market value of a finished product or service, and the latter foregrounds 'what is ultimately important in life'. For the purposes of the discussion here: value might be attributed to an AD car or a digital voice assistant, as commodities in present or imagined future markets; while values might entail feelings and experiences of trust, safety, and care. The way that Graebner connects value and values is to seek out the 'hidden level where both come down to the same thing'. Graebner explains this with reference to the example of commoditised labour and housework as labour (Graebner 2013: 224). With reference to emerging technologies, we might think of this in terms of the purchase and use of a digital voice assistant which has commodity value, in relation to the 'digital housekeeping' (Tolmie et al. 2007) through which people manage and use emerging technologies in the home, in this case, both are services. In existing work, Grabener's distinction has proved useful methodologically to develop a design ethnographic approach to revaluing (Pink, Fors et al. 2022), precisely because the concept of value/values enables us to make visible and intervene at the sites where market value or institutional agendas to create value and everyday values come into play. Neither values nor value are end points, but they are processual concepts and states of affairs, thus suited to being data futures metaphors.

Data have increasingly become understood as a digital asset. Its commodity value is clear in existing uses of data in predictive analytics in commercial contexts discussed above, where data are bought and sold and as Mark Andrejevic (2020: 2) put it, automated media 'anticipate the automation of subjectivity' in the form of 'for example, the familiar promise of data-driven target marketing: that with enough information, marketers can fulfill our needs and desires before we experience them'. As explored with Debora Lanzeni, data are also implicated in how tech designers and developers anticipate possible future markets and the anticipatory modes through which people store and save data on an everyday basis (Lanzeni & Pink 2021). This anticipatory stance is similarly found in larger institutional approaches to data storage, where Taylor reports that 'with bunkers being rebranded as "future-proof" cloud storage sites, their material, affective, and temporal intensities are being directed towards securing the future of digital data' (Taylor 2021: 77). In this sense, data have become a commodity not only for what it enables organisations and individuals to know now, but because it has potential to generate value in and for unknown futures, and because the very ways in which it is stored are part of risk mitigation strategies, relating to ensuring that the data itself is not lost. Other future-focused data initiatives reveal alternative modes of rethinking data futures, including for example initiatives like Earth's Black Box, which has been launched in Tasmania to collect data and document the process as the planet goes forward towards climate catastrophe (www.earthsblackbox.com/).

A project developed as a collaboration between the Emerging Technologies Lab and the City of Melbourne demonstrates how connections can be mobilised in order to imagine emerging technology data futures that are underpinned by shared values. In the City Sensing Data Futures project undertaken in 2021 (Pink, Vallentine et al. 2022) the intersection between commodity value, city, climate and everyday values came into play as the research team (myself, Bianca Vallentine, Robert Lundberg, Melisa Duque, Shanti Sumartojo and Ilya Fridman), our research partners from the City of Melbourne and participants in our ethnographic research and experimentation considered how city data would be experienced and used in the future, the value it would hold for the city and people as citizens, and the values that must inform this. Our project unfolded in Argyle Square, a park in the northern part of the city, which had already been fitted with sensors to collect data about human and environmental activity including usage of park benches, temperature, bin capacity and moisture levels.

Our design ethnographic research process created a set of key shared 'core organisational and public values of: trust, privacy, transparency, open communication and care' (Pink, Vallentine et al. 2022: 4, bold removed from original). These values

> were derived from three sources: values agreed in partnership with the City of Melbourne; public values and international case studies identified in the [our previous] *Experiences and Perspectives of Urban Sensing in Melbourne* Report (Sadowski et al. 2020); and values emerging during the ethnographic research process.
>
> *(2022: 49)*

These values therefore were the meeting point between the city, the participants, the knowledge we derived from the wider literature and also represented our own values as engaged and interventional researchers. They enabled us to create a design proposal that we believed would be ethical and meaningful for the City and for citizens and which therefore also formed the basis of our interventional design proposal.

The City Sensing Data Futures project followed three stages. First the team undertook ethnographic research in the park. They interviewed participants about their experiences of the park and their feelings about present and future data sensors, and used a 'if you were a sensor' method which we collectively designed, where participants (users of the park) were invited to role-play being one of the park-based data sensors, and to show researchers where they would be located and how they would collect, use and govern their data. These materials were analysed to produce new insights about people's experiences of the park and feelings about sensors and data, and began to indicate the core values noted above. On the basis of this, our design team developed a series of digital and mocked-up cardboard prototypes, which were tested with the collaboration of our City of Melbourne partner colleagues, with public participants during a series of tours of the park's sensors during Melbourne Knowledge week.

The idea of working with values emerged and coalesced as the project evolved, and eventually values became a core concept in the report we delivered to our City of Melbourne colleagues. The category of values provided a means through which to create a series of shared meanings around data – that is what I call data-values. Indeed, in the context of this project, by viewing data through the prism of values and value, as always present, we were able to ensure that we could align researchers, research partners, participants and place. In advocating for a design process that accounts for the plurality and locality of data, by which data are inextricable from place, Yanni Alexander Loukissas insists that 'accepting that all data are local means engaging with data settings instead of simply datasets' where 'today data are too often harnessed as discrete tools to enable analytical work at a distance' (2019: 23). The approach to designing data futures that I am calling for aligns with this, accompanied by a strong understanding of futures (as outlined in chapter *futures*) as contingent, uncertain and human.

The future of data futures

Data are everywhere, and data futures, as well as the emerging technologies they are inseparable from, need to be a core concern going forward. Not only academics are identifying a need to deepen our knowledge and action. In the business world, the UK based data, insights and consulting company, Kantar's, Insights 2030 report, based on 'hundreds of one-on-one interviews with business leaders around the world, as well as a global survey among more than 1,700 senior business and Insights leaders' determined (amongst other things that):

> The era of Big Data arrived several years ago with the promise of ever-more specificity about consumers in the marketplace. That promise has been fulfilled, but business leaders worry that the human experience of the person at the centre has been lost in the haystack of data and information. With disruption added to the mix, senior leaders believe that big ideas are needed to get full value from Big Data.
>
> *(Smith, J. W. 2021, November 9)*

In the data science field, the data feminism movement promotes human perspectives. The book *Data Feminism* seeks 'to describe a form of intersectional feminism that takes the inequities of the present moment as its starting point and begins its own work by asking: How can we use data to remake the world?' (Data Feminism 2020). Its proponents highlight that global power inequalities tend to be invisible in data science, where the powerful are 'disproportionately elite, straight, white, able-bodied, cisgender men from the Global North' and advocate for using data science 'to challenge and change the distribution of power'.

Social scientists similarly need to be engaged and involved with data and part of data futures, and to achieve this requires new modes of openness, shared values and collective improvisation with those other stakeholders in data futures. Anthropologist Hannah Knox rightly suggests that 'we need to find our way out of the trap of either treating data uncritically as direct signs of an underlying reality, or treating it critically as socially constructed representations' (Knox 2021b: 109). Knox asks what kind of action anthropologists should take, exploring the possibility of a route forward that does not take the traditional anthropological stance of remaining 'agnostic', or rendering the computational 'provisional', but instead take it seriously 'to allow other perspectives from outside the dominant techno-political order to appear' (2021: 110). We are not without initiatives in this direction, Lehtiniemi and Ruckenstein's (2019) engaged research with data activists is an excellent example, as is the important work of the indigenous *Old Ways New*'s Tracker Data project mentioned above. But, we need more.

As argued through this book, a collaborative and respectful interdisciplinary approach is fundamental to creating an interventional anthropology of emerging technologies. We need to apply this to the questions of data futures. To do this we need to extend social science accomplishments in critical data studies, toward participating in data futures. Data futures should be an interdisciplinary and inclusive field. We should continue to define and make visible the place of a design anthropology of emerging technologies as part of this.

AIR

Air is an inescapable facet of our planetary existence, and anthropologists have found it a productive category through which to consider fundamental questions addressed in this book: for Tim Ingold (2021) breathing the air is inseparable from how we know, live and move forward in the world; Tim Choy (2011), engages with air to consider 'relations and movements between places, people, things, and scales' (Choy 2011: 143); and for Bettina Hauge (2013a: 172) studying air entails understanding 'how we conceive the world and feel at home in it through air and air practices'.

In media and science reports, the COVID-19 pandemic has opened an opportunity for air quality to be studied by atmospheric scientists (Bourzac 2020, September 25) and has created the need for better air purification and filtration in indoor spaces. Australia is a good place to start this story, as a site where air pollution is a growing issue (Morawska et al. 2021: 10). A 'TechSci Research 2019 Australia Air Purifier Market by Filter Type' report (cited in Dahlgren et al. 2020) attributes Australia's deteriorating air quality to the smoke of bushfire events, and expects that this, combined with 'increasing consumer awareness about benefits of good indoor air quality' will lead to growth in air purifier sales in Australia. The rise in air filtration and purification has also been associated with the COVID-19 pandemic. However, there is still a need for clarity in this field since Digital Trends reported in 2021 (Hearn 2021, March 4) that while sales in filters grew 57% during 2020, 'a standard HEPA filter can't capture and destroy something as small as a virus' and a PECO filter, which 'can catch incredibly small items', '*might* make a difference, but only in a limited way'.

Emerging air technologies and moreover dominant narratives about the measurable qualities of air need to be connected with the realities of everyday breathing. What does this growing embedding of present and possible future automated air technologies and systems in homes, workplaces, schools and transport systems,

DOI: 10.4324/9781003182528-6

mean for social inequalities? Who gets to breathe the best air? Who is excluded from clean air? Or, how do people creatively engage with air? What does the future of air feel like from the everyday? How might we rethink the future of air through the prism of possibility, ethics and responsibility?

To respond to these emerging issues, I argue that we need to shift the focus and temporality on existing social science research towards air futures. For instance, what happens then when we bring insights from the most hyped emerging technologies – like autonomous driving (AD) cars (discussed in chapter *mobilities*) to consider mundane newcomers like the automated air filter? How and where might social scientists address the questions this raises? And how might we be involved?

Thinking with air

In Melbourne, Australia, in 2020 the air became contaminated twice. In early 2020, as our environmental crisis became perhaps more visible and experiential than ever before, the streets of Melbourne filled with bushfire smoke, people began to buy facemasks and monitor the air quality through a smartphone app, which datafied the environment and measured its safety, recommending when masks ought to be worn. The streets emptied, as my assumptions about how I would live in the city that summer rapidly changed. Overnight, the environment I had expected to inhabit was lost. The immediate future I had anticipated had dissolved into one where new ways of knowing, materialities, routines and expectations were rapidly assumed. My perception of the air around me shifted from a life where I barely noticed outdoor air beyond the ways of sensing and commenting on its texture, temperature which had become familiar over the eight years I'd lived in Australia. I had learned to anticipate the feel of the hot summer air that would hit me when I stepped outside from an air-conditioned indoors into deceptively windy summer days. In my life in Europe, I had always expected a breeze to be cooling, here the wind felt hot like a 45-degree early afternoon in Southern Spain. I had learned to recognise Melbourne's characteristic temperature drops, interpreted experientially as the wind changing to blowing in from Antarctica. But this was something new. I was on holiday in Tasmania when the fires started. The small city of Launceston filled with smoke, said to have been blown over on the wind from far away, making visible air's capacity to carry this ominous texture, otherwise so hard to capture and contain. Melbourne is no stranger to extreme weather events. In 2016, thousands developed breathing difficulties in an asthma thunderstorm, with nine deaths and over 10,000 seeking emergency services (Kenner 2018: 5; and see Department of Health n.d.). In our emerging future, will we need to reflect more on how we breathe? According to Alison Kenner 'Scientists predict that ... flash asthma epidemics will become more frequent as climate change progresses, as extreme weather events become more common, pollen counts rise, and allergy seasons start earlier and last longer'. This facet of climate change, combined with an increase in people with seasonal allergies, means that 'now more than ever we need to care for the place of breathing in the world' (Kenner 2018: 5).

There were masks for us waiting back in my house back in Melbourne. Smoky air is disturbing because unlike the fog, which it reminded me of visually from my childhood in England, it smells and to breathe it already feels unhealthy. On the worst day I masked up to walk through my neighbourhood. It was uncomfortable and unnerving. Later in 2020, when walking that same route through a leafy Victorian park in my neighbourhood, masked during the Stage 4 restrictions of the COVID-19 lockdown in Melbourne, I often remembered how wearing the mask had felt so incongruous as I had crossed the empty park in the smoky haze of January. By mid-2020, wearing a mask started to feel familiar, by 2022 I could forget to take it off. I thought back to participants in ethnographic fieldwork about urban car commuting in Sweden and Brazil (Pink, Gomes et al. 2018; Pink, Lacey et al. 2019), for whom leaving the home to drive without their smartphones was unthinkable. The facemask became a familiar sensory materiality of everyday life and part of the configuration of things that became a new kit for stepping outdoors. With colleagues in the United Kingdom, I was interviewing social workers online, about their experiences of using digital technologies in child protection social work during their lockdown (discussed in chapter *work*). Social workers visited children and families in person when necessary, the face mask becoming part of their safety kit. In our documentary *Social Work and Child Protection in the COVID-19 Pandemic*, based on research carried out by Harry Ferguson, Laura Kelly and me (Morgans, 2022), actors performed and spoke participants' experiences of entering homes, visiting families who might themselves be unmasked, their fears when children who were too young to understand social distancing and transporting children in their own cars, in the uncertainty of an airborne virus.

The idea of living in an everyday world on earth where the air is so contaminated that humans should not breathe it, is nothing new. Sheila Jasanoff suggests science fiction is 'a repository of sociotechnical imaginaries' which 'offer a deeper look into – possibly even predictions of – what harms societies are most desperate to avoid and what good they may achieve through foresight and imagination.' (Jasanoff 2015b: 337). Over a century ago, in E.M. Forster's science fiction story *The Machine Stops*, first published in 1909, when humans go out onto the earth's surface they must wear respirators to protect them from the dangers of breathing the air. One of the things that is striking to me about Foster's description, is how, for his protagonist, life in a world where contaminated air made it necessary to live underground, the precautions that one should take to survive above ground were so habituated. In Melbourne, in my experience, as breathing outdoors became increasingly understood and experienced as unsafe, new routines and activities were improvised to cope with these new circumstances. New modes of trust, anxiety and hope evolved and became sedimented as we learned to anticipate and imagine our present, immediate and far futures anew. New technologies became part of our lives: masks to filter the air; new smartphone apps; and air-quality data. With the bushfires, pandemic lockdowns and subsequent greater exposure to indoor allergens, possible and emerging technologies of filtration in homes, cars and institutions, emerged in new narratives, markets and materialities. I began to avidly follow the air news, as in 2021, a cargo of air filtration units to be installed in Victorian schools was flown in, and the uptake of domestic air purification and filtration technologies increased.

In the first two years of the 2020s, the public health and environmental crisis refigured the ways we experienced the air we breathe, how air technologies might become part of the sensory materiality of our homes and institutions, how we moved, and reshaped our future technological and social imaginaries of air and society.

Anthropologies of breathing

The substantial quality of air has been argued to lie in that 'it is always breathed' (Choy 2011: 155). Megan Wainwright's (2017) ethnography of 'the sensation of breathlessness' in people with chronic obstructive pulmonary disease (COPD) led her to conclude that rather than simply focusing on the experience of breathlessness inside the body, we should rather attend to the experience of sensing the environment through the lungs and breathing. Breathing is an inevitable and inescapable part of everyday life. It's something we need to keep doing, and, as if to emphasise this, many reports of COVID-19 cases in the news include statistics of the number of people who are breathing with the help of respirators. We are as such, as Choy and Kenner (who borrows the term from Choy) insist 'breathers' (Kenner 2018: 6). Breathing is not just essential to life itself, but it is the way that we move forward in life, from one moment to the next. If we stop breathing, then we stop living.

There are many clinical and existential questions and debates about the nature of life and death, including the roles of technology and ethics in this, which I do not address here. Rather I am concerned with how thinking about breathing can be aligned with a design anthropological theory of emergence, contingency and improvisation as outlined in chapter *emerging technologies*. Breathing is part of, and inseparable from, how we participate in the ongoingly emerging worlds of the everyday, and indeed where there is an airborne disease co-inhabiting our environment, potentially it is one of the ways in which we get caught up with its spread. What then is breathing?

For Ingold, breathing is not simply a physical matter, rather, drawing on the work of Maurice Merleau Ponty he insists that 'when we breathe, it is not just the body that takes air in, and lets it out' but that we must also account for how the mind is implicated in how we breathe, rather being 'left to float in the ether of the imagination' (2021: 254–255). Instead Ingold argues that 'we breathe with our entire being, indissolubly body and soul. Thinking is the breath of the soul and its sound is a murmur, an undercurrent on the verge of forming itself into articulable words' (2021: 254–255). Thinking, for Ingold (2021: 26), is akin to breathing; thinking is 'an active "taking in", akin to inhalation, which readies the thinker for further release into activity, just as breathing in prepares a body for breathing out'. In this interpretation we can understand breathing-thinking as an anticipatory mode whereby in Ingold's view 'every breath is new, of course, *but it is not a novelty*' (2021: 26, italics in original). As Kenner's analysis of breathing with asthma shows, this involves attunement and adjustment, she writes:

> Breathers work with the breath to stay calm and gain control over airways run amok, and also to assess the severity of the attack itself. They develop these informal breath control tactics over time, through experiences with asthma. Such tactics are anchored in attunement, in sensing the body in place, but they are sometimes also informed by breathers' past interactions with caregivers who coached them through attacks.
>
> *(Kenner 2018: 180)*

Just like the flow of the everyday, where familiar routines and tasks are repeated daily, in ways that are usually similar but never exactly the same, breathing is repeated but the same breath can never be drawn more than once. Equally, as the experience of the pandemic has shown us, the ways we breathe and the experience of breathing can change both rapidly and incrementally over time. Breathing is moreover inevitably part of how we experience our environments. It is particularly implicated in our perceptions of the materiality of air, in our understandings of the modes through which we access it and in how we seek to change or manipulate its quality. From Ingold, we gain a sense of how breathing is implicated in our very being in the world, where 'With every intake of breath, we draw the wind into a bodily circulation that deviates from, or even reverses, our direction of travel. But with every outbreath we release it again into the prevailing current' (2021: 51).

While Ingold focuses on breathing as a route to the fundamental question of how we know, move and participate in our environments, Choy invokes the poetics of air as a tonic for flailing theory. Suggesting that no single theory of the relationship between the particular and the universal can encompass a question so complex, he draws on the case of Hong Kong to suggest that 'the material poetics of the substantiations' of its air

> with its whirlings, its blowing through scales and borders, its condensations, its physical engagements, its freight of colonial, economic, and bodily worries about health and well-being, its capacity to link and to divide, its harnessing for simultaneously local and cosmopolitan projects—provide that reviving breath theory needs?
>
> *(Choy 2011: 168)*

Air again is proposed as the connecting thread of the universal and the particular.

The way we sense, know and live with our environments involves deep expertise and ways of knowing, which are moreover also deeply bound up with personal relationships and identities. For instance, in research about how people experienced motorway noise in Melbourne we found that often people living near the motorway had learned to not hear it, and that being able to live with noise sometimes became a point of pride (Pink, Lacey et al. 2019). Choy describes how similarly, when living, and doing fieldwork in Hong Kong, his relationship to air pollution was bound up with who he felt he was. He describes how 'we, like our friends, routinely avoided waiting or walking on busy streets because the air stung our eyes and throats'. But he 'consistently refused to comment upon or even to notice the air', in order to distinguish himself from United States expat business people, who complained about the air. Finally, though, Choy tells us, when his partner became ill from sinusitis three times in six months, they moved out to a village on the coast (Choy 2011: 141). Once a more dramatic series of events struck, their approach to air shifted.

As these works suggest, air is clearly not something separate from us or from any other element of the environment. Air is as much part of us, and of our sense of who we are, as is any part of our bodies, its relationship to us is experientially dynamic. Breathing air is not only fundamental to our continued existence, and to the nature of our being, thinking, and knowing. It is also part of the anticipatory modes of the everyday, it is what takes us forward, and what we go forward doing. Air is, moreover, always implicated with the politics, inequalities and ethics of societal processes and governance, a study of air shows up the relations of power, inequities and injustices of society. And air is part of how we relate to and care for ourselves and others. The future of air, the possibility to make it less polluted, fresher, and for whom is bound up in this. This makes air an ideal concept, experience and materiality through which to consider emerging technologies and how they come about in our present and future.

The datafication of air

In chapter *data* I examine data futures, to consider the everyday and institutional layers at which data is made, collected, analysed and used. The datafication of air is consistent with the promise of data to render our futures more knowable, quantify the risks that the unknown holds, to diminish uncertainties and to prescribe action, and one of the ways this is achieved is by measuring air quality. The ethics of the datafication of city air are as complex as those of data and emerging technologies across any domain of life, they crosscut debates about our safety, privacy, air and data 'commons' and communities.

Choy considers Air Pollution Index (API) data in Hong Kong, which he writes of as 'the ongoing tuning, tweaking, and reiterating of numbers, graphs, and maps'. He emphasises its affective and aesthetic affordances, in making risks that are otherwise hard to express 'visible and experienceable (or invisible and experience-able)', so that the API is not just a persuasive device, but rather the 'technical practice' of generating it 'brings air into sense and sensibility' (Choy 2011: 164). There are many modes and politics of measuring air quality, ranging from government reports to citizen science and community-based open data-sharing, including 'citizen sensing', which Jennifer Gabrys defines as 'an emerging range of practices for monitoring environments through low-cost and DIY digital technologies' (Gabrys 2016, March 24). A good example is the Smart Citizen Air Quality IoT kit (https://smartcitizen.me/) developed by a Barcelona-based group. Debora Lanzeni's long term research with this group shows how the Smart Citizen Air Quality Kit was underpinned by the 'idea that the production of technological knowledge about our intimate environments will no longer remain solely the domain of governments, scientific companies and academic researchers' (Lanzeni 2016: 51). Smart Citizen represents itself as: 'a community of passionate people who believe data is critical to inform political participation at all levels'. They 'develop tools for citizen action in environmental monitoring and methodologies for community engagement and co-creation' (Smart Citizen n.d.). In a subsequent study of digital assets, Lanzeni and I discussed the principles of this system. The Smart Citizen team believed their project and its data were safe, because they use open (rather than proprietary) code and software for the platform, meaning the code was likely to have been shared more widely, and because people had created their own platforms to use and often publish the data collected from the Smart Citizen sensors themselves. The community around this project, as one of the Directors explained to us, therefore supported its activity and sustainability (Pink, Lanzeni & Horst 2018).

While air pollution from carbon emissions remains a concern, air-quality data is increasingly associated with environmental threats and extreme events, including bushfires. For instance, in 2020 a *National Geographic* report based on experiences in the United States, points to the ability of air quality sensing both by government agencies and the general public, to detect bushfire or wildfire smoke, which it reports, can contain harmful particles even when we cannot sense these ourselves visually or by smell (Ehrenkranz 2020, October 2). One example discussed is the low cost PurpleAir citizen science sensor (https://map.purpleair.com/), which is also present in Australia. The *National Geographic* piece suggests that 'New air monitoring technology affords the public the ability to easily measure something that they couldn't access before', it suggests that as 'wildfires become more frequent, and microscopic pollutants continue to spew into the air, checking the air quality might become as commonplace as checking the weather.' Yet the growth in the practice of and enthusiasm for citizen sensing, as evidenced by a host of local projects across the world, does not necessarily signify a future where locally sensed air-quality data contributed by citizen scientist communities will seamlessly contribute to deeper knowledge about and ability to predict changes and risk related to air quality. As such developments move forward, we will need to consider how they become situated in mundane, everyday lives and worlds with other people and other species, institutions and power relations. Gabrys points out such developments will be situated. First, 'the specifically digital practice of citizen sensing, located within a particular participant's use of a device to gather real-time data on air pollution … opens out on a range of other practices'. Second, the notion of citizen sensing tends to have a particular vision of alignment between different agencies and institutions, but in reality, it actually just 'opens out on a yet-to-be-defined set of practices'. She concludes that: 'citizen sensing points to the ways that practice can remain in formation through relations of subjects, objects, environ-ments, technologies, organisms, and pollutants' (Gabrys 2016, March 24). More-over, we must also not forget, that as Lanzeni has pointed out, in citizen sensing, the imaginaries of such futures do not only imagine air quality technologies, but that such a form of citizenship itself is also a future imaginary (Lanzeni 2016: 59) and does not pertain to a real future everyday person.

These various modes of, visions for, and practices related to the present and future production and analysis of air data, and the emerging field of research around them point to an emerging field of concern, experience, practice and action. We have a responsibility to go beyond simply understanding air data and emerging air technologies as part of techno-solutionist visions for improving air quality through community engagement. We need to also ask how they come about in everyday life practices and imaginaries and importantly how they are entangled with what Kenner calls 'the slow and uneven violence that makes the world increasingly unbreathable' (Kenner 2018: 28).

The hope and the hot air

In recent years, air technologies have become increasingly prominent in public, institutional and industry narratives. The relationship between air technologies and COVID-19 as an airborne disease has been discussed and explored by scientists, science journalists, international organisations and the air technology industries alike throughout the pandemic. By 2021, the World Health Organisation (WHO) had published a *Roadmap to improve and ensure good indoor ventilation in the context of COVID-19* (WHO 2021, March 1). Industry organisations are also getting involved. In Australia, for instance, the HVAC&R News website – 'dedicated to bringing you the latest Heating, Ventilation, Air conditioning and Refrigeration (HVAC&R) industry news' – has reported on developments in ventilation in relation to COVID-19 across a wide range of contexts (https://www.hvacrnews.com.au). The real estate website – Domain – has explored the relationship between 'airtight' energy efficient homes which have little natural ventilation and air circulation and surfaces expert views relating to the use of air purification as an immediate measure, and surrounding the need for changes to the building code (Williams 2021, September 9). The Victorian Government has a statement about the roll out of 51,000 air purification devices 'to all government and low-fee non-government schools to remove potentially infectious particles – like coronavirus – from higher-risk areas in schools including staff rooms, sick bays, music rooms and other high traffic areas' (Premier of Victoria 2021, September 22), echoed in the industry tech news. Many media articles also focus on: air filtration and purification technology and COVID-19, concerning for instance, ventilation (Dow 2021, May 2) and indoor air-flow (Bourke 2020, November 16); the benefits of having them in quarantine hotels Dow 2021, May 2), as well as in schools; and internationally for instance in 2021 on the 'First Air Purifier from Major Brand Tested to Remove Live SARS-CoV-2 Virus from Air' (Business Wire 2021, April 12).

On a lesser scale, to their more glamorous airborne mobilities counterparts, like flying cars and drones, the mundane air purifier is following a similar route of hype and promise, as it becomes poised as a vital element in the suite of technological solutions to airborne disease. Yet emerging air technologies are also being brought together with mobilities technologies, in ways that are aligned with existing approaches to safety in the industry. Road safety has two key facets, involving safety from road accidents, often due to driver distraction by mobile phone use and personal safety (Pink, Gomes et al. 2018). In 2020, during the pandemic, car companies and automotive journalists turned their attention to air filtration and purification in cars, with reports on Geely's 'healthy car project', which includes antivirus functions (Harper 2020, May 1; Zhang 2020, March 13), and Tesla's 'HEPA Filter and Bioweapon Defense Mode', which, its blog notes protects drivers from air pollution, a 'statistically more relevant' hazard than collision (The Tesla Team 2016, May 2), and was upgraded during the pandemic in 2020 (Tesla n.d.). In 2020, the online launch of Geely's Icon SUV attracted the attention of the SAE website which reported that 'Before the digital launch concluded, 30,000 per-orders had streamed in for the turbocharged, 175-horsepower Icon' and attributed this partly to it having an air-purification system with advanced filters and 'certified to CN95 – the standard that approximates the same 95% filtering efficiency as a state-of-the-art daily N95 personal respiratory mask' (Berman 2020, March 30). A 2020 Bloomberg news article suggested the concept of safety in luxury cars was shifting beyond safety from crime and accidents, so additionally 'now safety concerns include a medical element both mental and physical' (Elliot 2020, April 23). The journalist – Hannah Elliot – quotes Gorden Wagener, an established figure in the luxury-car design field, as identifying a key issue for cars: 'The most important thing for a long time has been to know that you and your family are safe' and 'The important question now is how to protect your health'. Elliot documents a history of air filtration in luxury cars, to remove or kill pollutants, allergens, mould, bacteria and 'harmful gases' and add beneficial charcoal for removing odours and ground level o-zone. But she comments on the newness of the idea of a car completely purifying a significant quantity of air in ways similar to removing 'airborne allergens like car fumes – but would also work on a broader level than just the car itself, effectively and significantly cleaning the air immediately surrounding the exterior of the vehicle' (Elliot 2020, April 23). Other technologies include the Panasonic Nanoex air purifier, the use of which in cars is demonstrated in a YouTube video, claiming it can fill the inside of a car within two minutes, and 'offers a cleaner space with less risk to your loved ones' (Panasonic Malaysia 2021, January 13). In 2021, Panasonic announced this would be used by a Jaguar Land Rover car company (Jaguar Land Rover 2021, March 16), and installed in 150 GrabCar medical vehicles in Vietnam, 'with the aim of improving air quality, safety, and comfort during transport for recovered COVID-19 patients returning home from hospital, as well as medical staff and Grab driver partners' (Duc 2021, September 8).

Mobilities also have a spatial element and help us understand air and inequalities. For instance, in his study of air in Hong Kong, Choy asks: 'How are Hong Kong's air spaces distributed? Who gets to occupy those with the cleanest air? Who breathes the street? Who breathes mountains? Who breathes the sea? Who breathes flies?' (2011: 158). When air becomes accessible through car-filtration systems, we need to ask similar questions: who gets to breathe filtered or purified air in vehicles? What privileged modes of mobility and spatial access would the use of an air filtered vehicle afford? Could we imagine the wealthy gliding through virus inflicted suburbs kept safe from airborne viruses through the filtration systems of their cars? Would air-purified rideshares be more costly? These are all valid questions and highlight the need to think through the future of air tech and mobilities carefully. Yet, they also echo the often-dystopian imaginaries of what should *not* happen that frequently dominate critical debates in the social sciences and humanities. What if we were to instead take inspiration from the Nanoex example, where in 2021 'in Vietnam, 2,000 units of Grab cars in Hanoi and Ho Chi Minh City will be equipped with nanoeX generators, with the purpose of enabling clean air in mobile space and comfortable rides for Vietnamese people on Grab vehicles' (Van n.d.). The collaboration between Panasonic and Grab is exemplary in several ways, since it demonstrates how emerging technologies can be deployed in ways that are responsive to the needs of specific communities, and are responsible and ethical.

Collectively, the examples discussed in this section show that with the COVID-19 pandemic, emerging air filtration and purification technologies are becoming increasingly advanced. The datafication of air, discussed above makes the analytics of air quality and composition that participates in this. They are generating new commercial markets, which for instance in the case of the automotive industry connect with existing concerns relating to safety and luxury. They are also participating in the constitution of new fields of responsibility and humanitarian and ethical action, as new ways of offering access to clean and safe air to people who are likely to be exposed to the virus are created. These emerging narratives about the future of air purification and filtration technologies are associated primarily with concepts of safety, health and care. They suggest that we are on the cusp of a near-global air tech experiment, being embarked on differently by many nations. Yet, there remains a big gap in knowledge; none of the media, industry or institutional agendas discussed in this section, or that I have encountered in my research, attend to the feelings, experiences, practices or hopes and fears of the real people who would live with this technology and whose lives it is envisaged would be made healthier and safer by it. In the next section, I examine what happens when they are asked.

Imagining air tech in the future home

Existing ethnographies of air in the home reveal the cultural and environmental specificity of everyday life and corresponding air practices (e.g. Hauge 2013a, 2013b; Pink 2004). Bettina Hauge's (2013a, 2013b) fieldwork in Danish, English and Scottish homes, offers two key insights for considering emerging air technologies at home. First, that people are likely to already have sensorial and practical ways of understanding and engaging with air quality, safety and risk (2013a: 183), through reassuring everyday routines ensuring that the home is environmentally safe and healthy (2013a: 178) and ritualised actions, marking moments in the day or when returning from a trip (2013b: 181). Second, we should attend to emerging air technologies in relation to people's engagements with seasonal air outside, the feelings of sickness associated with polluted air and how 'air practices and air make us knowledgeable about the world and about our place in it' (Hauge 2013b: 184).

In Australia, the climate and public health crises have impacted everyday life in the home in unique ways. In 2020, there were two reasons to stay at home. First as cities and other residential areas filled with bushfire smoke, outdoor air became polluted, windows were closed, air conditioning went on. Participants in the Digital Energy Futures project who lived by the sea told me how they could no longer use the sea breeze which would normally flow through to cool their homes. Unable to dry their laundry outdoors in the smoke, or indoors in air-conditioned environments, they used the dryer. One family of five returned home from their holidays to find their neighbourhood full of smoke and themselves with two weeks' worth of laundry from their trip, causing a big spike in their energy use over the first few days back at home. A couple of months later, as the lockdowns started, the air people sensed, breathed and otherwise used was more intensely focused in the home, as a site where work, learning and living played out more intensely. Air technologies, and forms of everyday expertise about them were already strikingly part of everyday cultures in Australia – a country where air conditioning was already an expectation for many (Strengers et al. 2019).

The Digital Energy Futures ethnography, just after the bushfires and during the COVID-19 pandemic revealed that 'Households are becoming more interested in managing the air quality of their homes – especially to reduce exposure to bushfire smoke, allergens, moisture, mould, toxins, and unpleasant odours' (Strengers, Dahlgren et al. 2021: 7). In this context, where Australians already collectively spent more than AUD\$ 3.7 billion a year over the 2020 summer period (Diaz 2021, March 18), we found that participants' interest in managing their air quality had accelerated and many already used or imagined their futures with air purification units and their functions, dehumidifiers and humidifiers, as well as oil or smart diffusers (2021: 64). About 10% of households who participated had specialised air purification units and many others had considered buying them (2021: 65). With this background in mind, in 2021, the digital energy futures team (for this activity the team involved Sarah Pink, Kari Dahlgren, Hannah Korsmeyer, Yolande Strengers and Rex Martin) set out to discover more about what the possible futures of air purification and filtration might look like from the perspective of everyday life, by creating series of design ethnographic workshops with participants across Victoria and New South Wales. Two of our online workshops, with five women, aged between around 30 to around 50 years, all living around the same or similar rural towns in Victoria offer some new insights about the possibilities, anxieties and hopes people associate with the datafication, automation, energy demand and safety implied by emerging air purification technologies. Amongst other things, participants were invited to imagine and role play new air tech devices that would ensure that their future air would be healthy, safe and comfortable.

Participants were invited to create any healthy, safe and comfortable air tech, including air conditioning, and all five focused on air purification and filtration tech. This would provide air which is cool, clean, healthy, fresh, dustless, humidified, comfortable, odourless, not human/stuffy, pollen-free, and could have covid-safe filtration and ideally perform heating and cooling. They considered this important, in one participant's words, in 'keeping the air everyone's got to breathe as clean as it possibly can be'. They imagined three similar technologies. *SmartAir* is a bit like a current split heating and cooling system, which protects its household from: dust; pollution; toxins; thunderstorm asthma; smoke from neighbours' bonfires; germs/bacteria and viruses; and ideally simultaneously heat and cool. *CleanAir 2025* protects its household from pollen, airborne viruses and smoke particles, and is used remotely by family members who wanted to turn it on manually, along with an auto option whereby it would start when sensors detect unwanted air contaminants. *PureAir*, the third device, would similarly protect householders from dust and pollen as well as pet hair. Thus, participants identified a series of generic filtration needs, and specific allergens that they would like their own future air tech to offer protection from. As one participant put it: 'If you've got an illness in your household you'd want to be hitting that button that eliminates the virus', and be ready for 'out of ordinary types of things'. The specifications for the air tech devices were similar. They all used data sourced externally, and sensor technologies within the home. They protected their households from similar air risks or dangers and required personalisation to the specific needs of particular households, which included temperature control.

We next invited participants to role play from the position of the emerging air tech they had proposed. The facilitators interviewed them from the perspective of the energy grid, which was characterised as an optimised structure, doing its best to fulfil energy demand in its local area. Speaking as *SmartAir, CleanAir 2025* and *PureAir*, participants imagined the technologies as used seasonally and following everyday routines, most intensively when the household arrived home, from work and school.

In the future, they believed the air tech would become connected to other technologies like digital voice assistants, smart watches, self-tracking technologies, security systems and smartphone apps in limited ways. However, in contrast to the future visions of the connected home discussed in chapter *home*, their everyday imaginaries made human decision making integral to how the technologies would keep the future home safe, healthy and comfortable. One participant imagined, as her co-participant echoed approval, that if the range hood was not working properly *SmartAir* would sense the grease in the air and alert the householders via a visual or sonic smartphone notification. She saw no need for *SmartAir* to be connected to the rangehood. Speaking as *SmartAir* a participant rejected the idea that she might be connected to or have any autonomy to operate the windows, since she thought 'my family would be mad with me if I closed the windows and they specifically left them open for a reason'. Again, she insisted on 'an alert message, a notification … there's pollution detected in the house, you might want to close your windows'; 'definitely', concurred her co-participant.

Participants could imagine automation and greater connectivity between devices and external agencies in their future homes, such as automated systems for watering the garden, security systems, and music playing. However, resonating with the *Future Home Life* (Strengers et al. 2022) report and *Digital Energy Futures* documentary (Pink 2022a), participants felt compelled to keep their capacity to, as one expressed it, 'make those choices for ourselves'. She pointed out 'we need to be able to set for an air purifier exactly what we want the air purifier to do, rather than just having it running automatically'. Staying in control of household health and safety from airborne allergies and disease was paramount:

> when its hayfever season, I'd love to be able to say 'air purifier, right I want you to strip the pollen out of the air that's inside the house', and … if … my husband comes home and we've had, you know, some really bad Covid stuff, OK 'I want you to be able to strip the COVID particles out of the air in my house to minimise our risk'.

Control was essential because she envisaged a future where with too much automated air filtration and purification, the impact could be detrimental to health, by weakening our immunity to the viruses or bacteria outdoors.

While participants doubted the accuracy of weather data, they wished that, for example when a neighbour was having a bonfire (common in the country), or thunderstorm asthma was likely, the technology would alert them. However, far from the ideal of householders becoming citizen scientists, sharing data from their own homes, or connectivity to data in other homes, was uncomfortable. Participants suggested options similar to opting in to sharing self-tracking data with particular friends or being paid for sharing data. However, they set limits, feeling for example that allowing in-house air data relating to airborne viruses to be supplied to the government would be too intrusive. They knew the emerging technologies they were role-playing were unfinished and that there were uncertainties around the trade-offs relating to control, data and privacy.

Discussing future air tech with people who had such experiences to draw on, in circumstances where neither the technology nor the ways it would participate in their lives are completely shaped, offers a unique opportunity through which to examine their priorities, anxieties and hopes for emerging technologies. The workshops helped us to view possible everyday futures where our air might be polluted by bushfire smoke, carry airborne disease and where the energy available to keep air safe and healthy might need to be shared. Designing future air tech from these sites of the everyday would enable new ways to accommodate and design with the everyday issues that came into view, that is to put care, ethics, equity, privacy and choice at the centre of the agenda.

Ethical air futures

Air is simultaneously experienced and imagined as contaminated, as recent and possible future airborne viruses, bushfire and forest fire smoke, and other forms of pollution, infiltrate humans' and other species' oxygenous life source. Ultimately, this points to fundamental questions of planetary health and the need for collective responsibility. Zorana J. Anderson and colleagues highlight that

> The COVID-19 pandemic has painfully demonstrated the close inter-connectedness of a fossil fuel-based economy, climate change, air pollution and emerging infectious diseases, and provides compelling additional motivation for stricter air pollution regulation, as an integral and imperative part of post pandemic policies, ensuring more healthy and resilient populations.
>
> *(Andersen et al. 2021: 4)*

This context also requires careful consideration of how new approaches to technology use and design might participate. We need an approach which acknowledges the environmental costs of the design, production and use of emerging technologies intended to make our air safer.

We must also consider the best way to invest research funding in securing a safe air future. There is a contemporary urge to keep people safe from polluted, virus infected or allergen-filled air and in turn to cleanse air from any of these possible threats. There are also moves to create, circumscribe and sustain safe air places – including cities, homes, vehicles and other sites, by government, activists, institutions, organisations, communities and individuals. Alongside this, there is the opportunity to explore how our air futures might be better designed and developed to be equitable, responsible, ethical, inclusive and appropriate for the people who will draw them into their possible future lives. How might we bring together these agendas and perspectives towards collaborative and healthy air futures for all.

ENERGY

Energy is an invisible materiality, discussed in terms of the activities and experiences associated with it, labour (and often resource extraction) involved in producing it and infrastructures to distribute it. It is an intangible source of value that is monetized and consumed. It is bound up with multiple and diverse forms, visions and temporalities of futures. Energy – discussed here primarily in relation to electricity – like data and air, resonates through the chapters of this book, as it does through our lives.

The scientific realities and imaginaries concerning the relationships between emerging technologies and energy make compelling news across public, industry and science fields. The electricity grid – which generates, transmits and distributes electricity to residential, industry or business customers – is a significant non-human character in this story. Electricity grids are themselves emerging technologies, continually developed and evolved. The smart grid introduces increasingly digital and automated technologies into this system, often with the ambition of (amongst other things) better balancing – or optimising – the relationship between supply and demand of energy, and the promise of providing more personalised energy services for customers. In recent news the electricity grid is implicated in new relations with other emerging technologies; a drone was reportedly used to attack the grid in the United States (Barrett 2021, May 11). Grid relations to the climate crisis are also complex. While initiatives to involve the smart grid in processes of transition to decarbonisation seek to mitigate climate change, news media has highlighted how climate weather events can 'melt down' the grid (Bachelard 2019, December 17). The complexities of the relationship between emerging technologies and energy demand are also news. A *New York Times* article draws on research to suggest that the internet itself uses less energy than previously thought (Lohr 2021, June 24), whereas, according to Power Compare, Bitcoin has been said to use more energy that whole countries (Power Compare n.d.). A *Nature*

DOI: 10.4324/9781003182528-7

Communications article (Jiang et al. 2021: 1) suggested that 'without any policy interventions, the annual energy consumption of the Bitcoin blockchain in China is expected to peak in 2024' and its 'emission output would exceed the total annualized greenhouse gas emission output of the Czech Republic and Qatar'. Other technological possibilities around energy open up sensational futures seldom discussed, such as the development of new materials, which could be applied to produce sustainable energy for colonies on Mars (Young 2021, May 3), or if hackers could attack AI systems with the purpose to making them consume excessive energy (Hao 2021, May 6).

In a world of experience and debate that is more mundane and accessible, energy, emerging technologies, people and other species, societal, institutional and planetary futures are coming about in the present and in the imaginaries of government, organisations, activists and everyday life. In this chapter, I examine the implications of a design anthropological approach to energy and technology in the everyday. How do we surface the configurations of things and processes through which energy and emerging technologies come into being relationally with people, other species, weather events and climate? How can we imagine energy technology futures? And how might we go forward?

Everyday energy futures

The documentary film *Digital Energy Futures* (Pink 2022), made with Emerging Technologies Lab colleagues, Yolande Strengers, Kari Dahlgren, Rex Martin, Larissa Nichols and Jeni Lee, opens with my narration, inviting viewers to a possible future where their everyday is shaped by industry narratives about emerging technological possibilities:

> Imagine a future life where your smartphone, watch, airpods and your electric car were automatically charged without you even knowing. What would it be like to give up control to an external system which optimises your energy use, decides when a robotic vacuum cleans your home and even when your electricity is available? Or are these even realistic or desirable futures?

Existing and emerging technological possibilities relating to renewable energy sources, battery or device charging, control, automation, optimisation and personalisation dominate the contemporary energy and technology industry and consultancy concerns about and solutions for the future of energy demand (Dahlgren et al. 2020). With this backdrop, the documentary foregrounds the everyday, by making visible real people's experiences, everyday activities and values, and future imaginaries for energy and technology.

On one level the documentary intends a simple response by surfacing differences between how people envisage these technologies within their everyday life futures and the socio-technical imaginaries of the industry reports. Our wider ethnographic research demonstrated that industry claims for the future coincided with how participants envisaged their futures in only one subsection of the seven social practice domains we investigated with 72 households in Australia. Four subsections did not correspond at all, and the other six corresponded 'somewhat' (Strengers, Dahlgren et al. 2021: 10–11). Therefore, any viable 'realistic or desirable' account of energy futures needs to acknowledge how people view and are already moving forwards into their own energy futures. Understanding present and future energy demand is indeed important both for academics and companies that supply energy. A design anthropology perspective considers the relations between people, emerging technologies, automation and energy in possible everyday futures. How might we differently design energy futures with and for people, in ways that position human and planetary health anew, and enable people and planet (and all that constitute it) to actively shape this process?

There is no single answer to these questions and the politics, contested spaces and gaps in knowledge and practice they reveal are greater than the scope of this chapter. The enormity of the question is matched by the vastness of the field of energy studies. Recent anthropological works have surfaced on specific constellations of interests. For example, to focus on electricity (Abram et al. 2019), experimental approaches to generating energy futures (Maguire et al. 2021), the constitution of energy markets (Özden-Schilling 2021), and energy futures (Abram et al. 2022; Pink, Ortar et al. 2022). Here, I respond by following and drawing on a thread of collaborative interdisciplinary and multi-stakeholder research which centres, or encounters, electricity and emerging technologies in the everyday.

A key concern runs in parallel to Sally Wyatt's (2021) interrogation of metaphor in critical data studies: How should we speak of energy? Energy anthropologists reinforce this, James Maguire, Laura Watts and Brit Winthereik (2021), join Simone Abram, Brit Ross Winthereik, Thomas Yarrow and Anjan Sarkar's (2019) work, in emphasising the question: 'What languages must we adopt and develop to be able to account for the presence of electric forces and flows, and their impact on social life?' (Maguire et al. 2021: 23). Wyatt (2021) argued for abandoning metaphors from the resource extractive industries in our discussions of data (see chapter *data*). We also need to accomplish this shift in metaphors for electricity, a resource itself that has a long and enduring association with the extractive industries, which needs not only new terminologies but new relations, materialities and economies of production, supply, demand and use.

Anthropologies of energy and futures

There is a rich and fast-growing anthropology of energy, and scholars in this field have increasingly turned their attention to uncertainties and futures. These moves provide a promising context for considering emerging technologies in light of energy.

The co-authored and edited book *Energy Futures* (Abram et al. 2022) was created through a collaboration between the energy anthropology and futures anthropology networks of the European Association of Social Anthropologists, developed by Simone Abram, Nathalie Ortar, Karen Waltorp and me. Amongst other things, our approach insists that anthropologies of energy should account for the attention to contingency (advocated by a futures anthropology approach) and to how people improvise as they move forward in uncertain circumstances (Pink, Berg et al. 2022). In their contribution to *Energy Worlds in Experiment*, Endre Dányi and Michaela Spencer, James Maguire, Hannah Knox and Andrea Ballestero, in a similar vein, suggest that we may 'need propositions that are more self-conscious of their deranging potential – not as modernist risks to be avoided, but as constitutive turbulences that need to be embraced' (Dányi et al. 2021: 92). This turn to uncertainty acknowledges the processual, incomplete and indeterminate nature of life and all elements of our environment as we move forward. As an alternative framework through which to consider energy and energy futures, it aligns the study of electricity with theories of imagination, ethics and trust as indeterminate (chapters *futures* and *trust*) to suggest that to talk of electricity, and people's relationships to it we need processual metaphors that acknowledge the uncertainties and possibilities associated with everyday energy.

This turn invokes ethical questions. In earlier work, I propose we consider electricity – a tricky to define category – as an indeterminate 'thing/ non-thing', in an ongoingly emergent world where futures are equally indeterminate. Following this we might see our energy futures as consisting of the process and experience of 'moving into an uncertain future with an uncertain thing'. In a scenario as undefined as that I suggest 'if there is anything we can grasp onto it should be the ethics of responsibility' (Pink 2019) and argue for foregrounding ethics as central to how we traverse uncertain terrain. Ongoing work in energy anthropology has also emphasised the centrality of ethics. Introducing their volume *Energy Worlds in Experiment,* Maguire and colleagues argue that 'questions of energy are far more than questions of technology or policy: they are about values and ethics, culture, power and institutions (Boyer and Szeman 2014)' (Maguire et al. 2021: 21). They propose that 'energy and experiment must go together in the work of figuring new energy futures' emphasising processes of emergence and making (2021: 18). For them, working between anthropology and STS, 'there is an ethical as well as a methodological imperative' for researchers to become engaged (Maguire et al. 2021: 21) in this work, which resonates with the processual and creative urge that is at the core of design anthropology.

These recent interventions in energy anthropology are committed to shifting the agenda and its ethics, through experimental methods and opening up anthropology itself to new conceptual and methodological disruptions and renewals. For Maguire et al. (2021: 212) 'Experimenting with new forms of storytelling gives us hope that, in this era of climate change, we can build flourishing energy futures'. The contributions to Abram and colleagues' *Electrifying Anthropology* (2019) collectively show that 'a focus on electricity can entail a critique of how human agency has been neglected by the recent theoretical turn to new materialism, or can serve as a reference point in recent discussions of big data' (Pink 2019).

Collectively, this body of work sets the stage for ongoing attention to energy futures, as an ethical and always unfinished project. This, aligned with the ethics of shifting dominant narratives around emerging technologies, is a perfect starting point for thinking through the implications of emerging energy technologies.

Centering everyday electricity futures

Energy is at the centre of ambitions to transition to decarbonisation, and thus inseparable from the future of the planet and climate change. It is also impossible to be in, or participate as a researcher or consider design in, everyday life without encountering energy; over the last decade, I have explicitly or indirectly found myself doing 'electrified' anthropology (Abram et al. 2019) whereby electricity is always a concern as I've investigated how people live and imagine future technologies in their cities, homes and travel: how people envisage locality based urban sustainability; how people's energy demand is constituted in the present and possible futures; how might technology simultaneously enable them to use less energy; how people, data and technologies can become co-implicated in a transition to net zero; and what exactly constitutes a just, ethical and equitable transition to decarbonisation in Australia.

Energy is layered into everyday worlds. Electricity powers most everyday devices, from the moment we wake to check our smartphones, or whatever else people do on waking. In around 2016, a participant in a project about self-tracking technologies (discussed in chapter *data*) described to me how he kept his commitment to digitally recording the data from all his everyday activities, although some of his apps used up a lot of battery power, by ensuring he had charging points around his home. I return to batteries later in this chapter. Electricity is often invoked in research not explicitly about energy. The *Laundry Lives* documentary (Pink & Astari 2015) is about how people do their laundry and imagine their futures. The electricity supplies to their homes were completely bound up in this, as participants showed us how and when they switched their machines on and off at the wall, in moments that made energy visible. In research around the documentary *Smart Homes for Seniors* (Pink 2021), discussed in chapter *home*, participants were concerned about the cost of the energy for the 'always on' technologies that were installed in their homes, they wondered how to resolve their habits of always switching everything off at the wall when they went away, with the need to have the system started again when they returned. A Slow City I visited in Italy was already mobilising electric vehicles in the early 2000s, while others were advocating for low-energy light bulbs, as these small initiatives became visible I became curious about how people might live out sustainability in their own homes.

Bringing together my work on the home (Pink 2004) with a new interest in energy, I realised the way forward for such research needed to be interdisciplinary, and I began talking with engineers and designers in my university. I was inspired to learn there was already an agenda to research and bring about change around energy use in the home and joined my new-found colleagues in our successful interdisciplinary funding application to the UK research councils. The Lower Effort Energy Demand Reduction project (LEEDR), at Loughborough University ran between 2010 and 2014. The project was an exciting opportunity not only to develop new research in homes, but to bring together anthropology, design and engineering, to learn how each other worked and to create a design anthropological methodology through which to understand how people used technology and media in their homes, and how digital design interventions might help them to reduce their energy demand (Pink, Leder Mackley et al. 2017). The project, Roxana Moroşanu (2016) discusses, was framed by the need for the UK government to comply with targets to reduce carbon emissions, by reducing people's energy demand through digital interventions. This framing requires individuals or households to take responsibility for reducing energy demand, when in fact the reasons why their demand exists is more likely to be framed by structural issues related to policy and governance, than to their having 'bad' energy habits or attitudes that need to be reformed through behaviour change methods (Shove 2010). This critique raises some key questions about both how we might rethink energy futures in relation to emissions targets and how we might frame everyday life participation in energy transitions to decarbonisation. Our project enabled me to conceptualise, through design anthropological practice, how the relationship between everyday life, technology and energy might be better understood. What theories of change did we really need in order to comprehend how people move forward in their everyday lives at home (Pink, Leder Mackley et al. 2017) and how might we define futures (Pink & Salazar 2017).

The project also offered me an early opportunity to learn about how technologies and energy demand mutually came about through the anticipatory modes of everyday life. One of the most intriguing findings from the ethnographic strand of the project (which I carried out with Kerstin Leder Mackley and Roxana Moroşanu) concerned how participants used the standby modes on their devices in the early years of the 2010s, particularly television monitors. We found that while engineers tended to consider standby mode to be wasteful, a mode of a device being 'on' while not being used, and consuming a surprisingly high amount of energy, in fact in everyday use it meant something else. Some of our participants had appropriated standby mode as a function that played a role in helping them to sleep at night. For example, one couple, who in fact had ambitions to be environmentally sustainable and took measures to that effect, also had a young son, and amongst their key priorities, above saving energy, were getting him and themselves to sleep at night, in order to be fresh for the next day. Amongst other things, they drifted off to sleep with the television on. They didn't particularly care what was on but found that leaving the TV on a timer for 30 minutes once they were in bed would enable them to either fall asleep or become sleepy, after which they were not prepared to get out of bed and switch the TV off at the wall, so let it stay on standby all night (discussed in Pink, Leder Mackley et al. 2017). I've often discussed this example, because it pulls back several of the layers of how energy, technology and the routines of everyday life in the home become entangled. It is moreover illustrative of an anticipatory practice; the participants' aim was to be able to confront the following day, of caring for their son and their full-time jobs, and therefore they used the TV, the timer and electricity in an anticipatory mode. They trusted that they would fall asleep with these technologies and resources doing their work, and their actions were oriented to reducing the risk of being tired in the near future, of the next morning. Ten years later, on the other side of the world in Australia I am reminded of their story often in the accounts of participants in our Digital Energy Futures research. Participants who are concerned about saving energy are consistently willing to use electricity to get themselves and their children to sleep. For example, by engaging air conditioning and other digital devices to create sleep environments for children, or moving to sleep in separate rooms when one partner needs to use air conditioning and the other doesn't.

Energy in homes is used not simply in the moment to satisfy immediate needs, but rather energy demand, when conceptualised as what people do, what they feel and as embodying the hopes and anxieties that they have for their everyday futures, bridges the present and the near future. Energy demand is concerned both with how we feel now, and with ensuring that the routines of home, life and work can continue as we hope they will. Towards the end of this chapter, I return to how it also involves ensuring that what we value comes into being (such as getting a good night's sleep), and in making sure that we can live according to our values (such as being able to cope as a parent and in work tomorrow).

This very human, phenomenological involvement in sensing, feeling and knowing about our everyday environments, and aligning them to our near future needs and hopes is moreover fundamental to understanding our possible future relations to emerging energy technologies. Everyday priorities are always contingent, precisely because we don't know what will happen tomorrow, however much we construct routines and provisions in advance to ensure that life will flow smoothly. It should be no surprise that, as participants in our *Digital Energy Futures* documentary (Pink 2022) expressed, external control of their energy supply through an automated system, in which they would be excluded from participation in decision making about when their energy was available, could be difficult to contemplate, as discussed in chapter *air* research participants had similar sentiments regarding staying in control of future air technologies.

The datafication, automation and optimisation of energy

Electricity has long since been measurable as a monetized resource, and methods for measuring, monitoring and predicting its use have evolved as it has become datafied. The quantification of energy has formed part of initiatives to introduce energy metres into the home, an intervention that Yolande Strengers' (2013) work has shown people often did not engage with. However, smart metering continues in increasingly sophisticated, detailed and accessible forms, making energy use data available to people who do become engaged with it, for instance through their interest in and application of solar technologies.

The Digital Energy Futures report (Strengers, Dahlgren et al. 2021: 120) distinguishes between three categories of continuing or emerging/speculative energy technologies: energy management technologies; energy generation and storage technologies; and technologies for buying, selling and sharing energy. This includes technologies that directly address energy: smart metering, emerging home energy management systems, energy monitoring apps and portals, existing home solar photovoltaic inverters and emerging home battery storage and community batteries, existing feed-in or time-of-use tariffs and emerging virtual power plants, peer-to-peer trading platforms and microgrids. However, within and beyond these categories it also includes other tech which tends to be already used or imagined for future energy-related activities including existing weather reports and apps, digital voice assistants, and smart plugs, thermostats and other appliances, electric vehicles and wireless and automated charging as energy technologies. What is evident from this list is that a series of technologies are emerging that are specifically oriented towards energy management, storage and generation and use, but that energy technologies are also emerging everyday life technologies and that to bring together energy, technologies and futures we need to align them with other analyses of everyday and emerging technology futures. The use of digital voice assistants for household energy management, runs alongside, for example, their anticipatory uses, such as setting a timer for cooling champagne (in *Digital Energy Futures* (Pink 2022)) or simply playing music (as demonstrated by participants in *Smart Homes for Seniors* (Pink 2021)). Thus, energy futures become configured with the processes of datafication, automation and control that likewise are implicated in for instance, the future of healthy and safe air (chapter *air*) and mobilities futures (chapter *mobilities*).

The electricity grid is inevitably tied up with the way energy futures are imagined (which is one of the reasons why in the workshops, discussed in chapter *air*, researchers role-played the grid in our discussions with participants). Anthropologist Canay Özden-Schilling shares an anecdote from her fieldwork with energy engineers in the United States: 'An electrical engineering doctoral student studying the electric grid once told me, "The point of all we do is to better match supply and demand."' For Özden-Schilling, this statement 'came as a surprise given that, today, discussions surrounding the grid typically focus on the integration of renewable energy and communication technologies' (2015: 578). The supply and demand terminologies endure internationally when discussing how renewables and automation might be integrated with the grid. In 2021, Yolande Strengers, who has significant experience of the energy industry, suggested that we end a section of my narration of *Digital Energy Futures*, the documentary, with a point about supply and demand, to report that:

> Consultancy and industry reports envisage a 'set and forget' future where individual consumers receive personalised digital services operated by automated systems, making their lives more convenient and more energy efficient, by better matching the supply and demand of energy.

While the documentary goes on to show the complexities of achieving this through automation, the example is illustrative in that it reveals the persistence of the narrative of 'the supply and demand curve', which Özden-Schilling's history of electricity suggests has been an evolving element in the agenda from the outset and had 'garnered scholarly interest once again in the age of the smart grid' (Özden-Schilling 2015: 581). In these narratives, supply is the task of the energy companies, manifested as the grid, and demand is the activity of consumers of energy. The datafication of energy makes this visible, and not just retrospectively or even in real time, as people view their energy use as it evolves online. Predictive analytics means that datafied energy futures are possible. Indeed, it is also important for energy supply companies to forecast future energy demand in order to be able to meet or mitigate the effects of demands of and on the electricity grid.

In a technologically possible future, automated decision making, artificial intelligence (AI) and machine learning (ML) systems could constitute new and invisible relationships between people, their homes, vehicles and the grid. For instance, EVs could be automatically charged while on the move, at moments that were optimal to the supply and demand of energy for both the grid and the vehicle, without their drivers being consulted, using wireless charging technologies, paid for through secure blockchain transactions between trusted entities (e.g. Ketter 2019). As I have argued (Pink 2022a), such engineering imaginaries around future mobilities neglect to concern themselves with how people would experience such seamless technological 'solutions', or how they would combine with contingencies and uncertainties of everyday life as it actually plays out. In the home, this resonates with questions about automation and future air quality (chapter *air*), where the possibility they might allow their energy supply to be controlled by an external organisation, which would subsequently determine when they could access air purification or filtration, was difficult for participants to confront. Likewise, the idea of external remote control of energy supply was not a comfortable prospect for the *Digital Energy Futures* documentary participants. Yet in an engineering dominated narrative, it is precisely this control that can effectively optimise energy systems and increase convenience and comfort for energy consumers.

From a critical perspective, such automation and external control of human access to energy could lead to further inequalities and reduce the agency of households and individuals to manage their own use of an essential resource, and subsequently to shift their priorities in response to the contingencies of everyday life in climate change and possible extreme weather events. However, before going down the dystopian route, we should remind ourselves that energy futures are configured not simply by one-way power relations but by multiple human and non-human actors, and that moreover they cannot be rectified by equally simplified utopian visions. As the anthropologist Hannah Knox writes, if we wish to advance towards a better future we need to 'understand and map the actually-existing relations that constitute the energy system within which people are entwined' (Knox 2021: 81). Knox proposes that attention to data is significant because by tracing numerical or ethnographic data we can learn about 'the social geographies of proportional responsibility' of climate change. This, she argues, is a propositional mode: 'not because it proposes what the future should look like, but because it emerges out of the relationship between the articulation of what is desired and the destabilising potential of what might become apparent in the tracing of relations' (Knox 2021b: 84), and I add, as we imagine relations and the possible data traces they might create in to unknowable futures. Hopeful energy futures can make new data traces into anticipated futures; they involve modes of mapping out possibilities that are aligned with values that make sense for their proponents (as in the example of city data sensing discussed in chapter *data*).

Turning back to the present possibilities and concerns relating to the datafication of energy and the grid, the concerns (if not dystopian anxiety and dread) are already evident. In the first part of this chapter, I invoked the sensationalist possibility that the grid could 'melt down'. In more mundane terms, the grid is vulnerable, to future extreme weather events, as well as in relation to sudden or incremental changes in how energy demand is configured by households and industry. For instance, in Australia when the use of air conditioning rises in response to days of extreme heat, the grid can fail, meaning that vulnerable people, dependent on electricity for their health, will be in danger (see Strengers, Pink & Nicholls 2019). Dramatic change is exemplified through the COVID-19 pandemic, with the shift to working from home. This not only meant a radical disruption in how people lived and worked, as for social workers discussed in chapter *work*, moreover, energy demand at home increased because people needed to heat and cool their homes all day, cooked at home more often, worked from home using digital technologies, used more entertainment devices at home, and charged all of their mobile battery powered devices at home. Energy companies need to prepare for such shifts and have sought to do so through a range of energy demand management initiatives (Nicholls et al. 2021), as well through renewable energy sources for off-grid living (Bainbridge & Kent 2020, December 15). In these circumstances prediction is important. Quantitative energy demand forecasting is a core activity for organisations in the energy sector, yet it needs further attention to social futures (Strengers, Pink & Nicholls 2019), otherwise it runs the risk of missing the key complications that human 'data traces' bring into sight.

I have outlined how anthropology, electricity and emerging technologies are participating in the processes through which energy futures are conceptualised and imagined. I have argued for a processual approach, encompassing design anthropological attention to uncertainty and contingency in the everyday and in global, weather and climate and the politics of energy. Energy futures are unfinished and contingent, but comprehensible through the often shared but differently articulated ambition to secure ethical, equitable and safe energy futures. Such futures are also bound up with the sentiments of trust (chapter *trust*) and hope (chapter *hope*). I next explore how these two concepts might be mobilised to consider energy and technology futures design anthropologically.

Trust in everyday energy-technology futures

Özden-Schilling has argued that the nature of supply and demand of electricity, as a live dynamic and changing relationality, whereby the smart grid's 'temporal sensitivity to changing conditions in supply and demand' (2015: 583) makes it stand out in such a way that it challenged existing theories of 'commodities, economics, and markets' (2015: 579). The engineers Özden-Schilling did research with were trying to re-shape the market – that is, consumers – to the intentions of the smart grid. 'DSM researchers hope to turn us – as electricity consumers – into a new homo economicus, upgraded with new expertise and technological equipment and making decisions for a more balanced grid either automatically or deliberately' (2015: 586). As she discusses in later work (2021), engineers sought to optimise everyday energy use for consumers and for the grid – or energy supply and demand – in ways that enabled people to make optimal decisions, or to leave this to automation. Other scholars have personified these engineering, imaginaries, which are not only alive in the research Lab, but also in industry reports, as gendered optimised personas such as Strengers' 'Resource Man' (2013), Charlotte Johnson's 'Flexibility woman' (2020) and most recently Dahlgren et al.'s 'techno-hedonist' (2021). For these imaginary personas, who live seamless and predictable lives, the relationship between energy supply and demand is resolved by automation. Of course, for real people whose lives are messy, contingent and uncertain, the story is very different. One way to understand how energy futures play out in everyday life, and how this complicates industry visions, is through a consideration of trust.

The concept of trust is highly visible in consultancy, industry and policy reports and agendas, and its extraction – discussed in chapter *trust* – is fundamental to the task of optimization. The Digital Energy Futures review of 64 technology and energy industry reports (Dahlgren et al. 2020) revealed that a key claim of the reports reviewed was that 'Building consumer trust will enable environmentally and economically efficient digital energy futures'. Underpinning this claim were assumptions that 'Consumer trust in the energy sector is low'; 'Low levels of trust in the energy sector are a barrier to consumer engagement with demand management and acceptance of automation'; and 'Building trust requires increased consumer knowledge of the electricity sector'. The reports saw 'consumer' trust as being comprised of three elements: 'Trust in institutions and their management of technology'; 'Trust in the data collected by emerging energy technologies and how it will be used'; and 'Trust in the technology to function as intended' (Dahlgren et al. 2020: 37). As is evident from my discussion in chapter *trust*, none of these renderings of trust is aligned with everyday trust and how the ethics with which it is entangled are experienced. Instead, they support visions of the future in which consumers' (seen as rational actors, who will act in the right way when they have the right knowledge) trust is needed to induce their acceptance of and adoption of technology. They propose logics that fail to account for the everyday realities in which people live in the present, which might lead them to engage with particular technologies, and knowledge in ways that are contingent, and that the future will be shaped by equally contingent circumstances.

One of the key explicatory themes of the *Digital Energy Futures* documentary is precisely this point that everyday energy and technology futures are differently constituted and imagined, to the futures that predominate in industry narratives. As explained in chapter *trust*, trust is also differently constituted in everyday life and industry narratives. The point, which resonates across the chapters of this book, frames the documentary, as I narrate:

> In Australia, increasingly extreme weather, concerns about public health, growing levels of technological automation, and a society dependent on digital media are set to create uncertainty about demand for electricity in the future. The energy industry, and technology companies, are seeking to envision our futures and to plan and design new systems to suit them.
>
> In the meantime in their everyday lives people are inventing their own ways to live with emerging technologies. And they are imagining and planning for their own futures in ways that might complicate the ambitions of industry and policy makers.

The *Digital Energy Futures* documentary takes us into the everyday lives of five households in Australia, chosen for their diversity and their interest in participating in the documentary. All households had already participated in two stages of our online digital and visual ethnography and so knew our interests and members of our team. Let's return to the question posed from the *Digital Energy Futures* narration at the beginning of this chapter: 'What would it be like to give up control to an external system which optimises your energy use, decides when a robotic vacuum cleans your home and even when your electricity is available?' Nigel and Anna, two participants in our research and documentary, were committed to using and exploring automated technologies and systems, including their digital voice assistant, smart lights and a robotic vacuum cleaner. They had solar power, which they combined with energy from the grid, and were watchful and analytical of their energy data and billing; with Nigel working in IT and Anna an accountant, they had a sharp eye on the technologies and finances involved. Yet, while they were invested in automation, as I have noted in chapter *home*, as Nigel expressed it in the documentary, he could imagine more automation in the future, but on the condition of an 'override' button.

The robotic vacuum cleaner, looked at through the prism of everyday trust and ethics, provided the perfect example of why externally driven automated optimisation of energy doesn't necessarily even work for people who are keen to benefit from new energy technologies and automated systems. For Anna and Nigel, the automated vacuum cleaner was helpful, but they said it should not replace human responsibility for the home, Nigel's mantra was that if someone makes a mess then they should clean it up, and Anna pointed out how their children still had to clean the floor before the robotic vacuum cleaner could be used. The contingency around whether there is mess, or not, can scupper the best automated routines, and therefore the anticipatory modes of its use needed human intervention to account for this. But for this household there was additionally an ethics of responsibility in the home, which they shared and wanted their children to learn; you clean up your own mess. Moreover, Nigel's knowledge of technology also meant that he understood how the vacuum cleaner 'saw' and learned to clean their home visually. This created privacy concerns relating to the visual data that the machine had access to, and how this could be shared, which meant that they needed to be able to control the time of day and moment when it was used. As these examples show, layers of energy data, financial data, and unseen visual data can create everyday ways of knowing that engage people with technology but that complicate the possibilities of seamless technological solutions that optimise energy demand and make life more convenient. The robotic vacuum cleaner is but one example of how tracing the relationality between energy, data ethics, trust and safety at home can reveal otherwise hidden stories. But, collectively, the many stories that surface through ethnographic engagements with people in real everyday worlds and possible futures demonstrate a complex and contingent field of relations. They suggest that it is these sites, of contingency, uncertainty and everyday ethics that trust in emerging energy technologies will come about, and that trust will come about when we acknowledge the everyday as a generative site from which any understanding of the possibilities of automated technology need to emerge.

Hopeful energy and technology futures

Energy industry ambitions towards optimisation through automation are narratives of hope for the future, invested in the mastery of engineers, where they offer solutions to problems of energy supply and demand, and have hopes for a sustainable future involving renewable energy and new zero-emissions targets. But, as shown in the last section, they can be foiled when they do not align with everyday values, ethics and trust. As the *Digital Energy Futures* voiceover continues: 'people creatively tailor their technology use to suit their everyday lives, so to gain the benefits automation offers to the energy sector, we need to align it with their human futures'.

In chapter *hope*, I have discussed the idea of creating shared categories of hope. If, as suggested there, hope is concerned with living through our values, how do hope and values come together to create everyday energy demand? Earlier in this chapter, I outlined the example of how parents' energy demand was related to their acquisition of something they valued – a good night's sleep – and living to their values of performing well as parents and workers the next day – even when this meant leaving devices running when they were sleeping. Similarly, in chapter *air*, I discussed how people preferred to control their future air technologies themselves, according to their personal needs and values. If people are to engage with emerging energy technologies, then their values need to be accounted for, and they need to be able to invest their uses of technology with such values. In such a way they will be able to use new technologies with hope. In mundane everyday life, values and hope can be about things as simple as sleeping well, and the possibility that these achievements open up to anticipate what the next day will be like.

The principle of engaging anthropology to complicate, rather than critique, and as the basis for respectful interventions, is fundamental. It can involve collaborative interventions undertaken with industry partners (Pink, Raats et al. 2022), ongoing interventions with tech designers as they work (Pink & Lanzeni 2018), as well as everyday life interventions and experiments, often digital or technological (Duque et al. 2021). *Digital Energy Futures*, the documentary, is itself styled as an intervention, to engage with the energy industry in Australia and beyond, as well as with research engineers and computer scientists, other academics, students and wider publics.

To create hopeful energy and technology futures, stakeholders in these fields need to collaborate. This might involve accommodating multiple ways of under-standing the relationship between the electricity grid, automated systems and technologies and people. The immediate challenge is to create a relationship between different perceptions. On the one hand, we need to account for the hopes invested in the optimisation of supply and demand, their need to ensure that the grid doesn't break down in extreme weather events and moments of high demand, and their plans to incorporate clean energy and reduce carbon emissions. On the other, we must simultaneously acknowledge that the uncertainty and turbulence of demand is located in the dynamics of everyday worlds that are themselves uncertain, turbulent and indeterminate. Uncertainty, when viewed from the risk mitigating structures of contemporary societies, is a problem, but when viewed design anthropologically (Akama et al. 2018) as generative of hope (as discussed in chapter *hope*), the question becomes one of how to live with and harness uncertainty for good. Returning to the question of metaphors, a starting point might be to re-think the terminologies of supply and demand and consider terminologies that lead along new shared paths.

HOME

Chris Dancy, known as the 'most connected' person in the world, in an interview with Bojan Davinic (Bayer Global 2021, April 13) was questioned about the 'best' or 'most impressive' health tech he used. Acknowledging that he was about to answer this question differently to most people, who would probably say it was a fitness tracker, Chris replied:

> I think the most singly impressive piece of digital health technology I have is lights, all the lights in my home since 2013 have been Wi-Fi lights, so they automatically synch to the season, so you know if the days are getting shorter the lights, the lights get shorter, also you can change the colouring of them, so something as simple as having adaptive lighting that you don't have to think about, you know, normally lighting is either on or off, right, lighting doesn't live and I think we still have yet to truly understand circadian rhythm. So, I'd have to say that adaptive, smart lighting is the coolest health tech of the last decade.

I interviewed Chris a few years earlier, in Sweden, when I was researching digital self-tracking and body monitoring technologies. From Chris, and from a video hosted on his website at the time, I learned that his digital health project was not simply concerned with measuring his body, but that, in ways that are coherent with design anthropological thinking about the body and technology, he situated his body in relation to as complete as possible technological rendering of the environment he inhabited. In the video, Chris explained to the filmmakers, showing them around his home, how he used many sensor technologies – including 'ingestible, wearable and location-based sensors, voice-recording devices, apps and services, connected devices such as digital scales and every light bulb connected to the internet individually, a sleep monitor and more' to monitor as much of the detail of his life as possible. When he

DOI: 10.4324/9781003182528-8

checked, in 2014 – he told the filmmaker – 'there had been something like 20,000 things measuring his life' (Fors et al. 2019: 22). I concluded that he had not followed 'the conventional modes of smart-home design' but had 'created a home that is intelligent in the ways that he needs it to be and that he can control in the ways he wishes' (Fors et al. 2019: 109). Chris's connected home, named 'Casa Stuart' (www. chrisdancy.com/casastuart), goes beyond the standard definition of a connected home, which in his words would be: 'Any system that can connect to the internet or another system within the house' whereby 'In essence, electricity makes your home connected' (Dancy, 2016, January 21).

Chris Dancy's case is unusual, and his project of connectedness is beyond the bounds of most people's everyday possibilities. Yet, the way he has engaged automated, smart home technologies in his home offers a fundamental lesson and starting point for considering the relationship between emerging technologies and homes. Chris created a connected home and used sensors and smart devices that suited him, his body rhythms, and his needs, rather than conforming to industry visions of the problems that smart and connected home technology can solve. Around the same time the consultancy, McKinsey & Co. published *There's No Place Like (a Connected) Home* (McKinsey & Co. n.d. b), in which, based on 2016 research, they reported that while 'The vision of the connected home is finally beginning to come together', 'the market still has a ways to go before it reaches its full potential', telling us that 'Many consumers still do not understand connected device value propositions and early adopters face significant pain points that have yet to be addressed'. Specifically, research by consultancies such as PwC (PwC n.d. c) and McKinsey & Co. (McKinsey & Co. n.d. b) suggested that most people surveyed are not likely to buy a connected home yet. This dissonance between the vision of the future connected home and the reality is therefore played out in two ways. Chris' example shows how someone with the technology skills and interest evaded the vision through his own improvisatory practice in creating the home he needed, while simultaneously, the industry vision had failed to find its market in everyday life. In the latter case, I argue, because it has remained unaligned with the everyday lives and possible futures it seeks to create solutions for.

It's no surprise that connected automated homes with multiple smart home devices are envisioned as technological solutions to societal problems, and are being developed, designed, tested and trialled across the world. But what kinds of so-called problems are being identified and how is automated and smart home technology predicted to solve them?

In 2019, a *Time* article predicted that 'a decade from now, experts say, we'll move from turning the lights on and off with our voices to total immersion in the Internet of Things (IoT)'. The *Time* article outlined the small ways this would make people's lives better. With advances in AI, it says 'the smartest homes will be able to truly learn about their owners or occupants, eventually anticipating their needs', 'robotics will give us machines that offer a helping hand with cleaning, cooking and more' while 'sensors will keep tabs on our well-being' and data will be collected, analysed and used to create truly '"smart" homes' (Austin, 2019, July

25). By 2021, according to a *Forbes* article, the smart home was already becoming more ubiquitous, beyond 'the most high-end homes or saved for an upgrade year down the line – people are actually buying homes today with an eye on the existing smart home tech that's already included'. *Forbes* identified five of the 'biggest smart home tech trends happening right now': smart home tech is becoming more integrated with technologies communicating with each other; AI is increasing and IoT is making homes and their devices more connected; touchless technology is on the way up, particularly since the COVID-19 pandemic; smart thermostats were amongst the most adopted devices. Moreover, they tell us, smart health tech is becoming more advanced, including a rise in smart air purification and air conditioning 'to assist in elevating and maintaining air quality during this global health crisis', even 'smart doorbells are integrating temperature-taking functionality so that people can screen their guests for one of the most basic Covid-19 indicators before allowing them inside' and 'smart water filtration systems are helping with overall health' (Hirt & Allen 2021, September 14). These technologies are not simply seen as making life better at home for people who can afford them, but as the *Wall Street Journal* describes it, some such technologies are pitched as supporting energy transition, such as smart thermostats which can automatically ensure technologies are used when renewable energy is available (Holger & Chin 2021, October 6) and as such are seen as contributing to solving environmental problems. These reports are emblematic of contemporary dominant industry and consultancy narratives. In an analysis of 64 industry and consultancy reports, the Digital Energy Futures project found broader future claims that smart home technologies will 'enable studying and working from home' through 'improved telecommunications, virtual reality and augmented reality'; 'enable older people to be cared for within their homes'; introduce 'immersive household entertainment'; be accompanied by an 'increasing uptake of electric and AVs'; and 'manage increased energy demand from heating and cooling to deliver savings for both consumers and the energy industry' (Dahlgren et al. 2020: 56).

Social scientists are generally critical and wary of such promissory discourses about smart homes. In a 2021 analysis of 'the consumer technology industry's discourse about emerging smart home devices', Adam Richard Rottinghaus (2021: 45) identifies a shift in industry discourses in a 'move away from liberatory labor discourses toward management of work/life balance' (2021: 46). He proposes that the industry promotes what he calls a 'new white futurism' which is 'a discourse from companies that promotes emerging smart home technologies as tools for data-driven management of work/life balance in contemporary heteronormative, white, middle-class culture' focused on the possibilities offered by the Internet of Things. Rottinghaus 'suggests that intervening in the cultural imagination through Afro, Indigenous, and queer futurisms can focus collective attention on the emancipatory potential of technology and help reimagine cultural relationships to IoT smart home devices' (2021: 47). At the level of discourse, which is his focus, this is certainly a powerful response. However, there is more to consider, since it is not only by looking at these futurisms that we might examine the consequences of the dissonance between industry visions of data-driven automated homes and managed lives and social and cultural diversity. We should also account for this by investigating how diverse people actually live and engage with such devices and systems when they do encounter them. Rottinghaus concludes that: 'Though promising consumer convenience, new white futurism entrenches corporate power over domestic life. Consumers *must not* buy into such discourses and practices for simple conveniences' (2021: 54, emphasis added). The evidence is that in fact they very often *do not*, as discussed in chapter *energy*, householders visions for future home life with technologies tend to not be aligned directly with those of industry (Dahlgren et al. 2020; Strengers, Dahlgren et al. 2021). This is precisely because, as introduced in chapter *emerging technologies*, people are creative, improvisatory actors in the making and management of their own lives and futures with emerging technologies.

It is no coincidence that the various existing industry visions of home-entangled emerging technologies have either failed to deliver or appear unlikely to be able to realise their promises of a seamless, convenient, safe, happy, sustainable, automated and personalised home life. There are plenty of examples of failure, some of which reveal further issues, in typical scenarios whereby the technology is rolled out and subsequently regulation around its use needs to be invoked. For example, a 2021 case, far from the promise of the temperature-checking smart doorbell anticipated above, a man showed his neighbour, who was an Oxford doctor around his home renovations, revealing to her that his Amazon smart doorbell was videorecording activity in her property. She subsequently took him to court, in a case commented on across the mainstream news media. A BBC news article about the incident (Wakefield 2021, October 14) reported that the man had installed the technology in good faith, but that the judge found his particular system to breach UK data laws.

In this chapter, I focus on the circumstances through which emerging technologies are experienced, both as part of the anticipatory modes of home life and as how they are anticipated as part of the future home. First, I examine the concept of the home itself and how it becomes a site of anticipation and action towards immediate and far futures.

Defining (smart and connected) homes

Home is a tricky, contested and slippery concept, hard to define in terms of both what it is and where its boundaries are. As the example of the smart doorbell noted above shows, emerging technologies are not necessarily aware of the unspoken boundaries of home perceived by humans.

In everyday language, home is commonly associated with a house, apartment or other built environment dwelling. Yet conceptually it is a social, material, mediated, technological, affective and experiential space. In this latter definition, home is not contained within four walls, or even a particular locality but might be constituted and experienced in relation to things and processes situated elsewhere. This is particularly visible for the migrant, displaced people and diasporic communities, for whom homes may be dispersed or distributed geographically, carried in memories, things, practices, food or other sensory effects of everyday and ritual life. Yet it applies to everyone.

If the boundaries of home are flexible, they are not only closed down in moments where they are transgressed, but also opened to other people, technologies, species and elements. The data, air and energy discussed in chapters *data, air* and *energy*, flow through the indeterminate boundaries of home and participate in the very constitution of home. The home has become a site of the labour of both people who work from home, and those who work in other people's homes (Gregg 2011; Pink et al. 2014; Pink, Ferguson & Kelly 2021). During the pandemic, emerging technologies were seen to play new roles in homes and their connectedness outside their walls as people innovated to make themselves feel comfortable and confident as the world around them seemed to change.

The home is also one of the most intimate, creative, dynamic and mundane sites of the everyday. It is a place where people imagine their immediate and far futures, and renew, refresh and prepare for what they anticipate to be next. Its routines and rituals engender senses of familiarity, safety and trust and hope and the ongoingness of the patterns of the everyday, what social scientists have called ontological security. However, while life in the home often follows daily and weekly patterns, and its routines may appear to be repeated over and over again, yet they are not; they are always performed in ways that vary, that are responsive to the contingent material, technological, social or sensory circumstances of that particular moment. The activities people perform and the experiences they have at home shift and change, sometimes incrementally and almost imperceptibly over time, and in other cases more dramatically in relation to the need for a recognisable change (as described for social workers during the pandemic in chapter *work*). Therefore, temporality and spatiality of home are inextricable from the human activity, creativity and improvisation through which everyday life is lived (Pink, Leder Mackley et al. 2017). My research into how people live with technologies in the home over the last 20 years reveals how people engage and improvise with emerging technologies to participate in the routines, rhythms, feelings and sensations of life as lived out and in anticipated futures (e.g. Pink 2004, 2012; Pink, Leder Mackley et al. 2017; Pink & Postill 2019). This, I propose, is where we need to investigate to understand how emerging technologies might be implicated in everyday life in the home in the future.

Modes of improvising with emerging technologies in homes also participate in constituting the home as a site where close gendered and intergenerational relationships of love, care, violence or abuse playout, where inequalities can be clearly witnessed through research but where they may also be obscured from view. Emerging technologies become bound up with all these different inequalities and power relationships in ways that are as diverse as those relationships themselves. There is abundant empirical evidence of the dangers of smart home technologies being engaged or imagined as devices of domestic abuse and control, as Yolande

Strengers and Jenny Kennedy outline in their book *The Smart Wife* (2020: 198–204). Yet existing and emerging technologies are also implicated in relationships of intergenerational care, care for the family and home, and as ways of being together when physically apart, as an equally significant body of research has shown (Hjorth et al. 2020; Sinanan & Hjorth 2018). Emerging technologies do not generate, define or determine the nature and power differentials of these relationships. Rather technologies are engaged by people in ways that may purposefully or carelessly exacerbate or exaggerate them.

Emerging technologies in times of crisis

The COVID-19 pandemic can be seen as involving two modes of change. First, as a dramatic shift, where for many people overnight, or at least over the course of a few days, places of work, education, shopping and recreation closed, time spent outdoors was restricted and mask wearing was made compulsory. Second, as people learned to live with these shifts and the contingent circumstances they brought about, incremental processes of change came about at home and in everyday practice more generally. The improvisatory actions people took to engage with their new circumstances – also discussed in the case of how social workers began to work with technologies from home in chapter *work* – created new everyday life routines, sentiments and experiences at home. New and emerging technologies were implicated in these processes in multiple ways, including because people purchased new technologies during the pandemic. This has been reported on extensively. For example, the Australian edition of the Deloitte Digital Consumer Trends 2020 report (Deloitte 2021) found that amongst the people surveyed, 26% of their respondents had purchased new technologies 'as a direct result of being at home through the pandemic', and 'close to 10%' had bought laptops, smartphones and televisions. They also found that (along with 'students and young people') 'home workers, and technology enthusiasts' drove the 'majority of pandemic purchasing'. The ethnographic research which informed the Digital Energy Futures *Future Home Life* report also found an increase in the use of technologies as they stayed at home in 2020, and particularly increased investment in and simultaneously use of devices for 'household comfort, smart home technology, digital entertainment devices, and recreation' (Strengers, Dahlgren et al. 2021: 7).

Changing home life during extreme climate events and COVID-19 pandemic offers insight into how technologies emerge into markets and how they are constituted in relation to and in response to how people engage with these moments and processes. Publicly available reports, including the *Future Home Life* report mentioned above, suggest that many people imagine that some of the new working from home practices they had developed during the pandemic will stick, and that they were unlikely to go back to working full time from the office. Some improvisations evolved out of the intensity of life at home during the pandemic, as in the context of an abrupt change, parents learned to live and use technology differently. For instance, as computing or timing devices in the home-education that parents were expected to deliver during the pandemic, or as voice assistants to read children bedtime stories. Some of the techniques that they incrementally developed will likely become sedimented into everyday life going forward. The pandemic grew many living examples of how emerging technologies actually come about, or emerge, as everyday life technologies, such as the growth of air filtration and purification (chapter *air*) or the use of digital technologies in working from home (chapter *work*), the tablets which the seniors who participated in our *Smart Homes for Seniors* documentary integrated into their routines for communicating with their families during the pandemic (as well as for speaking with the research team) (Duque et al. 2021), and the emergence of the home as a hub for battery charging shown in the *Digital Energy Futures* (Pink 2022) documentary.

Conceptualised as a technology experiment, the COVID-19 pandemic has demonstrated perfectly that technologies do not simply land in people's homes to solve problems that engineers, policymakers and governments assume to exist. In the pandemic, people used technologies at home in new circumstances of uncertainty, but did so in situations they could trust sufficiently to support their priorities and needs, and in ways that corresponded with their hopes and expectations. I next explore in more detail how this happens through the two examples of how seniors learned to live with smart home technologies on the one hand, and on the other how techies have gone about installing their own smart home technologies and systems.

Smart homes for seniors

A growing field of research, stretching across anthropology, sociology and STS analyses, technology tests and trials, is emerging. These disciplines have varied interests in testing and trialling, mainly informed by their theoretical orientations and the analytical units they work with. As for the case of AD car testing, discussed in chapter mobilities, smart home technology tests and trials, can be analysed design anthropologically. They can thus be seen as opportunities through which to gain theoretical and ethnographic insights into how people live, learn and improvise with emerging technologies in two ways. First, as they encounter them in the real contingent circumstances of the unfolding of the everyday; and, second, as they implicate them in the near and far future anticipatory modes through which they live out their lives.

The example I discuss here, draws on the *Smart Homes for Seniors* (Pink 2021) documentary film, which specifically focused on how seniors experienced smart home technologies. In the case of *Smart Homes for Seniors*, the wider research project (involving 33 participants and 22 households in New South Wales, Australia), revealed two anticipatory modes: near future questions regarding the feelings of confidence, anxiety or trust that participants experienced when the technology became part of their homes and their daily routines; and far future feelings of hope and aspiration, regarding their own or other seniors' continued independence and wellbeing. However, as I emphasise throughout this book, futures and the ways they can be treated always need to be situated, and the case of seniors is illustrative here in reminding us that our perspectives on futures are also related to where we are situated in life. The way futures feel – that is how they are sensed corporeally and imaginatively – vary for people at different age and life stages. Emerging technologies and the future narratives associated with them can only be meaningful to the extent that people can make them complicit with their own situated possible futures.

Smart Homes for Seniors, the documentary, was an outcome of an award-winning interdisciplinary project (see also Duque et al. 2021; Pink, Fors et al. 2022; Strengers, Duque et al. 2021). The Emerging Technologies Lab collaborated with a not-for-profit aged care organisation – Mclean Care – and Deakin University to trial a set of smart home technologies with seniors in their homes and evaluate their implications for seniors' independence and wellbeing. The documentary is an example of design anthropological filmmaking (Pink 2022b) which seeks to foreground the improvisatory ways in which people engage with technologies in everyday life, and the need to engage with their lives and needs. Indeed, one of the key messages of *Smart Homes for Seniors* is to demonstrate precisely how people and automated technologies become co-implicated as the possibilities that technologies might have in everyday life become evident.

The wider project revealed many examples which are reported in applied and academic publications and in the documentary. One of the most powerful instances of participant improvisation with the technologies being trialled, which was further developed through the interventional design ethnography practice (Pink, Fors et al. 2022) of the team, involved learning use the digital voice assistants (DVAs) to create everyday meaning through music. In the *Smart Homes for Seniors* documentary, one of the participants, Robert, showed us how he asks the DVA to play hip-hop music for him, and Ken told us 'the music's fantastic, I like the classics I like the jazz, hip hop … swap from one to the other, you know'. Sitting at the table with his wife, Ken continued 'and Helen, she loves her classics and we put that on of an evening, you know, and it's just beautiful sitting there listening to the classic music isn't it?' Helen continued, to describe how 'I sat and read a book for about three hours the other, well actually four, four hours, just sitting listening to the music, which is so relaxing, just sitting there, you know, no cares in the world'. Other participants showed us how music brought to them by the automated systems and devices of the DVA, created everyday meaning, in two research events that we could not include in the documentary, but were amongst the most emotive moments of the fieldwork I participated in. In one household, Edna showed us how she asked her DVA to play her favourite tracks by the Dutch violinist and conductor, André Rieu, while she made the bed, and in another household Melisa Duque, co-researching with me, suggested that David could ask the DVA to play his favourite music by the Irish music ensemble Celtic Woman. These moments invoked the sensory and affective ways of knowing that characterise ethnographies of home, by revealing the constitution of the sensory home through music. In my earlier work, which led me to coin the concept of the sensory home, as a site that is known, experienced and imagined multi-sensorially (Pink 2004), I discussed how a participant living with her cousin, camping out on the sofa and putting her bedding in the cupboard at night, made the apartment feel like her own home for short moments. This was a time when she was alone in the mornings and could fill the rooms with her favourite music. Similarly, Edna's, David's, Robert's and Helen and Ken's uses of the DVA brought their environments alive with the sentiments related to biography, self and pleasure. As, following Melisa's suggestion to request music from the DVA, melodies of Celtic Woman began to fill their living room, Beryl commented that David would 'be delighted, he loves it … my husband was a bandsman, he used to, he was drum major for years, he played a couple of instruments over the years, yes this is a lovely one, he'll be very thrilled with that'. Her words invoked a whole lifetime of experience and emotion to that moment in their living room, shared with the researchers, their dog and the DVA.

Far from the industry imaginaries of smart home technologies themselves solving problems related to senior care, independent living and wellbeing, the film reveals how it is in fact within the relations between the human, technical, material and other species' relationships of home that these issues are addressed. The evidence suggests that rather than smart home technologies themselves being the solution to social and individual problems, they might better be seen as elements of everyday engagements combined with human-led services that could be tailored to the needs of seniors. Such future services might involve big data analytics, machine learning, automated systems and AI-enabled devices, but these need to be embedded in relations that involve other humans and which are designed in accordance with human needs and are sensitive and flexible to how these needs change over time. Again, as in chapter *work*, we see the question of how emerging technologies come about in everyday life is answered: in terms of how people will shape the ways technologies are used in everyday situations; and as technologies and humans create new socio-technical services, where the use of different levels of digital, automated or robotic technologies co-evolve in relation to the specific service being delivered. Rather than technologies impacting on a passive quotidian site, we should see them becoming integrated into the digital living skills, needs, services and imaginaries that constitute an active everyday world.

Making homes smart

Another example of the role people play in bringing emerging technologies into their everyday lives in their home, is the case of people who are sometimes called 'early adopters', often in association with Everett Rogers' early but influential theory of *The Diffusion of Innovation* (1962). As outlined in chapter emerging technologies, we need to go beyond seeing innovations as products that are finished and seeing people as taking them up for use as instructed or intended by their designers. Early adopters defined as such probably don't exist in real life, but there are people who have an interest in and tendency to buy and use emerging technologies before others, who are referred to as early adopters. In this section I explore how human creativity and improvisation meet smart home technologies in such cases.

Chris Dancy would be more likely to be classified as an innovator than an early adopter on Rogers' scale, nevertheless, his example is illustrative, since rather than installing an existing smart home system and using it to solve the problems it was designed for, Chris defined his own needs and used the possibilities offered by smart home technologies to design a system that supported him. Other people follow similar processes. For example, Murphy, was an engineer living with his wife and their four-year-old son and ten-month-old baby in a modern house in a quiet area of a regional CBD. When I interviewed him and toured his home with him on Zoom in 2020, he and his wife were still both working from home during the pandemic lockdown. For Murphy his job was 'not unenjoyable', but it was more of a 'pay cheque' than a passion, which amongst other things supported his interest in developing his own personal smart home system. During the pandemic, the family made some new purchases, including a TV for their children's room, and brought home monitors for work from his wife's work for which Murphy set up a 'hardwired internet connection to the desk'.

Murphy had used an Apple HomeKit home automation platform, which meant he could control his home technology through a smartphone app or voice commands. Yet, while he was committed to this automated system, like other participants, he was very involved in the decision making regarding how the system operated and in the fine-grained decisions that were actually taken on a daily basis, relating for example to his smart lights and heating and cooling systems. As discussed in chapter *energy*, my earlier research has also shown that for families with young children, a powerful everyday priority is to get a good night's sleep and technologies tend to be harnessed to achieve this regardless of the energy demand implications even when families are committed to sustainable living (Pink et al. 2017; Pink, Leder Mackley et al. 2017). Murphy and his wife's priorities were no different. My first question was about their daily routine, and he immediately described how, 'assuming the baby sleeps through, then we're generally woken up by the baby. We'll check our phones obviously then and make a note of when he did wake up', explaining that his 'wife likes a lot of control so we have a running log of all his sleeps and drinks and stuff'. Because the baby hadn't been sleeping through, they were doing 'literally everything we can think of to make him comfortable' and had recently even been putting air conditioning on all night in the baby's room to try to keep the temperature stable. This was part of the way that he used the platform, with which he said there was 'lots of interaction with the app to, you know, check room temperatures, what's best with his [the baby's] room temperature because that's the only thing we can control'. Going into more detail, it becomes clear, in ways that correspond with the stories of other participants, the more automated the home, the more involvement people had in its management, creating new modes of what media scholars have called 'digital housekeeping' (Tolmie et al. 2007).

Murphy had 'set up themes in certain scenarios', including to monitor his older son's room temperature, which would automatically come on, on particular days of the week, but he said that in reality 'a lot of the time we just use it manually'. For this family, using the automated technology manually involved ways of living and engaging with automation that enabled them to control how and when their systems worked, to anticipate what knowledge they would need, access that knowledge and use it to make their lives as comfortable as possible in the present, and to plan for the next day by doing their best to arrange things so they would get a good night's sleep. In Murphy's words: 'Typically what we'll do is we'll go oh it's a bit chilly in here, what's the temperature in the pool room for instance or the living room, we'll look at the sensor and it'll tell us and we'll go yeah that's a reasonable time to turn the air conditioner on'.

'Early adopters' therefore do not necessarily simply adopt emerging technologies. Rather, they mould the possibilities that are offered by the designs of emerging technologies into the materialities of their homes, their everyday routines, and their family priorities and needs. They remain in control of their homes, engaging automation to support them, rather than to determine their experiences and actions. Here, I have focused on one particular example to demonstrate how emerging technologies actually come about in everyday life in the home. A focus on what women might engage smart home technologies for, offers similar insights in terms of control (as does the *Digital Energy Futures* documentary more broadly), but demonstrates differently gendered approaches to managing technology at home.

Smart home complications

In examples, or smart home technology experiments, discussed in this chapter, we have seen how people have come to live with technologies. I have suggested how emerging technologies participate in people's routines, engage their emotions and subsequently contribute to how they create certainties about themselves and their lives. Emerging technologies thus become part of the processes through which people gain a sense of ontological security about themselves and their circumstances, how they anticipate their near futures, and feel confident about what might be next, that is they contribute to how people trust in their everyday worlds. This, I stress, does not constitute evidence that people trust smart home technologies! Instead, it provides us with an example of how emerging technologies can both come about through and become constituent elements of continually evolving everyday circumstances, situations and feelings in which people experience trust.

On his web site, Chris Dancy outlines how his 'home and it's systems are all linked to a series of triggers that make things happen automatically'. He describes how 'Upon waking, lights, music and temperature are adjusted. If I'm anxious, talking loud, my lights soften. Spending too much time sitting still, fast music plays. The beautiful thing about Casa Stuart is how much technology you don't see'. Indeed, for Chris 'Connected homes are not necessarily "smart homes"' because he writes: 'Smart homes have books, people and love' (Dancy 2016, January 21). Why does Chris Dancy trust his connected home? – most likely because he created it himself and he is in control of it; he is a software developer. A 2014 *Guardian* newspaper article interview with Chris, when he was at an event in London, quotes him as saying that there, 'Right now I feel pretty naked … because I can't control the room.' whereas his connected home environment 'automatically adjusts according to his mood and needs'. Subsequently, it is easy to understand why the Oxford doctor whose privacy was invaded, trusted neither her neighbour nor his smart home technologies. They were developed and designed by a company she had no connection with and installed by someone she hardly knew, without consulting her. These are two very different ways of living with automated technologies. As the *Guardian* describes it, in Chris' case

> Dancy claims this connected environment – which he calls "data-assisted living" – has revolutionised his life, helping him to lose 100 pounds in 18 months, and letting him live in a state of zen-like calm, safe in the knowledge that his every moment is being archived.
>
> *(Wainwright 2014, March 19)*

In contrast, the Oxford doctor, according to the court judgement, was left 'alarmed and appalled' and ultimately moved out of her home (Wakefield 2021, October 14). Research shows, likewise, that people generally seek to stay in control of their homes, the routines that are followed in them, and in what they anticipate or plan to happen in the near and far future of their homes: the *Digital Energy Futures* documentary concludes that most people are not interested in handing over the management of their home technologies or energy to automated systems of devices.

When considering emerging technologies and their relationship to the home we need to consider three essential points, learned from design anthropological knowledge about the home. First, *home is never bounded*: While the smart and connected home concepts are also based on the idea of the home as a specific unit in the built environment, inhabited by household members, it is of course not a discrete unit at all. If we see the home as an intensity of flows, of people, things, materials and more which constitute home as a place, in the emerging and possible future home these are accompanied by and entangled with digital, smart and automated things – algorithms, devices and systems. These similarly flow through the home, intensify their relationships with people and things in it, and continually co-constitute and configure the home anew. Second, therefore, *the home is always changing* in relation to the people, processes, things and experiences that constitute it. Third, as a site of change, the home is inevitably *a site for anticipation and human creativity and improvisation*, where people have innumerable ways in which to organise, direct, prepare for and imagine what will happen in their immediate and far futures.

These elements of home each challenge the promise of emerging technologies. First, automated systems of software and hardware digital data, algorithms and sensors using artificial intelligence, automated decision-making and machine learning are all

imagined to be able to optimise how the future home works, by automating its relationships with wider infrastructures, systems and services – such as the energy grid
(chapter *energy*) or the workplace (chapter *work*). But if we see the home as an
unbounded entity the internal (human and non-human) constituents of which are not
wholly consistent or predictable, the optimizable entity might be hard to define in
such a way that is aligned with the everyday. Second, future homes are imagined as the
sites where people will use connected smart devices, such as digital voice assistants,
robotic vacuum cleaners, smart lights, air filtration technologies and surveillance and
security systems, which could use machine learning to predict household behaviour.
But if what happens in homes is always contingent on the ways they themselves
evolve, future needs could be difficult to predict based on what has happened in the
past. Future homes may be seen as sites where *predictive data analytics* will be used to
optimise and control the use of energy and technologies to enable households to
accomplish their routines in the immediate future or support a sustainable energy
transition in the longer term. Yet, as suggested in the examples in this chapter, and in
chapters *air* and *energy*, householders might want to stay in control so that they can
make contingent decisions about when technologies are used.

Smart home futures?

As is evident from the discussion above, dominant smart home narratives do not
cohere with everyday life narratives. When we surface and foreground what prominent international technology experts, seniors in rural Australia, or everyday tech
experts are doing with technology themselves in their own homes, it is evident that
in common they successfully live with emerging home technologies because they
have the capacity to improvise, engage these technologies in the routines, priorities
anticipatory modes of their lives. That is, the technology accompanies them as they
plan for and step over *the edge of the future*. This is also the site from where home
technology futures need to be re-thought, with people more diverse than those I
have focused on in this chapter, towards new ethical everyday technology futures.

WORK

Nicci Rossouw (CEO of Robotics firm Exaptec) and Mark Pivac (CTO of FBR), speaking in a 2021 podcast, were wary of the hype of promissory or at least optimistic statements about the future of robots at work, often unrealistically made by the speakers who open tech conferences (Russouw n.d.). They were also both adamant the introduction of the kinds of robots they work with will not threaten anyone's jobs. Rossouw is in the assistive technology space. She interviewed Pivac about the story of Hadrian the robotic bricklayer (do not imagine a humanoid robot laying bricks), a technology he described as 'only just possible now'. While Hadrian just recently started to demonstrate its potential in the industry, like many tech inventions (Pink 2021b), it germinated over time. Pivac had been considering the possibilities of using optical surveying to create tech solutions to difficult and unpleasant work tasks across different industries since the 1990s, but realised that often there wasn't a global market for what he was proposing. In 2005, during a building boom and shortage of construction workers in Western Australia (WA), with the cost of construction worker salaries skyrocketing, things changed. The idea that Pivac said was 'sitting in the back of my mind, just waiting for the right application ... potentially big enough to be able to be funded to sort out the myriad of problems', came into being. In such moments, emerging technologies connect with their markets and in doing so, appear as the right solution to the problem they were waiting for; as Pivac points out 'The big issue with introducing new technology into the building industry is it's got to be a 100% solution you can't go there with ... even a 99% solution ... and that's what Hadrian does, it goes in there and solves all of their problems'.

By 2021, Hadrian, or rather the building-as-a-service model that Hadrian makes possible, was growing. To gain an idea of its implications, consider Pivac's comparison of it to a typical house building job: he tells listeners that typically to build a single house in WA it would take two to three workers between two to six

DOI: 10.4324/9781003182528-9

weeks. In FBR's video of Hadrian laying the bricks for a WA house, we're told the process took 29 laying hours (FBR 2021, October 15). In the podcast Pivac explains that, at the moment, using Hadrian involves working with ancillary staff whose role it is to develop and monitor the technology, although the machine itself only really needs two operators and ultimately it's likely to just need one.

Emerging technologies and the future of work

In contrast to the incremental and personal narrative through which Pivac describes the coming to market of Hadrian, in many dominant narratives the introduction of automated systems and robotic devices into the workplace has been heralded as leading to dramatic changes to the present and future of work. These are frequently promoted through accounts of utopian promise or dystopian dread. Both perspectives have more than a grain of accuracy in them; emerging technologies are already being used to exploit vulnerable workers for monetary gain in the service of capitalism; and they are also enabling people to work and live in ways that at the best save lives and at least generate wellbeing. But in the pursuit of powerful arguments through binaries we lose sight of the diverse everyday realities of how emerging technologies are actually experienced in the present, and of plausible and realistic accounts of how they may become part of the future of work.

According to the sociologist of AI Anthony Elliot, the evidence suggests we are in a one-way process of the increasing displacement of human jobs by automated machines and 'these jobs are not coming back' (2022: 94). However, Elliot warns against seeing this as universal job destruction, since the erosion of some jobs through the introduction of automated systems and robotic technologies will lead to new human roles and skills being needed. Hadrian the bricklaying robot is a case in point: Pivac is resolute that his company is not taking people's jobs away: 'Right now I can absolutely say that Hadrian has not taken any or put any bricklayers out of work and we've created up to 155 high tech jobs in WA'. This represents a diversity of roles, Pivac continues: 'we employ a whole range of people ranging from the people who build Hadrians, through to those who designed them, operate them, do the programming and so on'. In a context where there has been an 'undersupply of bricklayers in WA for years' and in 2021 a COVID-19 recovery building boom, Pivac thinks TAFEs (Technical and Further Education) will take a while to get up to speed, so they are training people internally, to offer Hadrian as a service; they are selling the bricklaying service rather than simply the technology. Pivac believes that they are on a 'growth curve where over the next years and decades it'll become ubiquitous' and eventually almost all building work will be done by robots.

Hadrian offers but one example of how people and machines might start to work together. Industry narratives about the future of work vary. Some seem to firmly believe that technology is the driving force and frequently speak in universals. Reporting on the findings of the Boston Consulting group, in 2021 ZDNet announced 'Technology will create millions of jobs. The problem will be to find workers to fill them' (Leprince-Ringuet 2021, March 20). Others put people first, earlier on in the pandemic in 2020, the consultancy Jones Lang LaSalle (JLL) reported that we were moving towards a more hybrid, digitally connected working model globally and proposed that future hybrid workplaces should be 'more human than ever to support employees' diverse, changing needs and work-styles' (JLL 2020, November 17).

Academic debate is still unclear on exactly what the implications of automation or robots will be for the future of work and of human wellbeing (Elliot 2022) or how our work lives will be impacted by COVID-19. The inevitable and inescap-able uncertainty about the future of work, and the impossible to answer questions of if or how dystopian or utopian predictions of future automated workplaces and robot workers will play out, form a highly visible backdrop to this chapter. But I argue we need to shift the focus to learn from the realities of the anticipatory modes and imagined futures of the everyday as automated systems and technologies ranging from robots to smartphone apps become implicated in the professional lives of differently situated working people.

In chapter *emerging technologies*, I identify emerging technologies as in the process of coming about. All technologies are in a continual state of emergence, which is contingent on how people who engage with them in real world situations and the evolution of the circumstances in which they emerge, as well as on the work of engineers and computer scientists who invent, develop or design them. The prac-tical question relating to emerging technologies and the future of work, then, is to ask how and where new technologies come about in the workplace. How are they differently imagined, and by whom? How and where do they emerge, and with what and whom do they configure as they come about? To do this I examine two examples of the kind which usually escape the attention of critical data and tech-nology scholars: automated and robotic technologies in the construction industry and digital technologies in UK social work during the pandemic.

Refiguring the question

There would be no point in being a critical scholar if your agenda wasn't to seek out things that are unethical, inequitable, unfair and downright wrong. Critical analysis and thinking enables the development of powerful arguments about what is wrong and why. Yet it frequently illuminates the worst aspects of society, taking attention away from the creativity and inventiveness of humans. This is no less the case for the future of work. According to the anthropologist David Graeber (2018) we live in an era of 'bullshit jobs' – which he defines as jobs that have no apparent meaning or purpose – alongside what he describes as 'shit jobs', which are con-siderably more unpleasant than the bullshit variety. Jathan Sadowski suggests we live in 'the age of Amazon' (2020: 25), the leading tech company which grew from its origins in online retail, and has also been extensively criticised by scholars (including Alimahomed-Wilson et al.. 2020, and contributors) and journalists (Sainato 2020, February 5) for how it has pioneered automated workplace surveillance systems. If Amazon is at the vanguard of the future automated workplace, the critiques of scholars such as Sadowski (2020) indicate that if other organisations follow suit, then the future of work is looking decidedly dystopian. Work in an era of emerging technologies and big data analytics has been problematised, and it is undeniable that there exist systems that exploit vulnerable workers, including gig workers, and exacerbate social and economic inequalities. But, just as the hype often fails its promise, technologically driven dystopian workplace futures are not inevitable or universal. I argue that we need to balance the analysis, to acknowledge these evident injustices, but to simultaneously create and illuminate the possibility of hopeful ways forward.

The COVID-19 pandemic led to growing enthusiasm for automated and robotic solutions to the multiple new challenges that arose in workplaces. However, this was not necessarily at the expense of humans. While there have been examples of uncomfortable uses of telehealth, others are focused on safety, such as a dog type robot developed to take patients' vital signs, which could potentially safely monitor COVID patients, and to carry a tablet through which doctors could speak with them (Trafton 2020, August 31). While the longer-term ramifications are as yet unknown, robots do not always take jobs 'away' from humans when deployed during the pandemic. In 2020, *The Wall Street Journal* reported (Smith, J. 2020, August 12) on how in a US company – American Eagle Outfitters Inc. – human workers managed multiple 'piece-picking' warehouse robots with 'mechanical arms, computer vision and artificial intelligence to sort through piles of apparel' to cope with growing online orders for comfortable clothes during the pandemic. Whereas before the pandemic new staff would be contracted to cope with growing demand, introducing robots was explained as a means of keeping workers safe in a situation where it was impossible or unsafe to hire new untrained staff. Robots also participated as tennis judges at the US Open during the pandemic where 'Hawk-Eye Live' made line calls 'to reduce the number of people on site' (Clarey 2020, August 3). Workplace robots are being developed to undertake multiple mundane tasks, such as workplace inspections in the case of the four-legged ANYmal (Anybotics n.d.), and working underwater in the case of the CageReporter robot which inspects fish pens and 'utilizes artificial intelligence-based algorithms to observe the behaviour of the fish, adjusting its movements in order to disturb them as little as possible' (Coxworth 2020, December 14). Robots that can get into spaces that humans cannot, and much faster, can potentially save lives – recently developed 'soft, wiggly roboworms can stretch up to nine times their own length and are capable of a form of proprioception', which 'could find applications in mining, construction or even in disaster relief to search for survivors trapped in rubble' (University of Glasgow 2021, September 6). There is evidently a lot of diversity in terms of how automated systems, robotics technologies and uses of digital data are becoming part of workplaces. Not all need to have dystopian ends, and most are not in the places where social scientists usually look.

It is not surprising that there has been so much academic and journalistic focus on Amazon; for Sadowski (2020: 25), it was impossible to write about digital capitalism without recurrently encountering the organisation. The case of Amazon is not only an example of how automation has been implemented in a mundane logistics and warehousing industry, but also a household name which continues to receive critical attention from journalists and academics. Conventional scholarship involves building on and dialoguing with the work of others, and contributing to high profile academic and media-worthy topics advances existing debates, *and* is effective in bringing ground-breaking and ethical arguments into public view. But the adverse effect is that many other more mundane stories, where automation and workplace robots are equally implicated, remain hidden. This includes stories where automated systems and robots appear not to represent the threats often associated them: in 2021 Reuters reported in an aptly titled article that 'The robot apocalypse is hard to find in America's small and mid-sized factories', that SMEs in the US aren't getting robots as they can't afford either them or the workers to use them (Aeppel 2021, August 2). Telling these other stories offers an opportunity to see what stepping away from the academic mainstream can reveal.

We need to focus on emerging technologies in the workplaces that critical social scientists of AI and ADM less frequently account for, to acknowledge the different temporalities of emerging technologies, whereby devices or systems established in one workplace may be absent or still at the cusp of becoming ubiquitous in another. Scholars have recently surfaced mundane everyday workplace worlds where new encounters are emerging between automation and people's everyday work practices, embodied knowing, sensory engagements, affective and social relationships and routines. Examples surface the mundane routine lives of office workers and the automated systems and 'assistants' that are appearing in their workplaces. For example, Stine Lomborg (2022) has demonstrated the disconnect between the metrics of automated work monitoring software and the ways professionals mix up work and life. Jakob Svensson (2022) shows how in the work of a daily news organisation in Sweden, rather than commanding workers' practices, automated systems freed journalists up from tasks and the algorithms became the site through which different professional priorities were negotiated between humans. Magnus Bergquist and Bertil Rolandsson (2022) show us how, when professionals bring automated technologies and systems into their work in health care, automation is used to support their work, rather than monitor their outputs.

In these contexts, emerging technologies and emerging work practices co-evolve, as people encounter new devices, algorithms and automated systems in the places they already inhabit. The oppressive regulatory and audit possibilities and tendencies of some automated systems can be dehumanising, objectifying people in the present and future through techniques of measurement predictive data analytics, and it is important to remember the inequalities and inequities through which people are situated as such (Benjamin 2019; Eubanks 2018). But collectively the work of those scholars whose investigations into the fine-grained detail of other possible working lives with emerging technologies reveals how they also become entangled with the everyday trust and hope and other anticipatory feelings through which we move forward in the world. I pursue this here by exploring emerging technologies in the construction industry and child protection social work.

Emerging technologies in the construction industry

The construction industry has been slow to digitalise and (while there are exceptions) there is little use of on-site robotic automation (Gharbia et al. 2020; Melenbrink et al. 2020). The continually changing and emerging environment of construction is a fascinating site in which to investigate human improvisation, trust and hope. The work that Hadrian the bricklaying robot introduced above performs is predictable because it is undertaken in a contained environment. But it is frequently difficult for robots to work on construction sites themselves due to the unpredictability of the material environment, and it is complicated to introduce new technologies due to the fragmented structure of the industry which has a high frequency of subcontracting.

Generally, automation and robotisation are seen as beneficial to the industry, for instance, in the journal *Automation in Construction*, Nathan Melenbrink, Justin Werfel and Achim Menges outline advantages of robotic automation for construction sites: 'reducing injury rates, handling repetitive tasks, and helping to enable construction in settings not currently feasible' (Melenbrink et al. 2020: 1). To realise this, they call for interdisciplinary research involving 'architects, civil engineers, mechanical engineers, computer scientists and roboticists', and suggest a greater focus on worker training in the industry (Melenbrink et al. 2020: 14–17). Typical of technology driven research in this field, the technological promise focuses on key issues for the industry, but does not account for the social, ethical and regulatory questions involved, nor the possibility that construction workers would have relevant knowledge to contribute to design processes, through Union representation, or through the filter of expert social science research. In visions of full automation, the knowledge and skills of or roles played by existing human workers become irrelevant, since the value added through robotisation is located elsewhere. For example: 'Replacing a drywall worker with a current state-of-the-art humanoid robot does not add value … Conversely, automating drywall hanging in a prefabrication factory could substantially increase productivity' (Melenbrink et al. 2020: 17). This view of the future of the industry also prevails in business circles. Just before the COVID-19 pandemic, in December 2019, an article by McKinsey & Co. suggested the future of the construction industry would be shaped by the automation of manual tasks undertaken on construction sites. On site, bricklaying and off-site modular construction would be done by machines. This would increase productivity and employment opportunities. They predicted that 'The key will be anticipating and preparing for the shift, in part by developing new skills in the current and future workforce'; envisaging future hybrid working practices where robots might undertake part of a task, and construction workers would accomplish technical tasks such as operating drones and using tablets (McKinsey & Co. 2019: 5). Examples of technologies which workers collaborate with on-site exist, including Hadrian the bricklaying robot and for example, the Hausbot – a wall climbing robot, whose company's website shows it operated by workers, in situations where they would otherwise have to face the dangers of working at height (https://hausbots.com/).

In these narratives and in the practical realities of the use of robotic technologies, the role of future workers is being carefully considered. In an analysis of over 60 industry reports and engineering- and management-focused academic articles reviewed by me and colleague Ben Lyall, we found an imaginary of a future: where automation and robotiscisation would impact workers. However, we found no suggestion of how workers might actively participate in a transition to an automated construction industry. The technology and industry driven vision is of future workers who are repositioned in the industry, companies who take responsibility for training them, and roles that Construction 4.0 will create for them. It implies a future where the industry will be transformed and subsequently the humans re-shaped to fit it.

However, existing ethnographic research in the construction industry paints a very different picture to this vision of passive workers, moved around and re-skilled by paternalistic or patron-like employers in order to fill new roles that have been created for them. Over 15 years, I have collaborated with colleagues in the UK and Australia, developing ethnographies to surface the experienced realities and everyday improvisation that construction workers engage in to stay safe on site. Like everyone, construction workers are creative and improvise. Reconstituting them into construction 4.0 workers is not so simple. Our earlier research has revealed how new technologies, from mobile phones to video and QR codes, have emerged in site construction work as safety technologies. While of a different order to some contemporary emerging technologies, in terms of their predicted capabilities, and impact on the industry, they exemplify how technologies actually come about in industry. The case of digital technology in the construction industry shows how the specificity of the particular structures, socialities, embodied ways of knowing, and material and climate-specific environments of an industry create the circumstances through which technologies emerge in particular ways. The very specificity of Hadrian as a bricklaying robot, custom made for the industry as part of a building as a service model is a case in point, very different to a self-driving car, which is a technological innovation searching for applications that it might not fit (chapter *mobilities*). The use of mobile phones on construction sites similarly shows how technologies emerge within work practices. The mobile or smartphone should never be thought of as a finished product because it is continually updated by software downloads and in new models; and it is only ever completed in use as it becomes part of socio-technical configurations (Pink, Fors & Glöss et al. 2018). Using mobile phones was banned on construction sites for some time, where

> For OSH [Occupational Safety and Health] professionals the relationship between digital media and OSH has tended to be formed around the problem of ensuring that people work safely *with* digital media and technologies, in order to prevent injuries attributed to the use of technologies (e.g., repetitive strain injuries, falls or traffic accidents if being distracted while using technologies), rather than on how such technologies might be engaged in the experience or performance of OSH.
>
> *(Pink et al. 2014: 337)*

However, our ethnography carried out on UK construction sites by Dylan Tutt, research revealed that here they were also being used in this context in ways that kept construction workers safe, in the coordination of complex processes (Pink et al. 2010). Later research with Jennie Morgan and Andrew Dainty found smartphones were also used for a range of coordination and safety questions by managers (Pink et al. 2014). The smartphone was being integrated into work practices on construction sites to support worker safety in ways that directly contested the dominant and regulatory safety narratives that viewed smartphones themselves as a threat to safety.

Later research about safety in the Australian construction industry, with Helen Lingard and James Harley (Pink et al. 2016), was undertaken where the smartphone had become a ubiquitous technology amongst construction workers and even introduced a new layer of digital safety technology. We collaborated with CodeSafe, a company founded by David Broadhurst, who, with significant experience of working in construction, had developed a platform-based system and method for workers to connect with safety knowledge through online video clips of safe working procedures, made using participatory video techniques with workers on sites, based on their expertise and experiences. Videos were accessed via QR code using smartphones, making them widely accessible to workers, who could identify with them much more easily than they could with written safety instructions. Our analysis explained how this system was effective precisely because through it 'safety is embedded in the work itself' (Pink et al. 2016).

In the wake of the latter stages of the COVID-19 pandemic in Australia, QR code has become part of the everyday life of the majority of the population, with the requirement to use it to check in. But when we were analysing CodeSafe's model, QR code was not prominent in most workplaces, or in the construction industry – known as a latecomer to most emerging technologies. Yet QR codes emerged in construction industry safety technology precisely because they were used in ways that were inextricable from workers' otherwise invisible values and ways of knowing. QR code came about in construction as it configured with smartphones and everyday expertise in a dangerous working environment where safety issues needed to be addressed in new ways. It empowered workers to take greater responsibility for their own safety.

The leap from QR code to bricklaying robots is dramatic, but there are some relevant similarities. Similar to the work of Hadrian as part of building as a service, the work of CodeSafe likewise involves the delivery of safety as a service. It is a platform-based service, which draws together human contact, tailoring to particular situations. Resonating with the examples discussed in chapter *home* and shown in *Smart Homes for Seniors* (Pink 2021), both cases evolved services with automated technologies that work with people.

There are many technological developments which have implications for the future of construction: automated and robotic technologies and vehicles, smart materials, digital twins, and increasingly advanced Building Information Management systems (BIM). These involve onsite and offsite automated construction, and construction in terrains and climate conditions inaccessible to humans, including in space. We can imagine more-than-human construction; where buildings may be digitally, but never physically, inhabited by humans but will bear relationships to other non-human species and environments. Yet even in such scenarios, human intent, involvement and ways of working collaboratively with emerging technologies are likely. How will people and machines co-shape the future of work?

Emerging technologies in child protection social work

The growing presence of digital and automated technologies in government and social services internationally has been greeted by an often-critical literature which has evaluated its relation to social inequalities (Eubanks 2018) and the extent of its correspondence with social realities (Henman 2018). The digital social policy scholar Paul Henman points to a 'history of digital technologies in government … littered with expensive failures' (2018: 84). Some failures have provided some high profile lessons, such as the widely reported Australian RobotDebt and the UK school leaver exams cases (Pink, Ruckenstein et al. 2022). In both cases algorithmic systems produced disastrous results for already underprivileged and in some cases vulnerable people. Showing where people are unaccounted for in the digitalisation of government services, in assumptions about technological possibility, their use in democratic processes, and in terms of human diversity and inequality, Henman emphasises that digital and algorithmic governance requires a nuanced understanding that 'technology does not simply replace human activities, but enables organizations to reconfigure their structure, operations and extend their activities' (2018: 84). With this in mind, we need to ask what we can learn from how the everyday actors in social services – in the case I discuss social workers and vulnerable service users – engage technologies within their own practices and how technologies consequently can emerge as part of valued services.

The COVID-19 pandemic participated in many reconfigurations of work, not least a remarkable shift towards working from home, predicted to endure with flexible and hybrid digital work for many. The shift to working from home came about for many people as if overnight, with little opportunity to prepare or plan for its new conditions. Working from home as a policy created what in STS terms could be seen as a massive 'experiment', on a scale that was inconceivable before it happened. With it came an unprecedented dependence on and new engagements with digital and emerging technologies for work, and consequently, many new forms of human improvisation and creativity emerged as people worked out how to live and work in new, unknown and uncertain circumstances. We were flung into work/life situations where the inevitably but often unseen uncertainty was immediately visible, and where we needed to rapidly discover new ways of engaging with other people, things and technologies. Analysing how this situation unfolded reveals how technologies already ubiquitous in everyday life continue to emerge. In contrast to the slower process through which smartphones and digital platforms became integrated in the construction industry, the COVID-19 pandemic created the possibility to study how such configurations came about at a time of rapid and dramatic change. In 2020, when the United Kingdom was in lockdown, I collaborated from Australia with the UK social work scholars Harry Ferguson and Laura Kelly, to research the impact of the pandemic on child protection social workers and how they improvised to cope with their new circumstances.

Child protection social work can be understood as an anticipatory practice, whereby social workers need to assess the situation of children and young people to determine which actions to take to ensure their safety. Thus, it is also an ideal example through which to explore how everyday professional anticipation plays out, and its relation to regulation and governance. As Ferguson's extensive research in the field shows, it conventionally involves a sensory and affective in-person practice, whereby much of what social workers know is based on their experiences of being there with children and their families in their homes (e.g. Ferguson 2018). Materiality, smell, visual and emotional cues underpin their evaluation practices and the confidence and trust they have in their assessments of children's safety and risk, and hence the courses of action they determine, involving 'continual movement between professional categories and sensory engagement as social workers anticipate what could happen next, and put processes in place to mitigate both their anxieties and risks to children' (Pink, Ferguson & Kelly 2021: 2). Therefore, shifting rapidly to working with families under circumstances where home visits were meant to be avoided and for some social workers who for reasons related to their own health, were not an option at all, presented many challenges (Ferguson et al. 2021) since the ways of knowing that underpinned the anticipatory foundations of their practice became largely inaccessible.

As social workers began working from home, digital technologies became increasingly central to their practice, with a combination of text messaging, video calls, and voice calls, using WhatsApp, Zoom and other platforms becoming fundamental to their communication with families and other professionals. We found that 'during the Covid-19 pandemic, home visits created new risks and anxieties and child protection social work was improvised and performed in new ways using digital technologies and media' (Pink, Ferguson & Kelly 2021: 2). Uncertainties about what could happen were exacerbated for social workers who could not engage their trusted methods, leading to anxieties about not being able to exercise good professional judgement. Simultaneously, while not downplaying the difficulties and complexities of the situation we found that 'the ways social workers sensed trust and evaluated safety shifted correspondingly' (Pink, Ferguson & Kelly 2021: 2). That is, digital technologies emerged within modes of practice through which social workers generally learned to trust in new sets of circumstances, through which they could confidently assess and take anticipatory actions with families and children.

Our research was anonymised to protect the privacy of all participants, and in the documentary film *Social Work and Child Protection in the COVID-19 Pandemic* (Morgans 2022) based on our project, actors perform a series of scenes which depict examples we discuss in our publications, for example where a social worker is close up to the camera communicating visually and verbally with a baby on her smartphone screen. These scenes bring viewers close up to the sensory modes of 'digital intimacy' (Andreassen et al. 2017; Dobson et al. 2018) with children and families that developed through the video calls. These situations enabled the social worker to trust in the circumstances she was working in, to assess risk, and also through her existing knowledge about the logistical barriers that people living in poverty face, to engage with the family empathetically in response to their text messages and drop off formula milk for them in person. What this, and many other cases from our research demonstrated was that in the circumstances of the pandemic smartphones, apps and platforms – things that are always unfinished and open to configure with other things – emerged as technologies of social work.

Our research showed that over time 'digital social work' – a hybrid practice which interweaves in-person and digital encounters into tailored engagements between social workers and service users (Pink et al. 2020; Pink, Ferguson & Kelly 2021) – became increasingly established in social work practice. In some cases, digital social work became a preferred mode of communication. Yet, during this period, the UK government Department of Education did not account for the possibility that new digital social work practices or technologies could emerge from the everyday sites of child protection social work itself. In the same vein that Henman (2019) identified more broadly, it made uninformed assumptions about socio-technical relations. In doing so it used outdated concepts, that the social sciences have left behind for good reason, stating that:

> During periods of national lockdown, the use of virtual visits should be the exception and can be used as a result of public health advice or when it is not reasonably practicable to have a face-to-face visit otherwise for a reason relating to the incidence or transmission of coronavirus (COVID-19).
>
> *(Department for Education, 2021)*

As noted elsewhere, social scientists have long since realised that the concept of the 'virtual', as internet scholar Christine Hine has put it, is 'no longer helpful' (Hine 2015) and bears little relevance to how digital and automated technologies are now part of, rather than separated or distinct from the everyday. We found that

> The UK Department of Education's conceptualisation of 'virtual' social work visits (Department for Education, 2021) does not account for or properly acknowledge the value of the new forms of social work – which flexibly combine in-person visits, video calls and other digital practices.
>
> *(Pink, Ferguson and Kelly 2021: 2)*

This project created a chance to see technologies emerging as part of work practices – not technologies that didn't exist, but always incomplete technologies that emerged into new markets and new practices, in a moment of dramatic change. Social work was *already a service* and here we have seen how rather than offering a new technology driven service, the technology successfully emerged because it was carefully and thoughtfully integrated into a service that humans already provided, and which was already imbued with care.

Safe working futures?

The construction industry and child protection social work have both been slow to engage with digital transformation and everyday workplace automation, and are both concerned with safety and risk mitigation in environments of uncertainty. The construction industry is one of the most dangerous places to work and worker safety is therefore inseparable from any task or practice performed. Child protection social work is concerned with the incredibly important task of keeping children safe. Worker safety in the construction industry is governed through extensive written safety regulations and manuals, which research has documented that it is difficult for workers to engage with. Child protection social work in the UK is characterised as 'constrained by excessive levels of case recording and other bureaucracy, tight timescales for completing work, high caseloads, and compliance with procedures and management dictates' (Ferguson 2017: 1009). These frameworks do have the important intent of keeping workers and children safe, but they also serve to ensure institutional accountability in the face of risk and future uncertainties (as also in the example of university research ethics committees and others discussed in chapter *futures*). However, as the philosopher Onora O'Neill (discussed in chapter *trust* in more detail) argues, increasingly fine-grained governance and regulation alone cannot make institutions more accountable (2017: 403).

My collaborative research has shown that safety is also rooted in workers' abilities to trust their own judgement, based on their own and other workers' collective expertise and ways of sensing and knowing what is safe and when risks are too great (Pink, Ferguson & Kelly 2021; Pink, Lingard & Harley 2016, 2017). The expert knowledge of social workers and construction workers, practising in variable and unpredictable environments, has been crucial to ensuring their own and others' safety. When new technologies have been introduced, both slowly and in moments of dramatic change, this has been achieved successfully because they became embedded in relationships, materialities and wider circumstances in which both construction workers and social workers trusted.

As this chapter has shown, particularly when we look at diverse workplaces, and specifically those that social scientists of digital technologies and media frequently bypass, two things are evident. First, in some workplaces, smartphones, apps and their platforms are the emerging technologies we need to focus on, rather than those that are most hyped. And second, even in sites where new AI and machine learning driven robotic technologies, with the latest machine vision capabilities are being applied, they do not necessarily eliminate, impoverish or oppress the humans who work with them. These realisations do not answer all the questions about the future of work in an era of growing automation and robotisation of work, and they certainly don't provide direct solutions. However, they offer us the basis for thinking anew about what future workplaces could look like and to propose a new research agenda surrounding what we need to know when we start to investigate what it would be like to work in the kinds of future workplaces that are technologically possible.

To understand how automation and robotisation will become part of the future of work, we must acknowledge and attend to the complexity, diversity and continually changing dynamics of the present, as well as the contingency of futures. Mapping out dystopian possibilities is a useful task in suggesting what the logics of capitalism could (and sometimes already do) imply for those who are least powerful in its systems. But we must remember that while emerging technologies do empower certain elements of capitalism, it is capitalism, rather than automated systems and devices, that is the problem. Dystopian narratives often neglect to seek out the examples of human creativity and improvisation which also drive change, constitute resilience to capitalism and also make automation work in ways that are meaningful and useful. They also miss those cases where automation just doesn't happen, or doesn't happen as intended. When we ask how people participate in how emerging technologies come into being, it becomes clear that there are no certain or predetermined ways in which the logics of automation and connectivity will play out. It is not a linear process, and the reality that some existing automated workplaces and systems have been heavily criticised does not mean that others will necessarily follow the same path. One of the potentials of an interventional social science is to participate actively in the processes through which automation becomes part of an ethical future of work.

MOBILITIES

In a 2021 interview published by the consultancy McKinsey & Co., Bonny Simi, the Head of Air Operations and People at Joby Aviation, described our possible future with electric vertical takeoff and landing vehicles (eVTOLs):

> Imagine waking up in the morning and thinking you could drive your car to work – but that might take an hour, an hour and a half. Instead, you just open up an app. A car picks you up and brings you to a heliport five minutes away. You ride in one of our aircraft. The flight takes ten minutes. At the other end, there's a car waiting for you. The entire ride is seamless, convenient, and affordable.
>
> *(Riedel 2021, November 19 a)*

Whether or not all eVTOLs will technically be flying cars – one of the most glamorous and long-awaited emerging technologies – is debatable. Yet they begin to fill a space long since invoked in popular imaginaries. According to a report from the engineering company Capgemini 'Today, there are over 100 VTOL projects under development worldwide, all seeking a stake in the game' (Altran 2020) and in March 2021 *Digital Trends* identified '14 awesome flying taxis and cars currently in development' (Glon 2021, March 20). As well as the urban air taxi, there is a growing range of iterations of eVTOLs, including the Airspeeder racing model (https://airspeeder.com/race-series). Personal aerial vehicles (PAVs) are another possibility, having 'control dynamics that can be learned and used relatively easily which might be effective for non-expert pilots trained at a level comparable with an average road vehicle driver's license' (Fleischer et al. 2019), more like personal flying cars.

Simi (above) described a small aircraft, deployed within a platform-based Mobility-as-a-Service type system, accessed via an app and involving other vehicles on the ground, and set up as a ride-share air-taxi. Safety is also high on the agenda for

DOI: 10.4324/9781003182528-10

Joby Aviation. Their aircraft, set to be running as urban air taxis by 2024 have pilots: 'it's very safe and it's easy to incorporate into the existing air-traffic system' says Simi. Such narratives of the urban air taxis may appear to point to an exclusive service for the wealthy commuter. However, further future industry visions tend towards an inclusive model, driven by new technological possibilities offered by autonomous eVTOLs, in Simi's words: 'to be truly ubiquitous we'll need to have autonomous aircraft'. Likewise, for another eVTOL company, Lilium, which plans to open up flights to consumers in 2024, eVTOLs will initially have pilots on the jets. But, Daniel Wiegand, the company's CEO said, in another McKinsey & Co. interview:

> Over time, we'll develop autonomous technologies ... we're envisioning a gradual shift from a fully piloted service to a more or less autonomous service. As we shift to autonomy, the number of aircraft that one pilot can operate [from the ground] will simply increase.
>
> *(Riedel 2021, November 19 b)*

Another company, Volocopter, seen as a front runner in flying car development in mid-2021 (Glon 2021, March 20), announced in a press release that it was 'the first and only electric vertical take-off and landing (eVTOL) company holding both the required design and production organization approvals ... to advance its aircraft toward commercial launch' (Reichman 2021, July 6).

More broadly, emerging air mobilities technologies have increasingly come into focus. One of the 2020 top ten emerging technologies was electric aviation, which *Scientific American*, in typical emerging tech hyperbole tells us 'Could Be Closer Than You Think'. The hype is that:

> Electric airplanes could provide the scale of transformation required, and many companies are racing to develop them. Not only would electric propulsion motors eliminate direct carbon emissions, they could also reduce fuel costs by up to 90 percent, maintenance by up to 50 percent and noise by nearly 70 percent.
>
> *(Hamilton & Ma 2020, November 10)*

The promise of possible future electric planes presents a new possible materiality upon which to pin our hopes for a decarbonised future. But the other, by now expected, news is that there still remain a series of technological challenges before air travel as we know it today (or knew it before the COVID-19 pandemic) would be possible, since like other emerging mobile and mobility technologies, electric planes will need lighter and more powerful batteries to be able to travel long distances.

We do not yet know what their story will be. When will autonomous urban air taxis fill the skies? Will electric planes, like electric cars, remain pivoted to take off for over a century? Will they become a low-cost, democratic and ubiquitous technology in which we will all be flying between or over our cities or across the world, or might this privilege be reserved for the very small percentage of the global population who can afford it? Will people trust and feel safe in them?

Emerging mobilities technologies

Many emerging mobilities technologies have been on the horizon for much longer than eVTOLs. Amongst the questions they raise include: when will electric vehicles (EVs) finally become the norm? When will Autonomous Driving (AD) cars be on our roads? And when will algorithms be planning seamless journeys, using apps connected to Mobility-as-a-Service platforms incorporating any combination of these emerging moblities technologies along with autonomous trains, shuttles, e-bikes, e-scooters and even some conventional walking thrown in? Design anthropologically we may ask: will they fulfil their promises and societal hopes by bringing with them safer, cheaper and environmentally sustainable solutions to our lives and our planet? How will these new autonomous mobilities technologies live with other species in our skies, land and waterways? How will they play out in a world of existing and likely future inequalities?

The field of emerging mobilities technologies is a dynamic space, occupied and invested in by stakeholders ranging from government, international organisations, the consultancies, global corporations, start-ups, disability activists, everyday enthusiasts and of course researchers from across all academic disciplines. Electric, self-driving and flying cars have occupied popular and technological imaginaries for over a hundred years and are implicated in new cycles of hype. It is a highly visible field, across technology journalism, media and the promotional strategies of organisations. Technologies of movement and mobility services, and visions of their roles in social, regulatory, infrastructural, environmental and economic futures are also an interdisciplinary concern, for anthropology, STS, sociology, human geography, lawyers, engineers, computer scientists and technology designers. Emerging mobilities technologies are pivotal in industry and government planning and investment and consultancies produce many reports concerning their futures. Mobility is a fundamental mode of being in the world. The mobilities of people, other species and organisms, technologies, minerals, materials, air, data, energy and more, continually reconfigure the sites, places, relations, experiences and trajectories of life itself.

Emerging mobilities technologies also take many forms and do, or would, participate in everyday lives and environments in diverse ways ranging between the glamorous futures of urban air taxis, the familiar examples of AD cars and trucks and EVs, and less frequently reported AD boats and ships (for example: Jamal 2021, June 16; Paleja 2021, November 22) and tractors, to the dirty heavy work done by emerging autonomous technologies for demolition, digging and removal of debris and earth for construction site preparation in areas inaccessible, dangerous or impossible for humans to work in (Melenbrink et al. 2020), to a Mars rover that uses automated navigation systems (JPL 2021, July 1). I have followed this field for much of the last decade, including debates on the promise of the eVTOL or doing ethnographic research around AD cars and EVs, the three technologies whose trajectories I consider in this chapter.

Emerging technologies in unfinished worlds

A key characteristic of emerging technologies, illustrated by the example of auto-mated and connected transport mobilities, is their incomplete and unfinished nature, always in progress (Pink, Fors & Glöss 2018). Stefan Krebs's analysis of the history of the automobile suggests that this has always been the case: 'cars cannot just be bought, driven and eventually sold or scrapped; they are in constant need of regular servicing and, in the event of a breakdown, of repairs in order to preserve their functionality as automobiles' (Krebs 2021). Beyond this, the very use of cars is a creative process through which their unintended unfinishedness becomes obvious as they re-emerge as relational to other technologies, such as the smartphone (Pink, Fors & Glöss 2018). Emerging transport mobility technologies are, by definition unfinished, even though they stabilise in products, in what Tim Ingold and Eliza-beth Hallam (2007) call after-the-event innovations. This, as I unfold below, is characterised by cycles of research, development and hype, which themselves intersect with problem and solution formation.

When automated mobilities technologies and services are conceptualised as fin-ished products, which are subsequently launched into a capitalist economy where their monetisation is a priority, it is easy to imagine how dominant corporate interests and oppressive modes of governance will impact their future management, regulation and adverse impacts on future people. The case of the connected car is a good example, since it brings together three important elements of present devel-opments and future imaginaries of automated mobilities: the vehicles themselves, data and services. For example, in critical data studies, Mark Andrejecvic suggests viewing AD cars through the prism of their capacity as 'media technologies or interfaces' that track things as diverse as our digital technology and media use to our speed and generate an immense amount of data. 'Further down the road', Andrejevic proposes, 'the creation and deployment of autonomous vehicles will transform cars into fully mediated devices, packed with sensors that collect and process a growing range of information' (Andrejevic 2020: 29). There are ample horror stories around how data might be mobilised in relations of power. For instance, Jathan Sadowski describes a series of incidents reported in the *New York Times*, where people who had purchased their cars on payment plans in the UK had defaulted on their loans and had their cars remotely deactivated by a 'starter interrupt device', in situations where their personal and road safety or comfort was compromised (Sadowski 2020: 75–76). Sadowski argues that 'The starter interrupt device is an extreme example of how disadvantaged people are now exported in new ways. Lenders cynically use the language of fairness and opportunity to justify a system that strips away privacy, autonomy and dignity' (2020: 77). He sees con-tinuities between these surveillance technologies and growing uses by car insurance companies of data collected from cars or smartphones which can be analysed to detect and rank driver safety (2020: 79). This thread of theoretical scholarship warns us of the potentially dystopian consequences of the connected car, which, as Sadowski points out, are already here, rather than being predicted futures.

However, there is another way to consider this: the already-here-ness of these technologies invites us to a further theoretical twist, whereby they are always unfinished, breakable and repairable; and to ask what kinds of practical engagements are needed, to instil hope in how we imagine them into the future. Do surveillance technologies that detect drunk driving (e.g. Yen & Krisher 2021, November 10) necessarily have negative outcomes? Might technologies that enable parents to monitor teenage drivers (e.g. Stenquist 2020, November 19) offer welcome modes of care as they do with smartphones (Hjorth et al. 2020)?

There are many examples of how unscrupulous organisations monetise the data of vulnerable people, which we need to learn from and avoid going forward. But enduring and evolving markets are not always constituted only on the basis of the extraction, monetisation and exploitation of data resources, and there is a growing recognition in industry that the technological possibilities data offers need to be brought together more closely with people. In fact, in 2021, the consultancy McKinsey and Co. reported that the monetization of connected-car data had not developed as rapidly as they originally predicted in 2016 (Bertoncello et al. 2021, February 11). They assess that original equipment manufacturers (OEMs) 'have struggled with connectivity or related software developments, resulting in poor customer reviews and delayed start of production. Only a few get the software-defined car right, and even fewer fully monetize vehicle data'. The limitations they point to are two-fold. 'Few customers now buy OEM-connected services or sign up for insurance-player-connected offers, such as usage-based insurance'. But everyday customers are not the only limitation in this field, additionally 'OEMs and data marketplaces typically find few B2B [business to business] customers today who are willing to purchase data'. For McKinsey & Co., this means 'Car-data monetization at the tipping point'. They urge companies to 'act now' to benefit in this fast-moving space, and one of the steps they recommend is to develop a more customer-centric approach, resonating with the consultancy Kantar's insight that big data is not telling companies enough about consumers (noted in chapter *data*). This kind of space, where emerging technologies are 'broken' or limited, offers moments for reflection for industry, where the consultancies might propose new monetisation strategies for organisations. But it also opens up moments where we might think design anthropologically about how and where alternative modes of designing and intervening with emerging mobilities technologies, data and services might come about.

Stories of emerging mobilities technologies, data and services are frequently propelled by a solutionist paradigm of innovation, which exacerbates existing power inequalities, sustains capitalism and takes the extractive approach toward trust and ethics discussed in chapter *trust*. But is this always the case? Importantly, *does it have to be the case*? And what happens when people simply don't sign up for the technology? Emerging mobilities technologies promise environmental sustainability and to democratise access to safe mobilities, reduce inequalities, make transport more equitable and affordable, and create new jobs. How might they better participate in the constitution of such scenarios. How might they be engaged and embedded in relations of care? – of humans for each other, other species and the environment? How might their participation be enabled and constituted through the hope and trust advocated for in chapters *trust* and *hope*. I next respond to these questions through a discussion of the emergence and possible futures of EVs and AD cars.

The electric car

A 1977 item on the electric car, shown on the United Kingdom's Thames TV's 'Drive in' programme (Thames TV 2018, September 13) invokes a moment of hope in the promise of EVs. The presenter, Shaw Taylor, explained how, with estimates that in accordance with the consumption levels at the time, there would be 200 to 300 years of coal left, it looked 'very much as if 21st century motoring will be electric motoring'. Taylor interviewed Dr David Porter of the Electricity Council who already drove an EV. The car had a range of about 40 miles which Dr Porter found 'adequate for my particular purposes', whereby – in a gendered narrative (see also Scharff 1991) – his wife took and collected him from the station to commute to work, and then used it for her shopping during the day. The prospect was for an increase in range up to about 150 miles, with a new type of battery being developed, and Porter noted that 'in the first instance, we see this battery and the EV market developing in the commercial vehicle area'. The interview also covered acceleration, driving up hills, and maintenance which Dr Porter said would be very low. On balance, he suggested that the costs of an EV would be about the same as petrol cars.

EVs, a technological innovation of the late nineteenth/early twentieth century (Høyer 2008) occupy a curious place in academic scholarship, as an object of interest for disciplines across the social, engineering and computing sciences since the 1980s. In these discussions, the question of battery power has frequently taken centre stage. In 1987, Michel Callon, a sociologist of innovation, proposed reading the failure of EVs to gain a mass market as a sociological 'controversy'. In his analysis of the work of engineers developing EVs for the French electricity company (EDF) in the early 1970s, Callon (1987: 80–81) argued that their vision was aligned with the theory of the French sociologist A. Touraine, which proposes that industry manipulate consumption by responding to the needs of popular protest in ways that serve their own ends. In contrast, he proposed, engineers working for Renault who supported the traditional car followed arguments consistent with the sociologist Bourdieu's theory (1987: 86) whereby consumption remains autonomous as 'goods and services, whatever their intrinsic characteristics, are ineluctably reinscribed by consumers into the logic of social distinction' (Callon 1987: 82). According to Callon, Bourdieu's logic prevailed, making a mass market impossible since the EDF's engineers realised that their EV 'needed batteries whose performance was sufficient for the average user and this sort of battery might be too expensive to produce for a long time to come' (Callon 1987: 84–85).

The focus on the battery has endured, and battery lifetime and availability of charging infrastructures have become represented, in popular and engineering narratives in terms of a human sentiment labelled 'range anxiety'. There are many examples. Recently for instance, in a 2021 ABC news article, range anxiety – 'the fear of running out of battery charge before you can find a charging station to recharge' – is blamed for hindering the uptake of EVs (Medlen 2021, October 17). Amongst researchers specifically focused on user acceptance and adoption of EVs two key barriers are frequently identified: EV drivers' assumed range anxiety about the distance an EV can travel without being charged, and the availability of charging infrastructures viable for both electricity suppliers, and commercial and/or individual users and customers. Drivers' relationships with EVs have been characterised as 'emotional' or affective in the Human-Computer-Interaction (HCI) literature (e.g. Row et al. 2016), particularly in relation to the feelings associated with the risk of breakdown due to low battery charge (Cahour et al. 2012). Various solutions to range anxiety are proposed in existing HCI literature and business consultancy reports, some of which must be read as country specific. For instance, in a 2019 Infrastructure Australia report it is suggested that 'establishing a network of fast-charging stations on the national highway will help to overcome the "access to charging facilities" barrier and reduce consumer anxiety about EV range' (2019: 51), responding to the long distances Australians might drive regionally or interstate. However, even in countries with shorter driving distances, range anxiety is flagged as a barrier. A UK House of Commons Business, Energy and Industrial Strategy Committee report saw range anxiety as a 'significant deterrent' to EV uptake (2018: 3). In a Norwegian study, Marianne Ryghaug and Marit Toftaker found stakeholders in EV futures 'believed users to be very concerned about having local "charging stations" available' and diagnosed potential users with 'range anxiety' which they believed was an irrational emotion that 'would disappear with more experience and as drivers realised that their home-charging access would cover their needs' (Ryghaug & Toftaker 2016: 122). Defining range anxiety as 'as an emotional property' the stakeholders suggested the technical solution of installing faster charging facilities (2016: 124).

But what exactly is range anxiety and who suffers from it? And was it really the inadequacy of the battery that impeded the emergence of the EV? In the UK, Dr Porter of the Electricity Council had found the battery to be perfectly amenable to his and his wife's routines and alluded to the promise of better batteries to come. In the continuing discussion of the French case from the 1970s, Kartsen Marhold (2021) has analysed initiatives by the French state power company – Électricité de France (EDF) – and the German Gesellschaft für elektrischen Straßenverkehr (GES). Marhold explains how in these cases 'It had been expected from the outset that batteries would be a delicate issue, and tests confirmed that they were indeed the most crucial and problematic component of the vehicles'. This had meant that

'Engineers at both companies framed the problem above all in terms of battery lifetime' (2021: 169) as well as a series of other issues including the amount of maintenance work this implied in changing and/or charging batteries, and the time and costs of training of staff or outsourcing services. Marhold's point is that if we look at this historical case differently, we need not necessarily understand the batteries as a discrete entity which was 'the problem' requiring improvement, or solution. Why not instead focus attention on performance or carrying capacity first (Marhold 2021: 178)?

When we start to interrogate what 'problems' batteries raise in everyday worlds, it seems that, like Dr Porter in the late 1970s, people who actually use EVs in the twenty-first century have often not been that concerned about their range, let alone being anxious about it (irrationally or not). Indeed, Ryghaug and Toftaker found, the 'imagined publics and imagined lay persons, that stakeholders [in the EV field] refer to … may bear no or little resemblance to real people' (Ryghaug & Toftaker 2016: 120). Several recent studies of how EVs become part of everyday life from global sites where EVs have become integrated sooner, indicate that drivers of EVs innovate in everyday life contexts and create new practices of driving, with consequences for energy demand, and everyday mobilities. Research in France (Magali et al. 2011) and Norway suggests that electric-car use changes driving practices, meaning socio-technical relations develop, different to those involved with conventional cars. Heidi Gjøen and Mikael Hård (2002) have shown how EV driving was 'domesticated' by users to constitute new everyday practices in Norway. Their research suggests that such 'users' still partly follow the engineers' script but 'inscribe their own visions about use into a certain technology and … bring these visions to bear on how a technology is interpreted' (2002: 267).

The evidence suggests that EV's become part of people's lives and their imagined futures in such ways that neither range nor charging are the issue, but rather that the difficulties, and indeed inequalities become visible when charging infrastructures are not in place. The digital energy futures project suggested that EVs have been fitted into people's lives in such ways that range anxiety is not relevant, where they are used for local and regional trips that are well within range (Strengers, Dahlgren et al. 2021). Indeed, the participants in the *Digital Energy Futures* documentary (Pink 2021) had existing routines, or clear visions of how they would charge their EVs in the future. What made it hard for people to have EVs was not anxiety about range, but rather the practical difficulties relating to cost and apartment living with no charging facilities. In brief, for people without access to renewable energy, and with no charging facilities at home, EV charging is likely to be both more expensive and more inconvenient, often making EV ownership inaccessible. Moreover, for those for whom it was a possibility, concerns about EVs seem just as likely to be social, as necessarily about range.

When I interviewed Peter, a participant in the wider Digital Energy Futures project, in 2020, he was in his forties, a consultant in the energy and buildings field who lived alone and worked mainly from home in his apartment in a Sydney beach suburb. He owned two cars, and we talked about the contingencies around possible future EV ownership for him. I asked him what would push him over to changing his sports car to an electric car? He first joked, 'a rapid charging station at the race track' but went on to explain that 'in all honesty both of my cars could be electric, for the type of travel that I do' since his longest 'semi-regular' travel was to see his brother in Newcastle, which he thought was within the range of current EVs and definitely a Tesla. For Peter, rather than concern about the car not getting there, he suggested 'there's also an awkward social interaction I think: ... hi, I arrived, do you mind if I plug my car in and you pay to fill my car'. Although he could envisage having such a conversation with his brother, he continued, 'I can't, you know, you go into a friend's place and just go, oh sorry, my car's run out of electricity, do you mind, you fill my car for me?'. It was the social awkwardness, rather than the cost, since, he said, 'You know it's not going to cost you a lot, but it's still a bit weird'. Presented with this problem, we turn to speculate about how it might be solved. I wondered out loud 'if in the future people could solve that by using, kind of, energy trading currencies I suppose?' Peter thought that sounded like 'an extension of smart metering where the smart meter in the house communicates with the car to say, this car has used this meter to charge itself, and then that car is registered to a person like your phone is registered to you'. He concurred, 'You know there's an idea, there we go'.

Design anthropology encourages us to go against the grain, to listen to what participants in research tell us. In the case of EVs it suggests to me that a rethinking of how EVs already, and will in the future, fruitfully participate in people's lives, how they will become embedded in social relations and where they will give us hope for environmental sustainability. There is certainly a current focus on EVs, across governments and industry, differently manifested across diverse national contexts, whereby in the early 2020s EVs were still expected to become increasingly ubiquitous. In 2021, McKinsey & Co. stated 'Mainstream EVs will transform the automotive industry and help decarbonize the planet' and 'By 2035, the largest automotive markets will go electric' (McKinsey & Co. 2021, September 7). It feels risky to say that it looks more likely than ever that the promise of EVs to become ubiquitous, and work towards decarbonisation would finally be realised in the next ten or so years. But, as is becoming increasingly clear, it is not the size or endurance of the batteries that will make this decision, but rather how EVs become part of our lives, routines, socialities and mobilities.

Autonomous Driving (AD) cars

In 2021, *The Financial Times* reported another in a series of undelivered AD car promises. The topic was the robotaxi – a fully autonomous taxi service that had been expected to be operating by 2021: 'Waymo prepared to order 82,000 such vehicles in 2018, Uber projected it would have 100,000 on the road by 2020 and Lyft divined that a "majority" of its rides would be autonomous by 2021' (McGee 2021, July 19). By 2021, ubiquitous robotaxis were not in sight. The story is unsurprising. AD cars hype has been immense (Stilgoe 2020). In 2015, they were the most hyped emerging technology (Korosec 2015, August 20), predicted to be on the roads by 2020, when my colleagues and I planned to do ethnographic fieldwork with people as they rode in them.

The emergence of AD cars is envisioned in industry accounts through five levels of autonomy, defined by the SAE (SAE 2021, May 3) international classifications, from driver assist modes where the driver uses some autonomous features, to full automation and to connected vehicles. In 2021, a *New York Times* article (Ewing, 2021, July 14) suggested that with new legislation, Germany might be getting ahead of the United States in the race to get AD vehicles on the roads, reporting a member of the German Parliament's comment that 'Germany can be the first country in the world to bring vehicles without drivers from the laboratory into everyday use'. This would involve the roll out of Level 4 AD Vehicles, which can drive autonomously with a human ready to take over (the German case involved humans remotely controlling the vehicles). This news contributes to a long and intense story rippling across diverse news and media platforms and industry reports, which cover technological, legislative shifts, investments and business news and political statements. The protagonists of these news stories are the next 'first' country, company or entity to take AD one step further. Yet such narratives seem distant from the actual everyday realities, contingencies and lives that AD vehicles might ultimately participate in.

Over the last years social scientists and designers have consistently complicated the hopes represented in industry visions of AD futures, from legal, regulatory, ethical, trust and people-focused perspectives. They have revealed the socio-technical imaginaries (Jasanoff 2015a) of AD and the flaws in these visions, (e.g. Forlano 2019; Stilgoe 2020), and it became unsurprisingly clear that AD cars were unlikely to deliver their promised benefits and solutions such as safer roads, reduced carbon emissions or more quality time for drivers without a deeper understanding of how AD might fit with human futures and other evolving systems and processes.

A consideration of the 'trust problem' outlined in chapter *trust*, which is of particular relevance to AD cars, helps surface the issues. In 2020, a 'new AAA survey on automated vehicles' reported that 'only one in ten drivers (12%) would trust riding in a self-driving car' (Edmonds 2020, May 3). This trust problem means that the automotive industry, consultancies and policy makers are keen to get AD ethics right. Worryingly, with respect to this the 'trolley problem' (an abstract philosophical ethical dilemma) has been appropriated by industry and engineers to talk about the human and ethical dimensions of automated transport mobilities. Solving the trolley problem entails a technological solution intended to make AD cars ethical and trustworthy for people. Originally 'conceptualised through the ethical dilemma faced by a trolley driver who experiences brake failure when going down a valley and has to choose between one or another accident scenario involving people in the trolley's path', the trolley problem has been avidly applied questions relating to AI and ADM across industry and engineering (Pink 2022). For instance, an IBM article (IBM n.d.) on 'Building Trust in AI' engages a version of the trolley problem to ask how 'we can trust that it [AI] reflects human values', whereby we are invited to: 'Suppose there's a bus coming toward a driver who has to swerve to avoid being hit and seriously injured; however, the car will hit a baby if it swerves left and an elderly person if it swerves right—what should the autonomous car do?' The trolley problem has particularly been foregrounded by a 'Moral Machine' experiment developed by a group at MIT (Awad et al. 2018) which tested out a series of scenarios through an online questionnaire and collected '40 million decisions in ten languages from millions of people in 233 countries and territories' (Awad et al. 2018: 59). Computer scientist and psychologist Jonathan Gratch at USC has since sought to extend the model to account further for the social element of decision making (Blumenthal 2021, February 24).

The trolley problem, including the MIT experiment, has been critically dissected, extensively, and critically by scholars from across the social sciences and humanities (Ash 2018; JafariNaimi 2018; Pink 2022; Pink, Osz et al. 2021; Stilgoe 2020). Its inability to engage with the realities of everyday life, the contingency of human decision making, and the situatedness of ethics and trust make it difficult to take any evidence accrued from surveys that present the trolley problem to respondents. Moreover, it is complicit in an extractive approach to ethics, seeking to extract human ethics from society through a questionnaire to invest them in AD, assuming that making machines ethical, makes them trustworthy, and humans will trust and accept them, allowing the societal benefits offered by these technologies to be reaped.

There are moreover other problems with seeking to isolate AD ethics from the circumstances in which they emerge. From a legal studies perspective, Jake Goldenfein, Deidre Mulligan, Helen Nissenbaum and Wendy Ju (2021) demonstrate a further complication to how the relationship between human and machine responsibilities and ethics for AD cars is further situated in relation to the levels of automation and connectedness of the AD car itself and the system of which it is part. They point out that each SAE stage configures the relationship between people and AD cars differently, has different implications for questions such as policy, regulation and privacy, and thus the ethical implications play out differently. The goal to get AD cars on the road is therefore not only confronted with the problem that machines themselves cannot be made ethical through engineering solutions alone, but their ethics are not constant.

So, what are the alternatives to extractive approaches to AD ethics and trust? Jack Stilgoe and Tom Cohen focus on the social. Stilgoe and Cohen (2021: 4) have critically outlined a dominant 'framing' of the AD 'problem', by technology developers and policy makers whereby 'the challenge is seen as first public awareness, then public acceptance, and finally public adoption of new technology' (2021: 8). They argue that by framing publics within a discourse of the inevitability of technology being held up by barriers to its acceptance, possibilities for enabling publics to imagine alternative technology futures are restricted in situations since 'innovators' genuine interest in understanding what the public might accept slips into a normative project of seeking to build acceptance' (Stilgoe & Cohen 2021: 3).

Stilgoe and Cohen helpfully suggest overturning this paradigm, to attend to public values (similar to city data sensing values in chapter *data*). Where emerging technologies are unfinished or not constituted socially, and their benefits unproven – as for AD cars – they propose asking 'whether technological systems are willing to accept public values'. They argue for public dialogues (beyond the 'one–off exercise') whereby AD governance might take place '"in dialogue", demanding ongoing conversation with the general public'. Involving values sourced from dialogue rather than extracting values through surveys is an important shift. But I propose taking this beyond the category of publics. The question of trust demonstrates why. For Stilgoe, 'trust is out of the control of innovators and regulators' and he argues that although they 'can design for trustworthiness' in fact '*trust is a gift of the public*, hard-won and easily lost' (Stilgoe 2021: no page numbers, italics added). Millions of the dollars and euros invested in designing trustworthy technologies may have been mis-invested precisely for this reason (chapter *trust*). Yet, the limitation of attributing the power to trust to the public, is that it is unclear how the public as a category or entity has the capacity to give or take away trust. The public is an analytical construct as much as it is the social imaginary of government and policy makers. Stilgoe and Cohen comment how 'Institutions and members of the public may have contrasting ideas of the public-in-general and publics-in-particular (Michael 2009)' (2021: 2–3). Moreover, if trust cannot be captured or objectified either to be extracted from publics and invested in trustworthy technology (see also chapter *trust*) it also cannot be given or taken away by publics (or anyone else). To understand trust in AD we must ask how it is emergent from the fine grained sensory, affective everyday of the present and how we sense its possible futures.

As in the case of EVs, we need to attend to how markets evolve in relation to people, and recent reports on the AD market have similar implications. The 2021 *Financial Times* article about the fate of the robotaxi goes on to discuss this in light of two different business models for AD cars, one aiming for fully autonomous systems of the robotaxi kind, the other being what has emerged since the middle of the second decade of the 2000s, when it became apparent that AD cars were on a slower boil, which has meant the proliferation of Driver Assist AD technologies, for which markets are growing. The *FT* analysis suggests that if this second 'evolutionary' model were to succeed, then 'the world's biggest, most sophisticated companies – Alphabet, Apple, Amazon and Microsoft – would have all backed the wrong horse' because this scenario 'would entirely flip the script'. Five years ago, when it was thought that tech companies would lead in this space and 'carmakers felt under siege from tech companies that were going to displace them at the top of the value-chain', but now the *FT* suggested car companies might be back in the picture.

Put another way, speaking design anthropologically, my interpretation is that the step-change that had been envisioned, involving the introduction of a dramatically different technology into people's everyday worlds in cities might be less successful than an approach that has incrementally developed and implemented the autonomous driver assist capabilities of AD cars in ways can become available to people in everyday life. There are various different ways emerging technologies might come about in everyday life and all of these are contingent on specific circumstances. In chapter *work*, I showed how existing smartphone apps, 'ready' or open to new practices, had rapidly been appropriated as technologies of social work in a disruptive – almost overnight – moment of change during the pandemic in the United Kingdom, and how a robotic bricklayer, a concept that had been on the boil for years, came to fruition in a situation of employment shortages and new material possibility in Western Australia. An ethnographic focus on emerging AD technologies, as part of the road towards possible future full AD, likewise shows how, by appreciating how people live and learn with emerging technologies, the AD 'trust problems' dissolve. Design ethnographic foresighting, led by my colleague Thomas Lindgren (Lindgren et al. 2021), suggests that AD assist technologies and a sense of trust emerge together with people as they engage with them in everyday life situations. These entangled processes of emergence are themselves in forward movement. They are both anticipatory sentiments *and* they are in progress, not static, and not extractable from the always shifting and evolving narratives through which people drive through the everyday and move from one moment to another in everyday life.

Other speculative approaches imagine AD beyond the established socio-technical imaginaries that associate it with safety, carbon emission reduction and quality-of-life benefits. Rather than seeing the AD car as a 'solution' such approaches create generative possibilities. Design researcher Laura Forlano (2019) discusses the 'Driverless City' project in the United States. Forlano's speculative work responded to the narratives of safety as part of linear technological advancement, which she found in experimental AD testbeds and AD advertising media. She shows how 'speculating and fabulating alternative possible futures can interrupt these narratives, offering opportunities for resistance'. In one example, Forlano and colleagues created a scenario concerning the 'disappearance of roadkill, the overpopulation of certain species, and the emergence of a new economy around seasonal hunting and trapping to replace lost jobs in trucking and warehouses' (Forlano 2019: 2828) to pull out the tensions in the dominant narratives. Design researcher Laura Boffi has also sought to introduce new speculative techniques into the exploration of AD futures (Boffi 2020; Boffi et al. 2020: 180). Boffi and colleagues discuss 'the possibility that autonomous driving might enable new social, human-to-human relationships' rather than simply the human-machine relationships upon which existing assumptions about trust in AD are based. Their Co-Drive speculative design experiment involves semi-AD cars hosting 'remote passengers as virtual avatars beside the human driver' (Boffi et al. 2020: 180).

Like Forlano, I believe we need a 're-think' (Forlano 2019: 2832). We need to acknowledge that both EVs (above) and AD need to emerge as part of a shared human, interspecies, planetary and sustainable future. Does the present moment of crisis offer us a moment of not only reflection, but the possibility for intervention and action? What is required?

Emerging mobilities technologies for times of crisis

The stories of EVs, AD and eVTOLs have long and entrenched narratives, which commenced long before the 2020s. Their technological promise has offered hope for net-zero-emissions energy futures, for democratised safer travel on our roads and air purified vehicle interiors (chapter *air*). Yet they may also exacerbate privilege, social inequalities, the extraction of resources needed for their production and the data storage needed to run them, and share our personal data. In response, critical design research, anthropology and STS scholarship collectively debunk many future mobilities promises. This work invites us to tell new stories, by opening up the possibilities of emerging electric and automated mobilities to publics, speculative design and experimental futures ethnography. Its proposals can be fruitfully aligned with commentaries from mobilities scholars, like Peter Adey and colleagues (Adey et al. 2021) and Mimi Sheller (2021).

Mobilities scholars centre mobility in their analysis, rather than seeing it as an outcome of other activities. They attend to technological, human and more-than-human mobilities, and have emphasised the need for both 'a transition to lower carbon forms of mobility' and 'to make such a transit with an eye to issues of social justice' (Adey et al. 2021). Sheller (2021) asks how we could 'kickstart the transition away from fossil fuels' in our current situation of COVID-19 in the context of the 'global climate emergency', arguing that we need new mobilities narratives, and new sustainable mobilities systems (2021: 18).

Similar to how societal problems will not be solved through the roll out of EVs or AD cars, Sheller warns against relying on the 'transition' to new sustainable mobilities technologies – which Adey et al. also note 'considerable hopes [are] being pinned on ... to enact a transition to a decarbonised mobile future' (Adey et al. 2021). Sheller (2021: 1010) emphasises that mobilities are entangled with political relations and Adey et al. insist on a socially just, equitable, democratic and accountable mobility transition away from fossil fuels (Adey et al. 2021).

Can we, at what mobilities scholars see as a pivotal moment for change, shift the cycle of technological promise and hope? Along with the speculative interventions of design researchers, and the design anthropological urge to intervene, these calls invoke the need for something more. It is time for a connected and coordinated, engaged, interdisciplinary social science, future-focused approach to shifting the narrative – through STS dialogues with publics and policy, design research speculation, and design anthropological engagements in the everyday and across organisations, in concert.

LIFE AT THE EDGE

Emerging technologies come about in ways that are contingent and uncertain, they are unfinished and indeterminate. As such they offer the possibility of hope. By which I mean a form of shared hope for a collective engagement towards making an ethical, trustworthy future life, world and planet where people, other species and emerging technologies live well, healthily, safely and sustainably together.

To achieve this, we need new ways of co-conceptualising not only emerging technologies, but the ways in which futures will come about. We need, I argue, to better understand *life at the edge*, that pivotal moment which so many commentators from so many diverse fields believe us to be in. Through the chapters of this book, I unpack how this moment is being realised. The consultancies offer strategies for private and public sector stakeholders moving forward. They portray technologies as poised to grow their markets, urging organisations to be ready for when they do. Scholars urge us to act in this moment of crisis. The unerring waves of a global pandemic confronted us with the question of whether the radical changes associated with it have given us a pause, an impetus, a wake-up call, or a new impulse to invent responsible ways forward.

In all these respects, we appear to be experiencing what it means to be in *life at the edge of the future* in particularly intense ways. Yet in fact, this is where we always live, about to go forward, feeling trust, anxiety and a host of other things, hoping, fearing or otherwise anticipating what might be further ahead. Improvising, adjusting and familiarising ourselves as we go on, always into uncertainty, but usually with a sense of what is likely to happen.

In the moment

Emerging Technologies / Life at the Edge of the Future involves an encounter with this moment. I have examined multiple ways of living at the edge of the future, across different countries, and domains of activity and experience. This experiment in

DOI: 10.4324/9781003182528-11

research and scholarship has followed hunches and sparked ideas as I encountered possible futures, emergent, contingent, coming about alongside each other. In place of the traditional ethnographic practice of the lone anthropologist immersing themself deeply in one site, my trajectory is woven across nine interconnected research fields, emergent from ethnographic, interdisciplinary and stakeholder teamwork. This has brought diverse instances of the specific into play with the general.

To learn and know in, and about, a broad configuration of things and processes, I have followed the emerging technologies media, industry and government narratives, everyday life stories, experiential environments and the possible futures in which the interests of all these converge. This involves seeing the ethnographic site as expansive and flexible, with its encounters encompassing technology news, consultancy reports, everyday life experiences, workshops, discussions and auto-ethnography. This site is not fixed in one place, temporality or one medium; it is digital, online, in-person and encountered through video, photography, documentary making and writing. This extends to after this book – and to the as yet unknown ways it will be read.

Both life and research happen at *the edge of the future*, and my argument is for a future-focused practice on two counts. We inhabit a site of uncertainty where we can never know or predict what exactly will happen next. As the case of emerging technologies – which continually fail to deliver their promise – confirms, this is a general state of affairs. Given these very fundamental limitations, critical analyses and visions of what might possibly happen, go right or go wrong, encourage or warn us. But they do not show us how to go forward. Therefore, I argue, we need to go beyond these conventional scholarly practices to focus our efforts on *how* things are most likely to come about and how we might participate as they do.

Telling stories forward

In this book, I am concerned with understanding how things and ideas emerge and the *possibilities they move forward with*, rather than with the debates they might refer *back to*. The study of emerging technologies taught me the importance of creating an anthropological and social science practice of studying forward.

Studying forward is a technique of hope and entails an invitation to others to join. It contrasts with the practice of retrospectively constituting the 'history' of a field of study in order to endorse its proposed future, which is a technique of seduction. Writing the past to justify the present constitutes a linear narrative and it closes down what could have happened. Studying forward opens up what could possibly happen. As opposed to traditional works of excavation, *Emerging Technologies / Life at the Edge of the Future* suggests a scholarship that does not look back, to survey and then contribute to an existing field. To cut to the core, and explicitly address the questions of concern, means taking a leap of faith and/or the preparedness to follow in a what-if. And the illusion of there being firm foundations does not necessarily support such moves. It was recently reported that AI is better at telling stories backwards once the end point has been set than telling stories forward (Sparkes 2021, December 15), but we, I propose, do need to hone this latter skill.

I argue that we need to take such steps because at this moment the social sciences need new theoretical and methodological modes of going forward and imagining possible futures. This should entail both working with participants in research, and with other disciplines and stakeholders. Like dominant narratives about electric cars, autonomous driving cars and workplace robots taking away our jobs, academic disciplines have been telling the same stories for too long. We need to 'complicate' existing stories, in part through exposing them to new stories.

This involves creating a hopeful narrative, an alternative to theories that we are on a downward spiral towards an automated dystopia. There do remain grave issues to be resolved in relation to the power relations and injustices of uses of emerging technologies in capitalist economies and the inequalities associated with this. I do not want to downplay this fact. However, it is salient to note the remarks of the anthropologist Hirokazu Miyazaki (2006: 149) that social theory was increasingly unable to hold critical sway in emergent forms of capitalism at the beginning of the twenty-first century. It is unsurprising that this state of affairs might continue into the present, since when social theory is a top-down, masculine endeavour, tasked to prove one idea to be better than another, it becomes competitive rather than collaborative. In this spirit, we need to temper theoretical declarations that are singular in their linearity and insensitive to the sway and flex of life as lived, to the creativity and improvisation of the everyday and to the possibility that people, organisations and other entities might weave new paths through futures. When, in contrast, theory is developed in dialogue with ethnographic attention to the everyday present and possible futures, to listen to sense and account for the environments we are in, then it has greater potential to connect. It is as such that we equip ourselves with the capacity to create and concepts which are shared and might generate modes of complication, learning and intervention, new modes of trust and hope become possible.

Therefore, while we must be attentive to ethics and justice, we also need to be alert to hope. We should engage with industry, public sector and not-for-profit research partners who share our agendas to better understand people, human and planetary futures. There are many of them. We should be encouraged by media reports that bring people into view. In December 2021, the *Wall Street Journal* published an article titled 'Tech Companies Bring Back the Human Touch; From online dating to social media, algorithms are getting more assistance from humans'. The journalist, Laura Forman (2021, December 13), detailed a series of examples of tech companies – for instance in online dating, online styling, food delivery platforms, and social media – who are introducing 'human' elements into their digital services, suggesting this will 'prevent the worst outcomes and to enhance the best'. In re-inventing our resources, expertise and practice as social scientists, we also need to nurture the ability to tell human stories forward. When we do, we will be better equipped to open up further to and steer the 'best' ways forward. As I have shown through this book, working with anticipatory concepts and everyday imaginaries offers a way to create anticipatory narratives ethnographically and

collaboratively. Existing research has shown that anthropologists are excellent at producing new stories that are not usually surfaced in technology research fields that are
dominated by engineering, showing that things really happened differently to what is
envisaged. But we need to go beyond this. We rather require anthropology to create
stories forward that are new to the discipline, and that can give anthropologists new roles
in interdisciplinary scholarship.

Anthropology, perhaps more than any other disciplinary practice, happens very
obviously at *the edge of the future*, as we seek to encounter people in life's flow as it goes
forward, and to accompany them in their trajectories. We now need a movement in
anthropology, of scholars who wish to go forward anew, into the uncertainty of the
anticipated, imagined and hoped for, both with participants in research and with
research partners from other disciplines and non-academic stakeholders.

Theories of *futures* as entailing uncertainty and possibility and anticipatory concepts of *trust*, and *hope* offer a beginning for such engagement and collaboration.
The case of emerging technologies provides a set of starting points which reveal
where meeting points for collaboration, collective categories and imaginaries may
be achieved. From these we might present new stories, complicate existing ones
and craft new modes of hope and trust.

No solutions

This book is not a solution, but a commencement. It is a call to do scholarship
differently and to do it in a new temporality and on a greater scale.

Big visions, step changes and end points/steps on the way that we see as desirable and which we hope for, are part of our worlds. Without them, other disciplines with whom I collaborate, – such as transition management with goals to
reach net-zero emissions – would not have goals or challenges to respond to.
Anthropology shows us that the straight lines to the ambitions of big visions are
hard to follow in reality. The stories of the bricklaying robot in chapter *work*, and
the gas sensing capsule in chapter *data* show how technologies emerge over time,
with twists and turns. The story of AD cars in chapter *mobilities* suggests that the big
linear visions that put fully AD cars on the roads in 2020 was replaced by another
story where we see AD cars as meandering through history towards different
applications of AD features and some autonomous vehicles in specific uses.

The idea that it is impossible to know what will emerge from research underpins
anthropology. It involves understanding that we work in a continually emergent
world. We need to better learn how to strategically engage this knowledge in ways
that are workable for influencing change initiatives. The incremental changes
through which we arrive at new ways of being are the domain of anthropology,
but I argue they should not be its only domain. We need to join others in their
pursuit of big visions, to reshape these visions, and to ask new questions.

REFERENCES

Abdilla, A. (2018) Beyond Imperial Tools: Future-Proofing Technology through Indigenous Governance and Traditional Knowledge Systems. In J. Harle, A. Abdilla & A. Newman (Eds) *Technology as Cultural Practice*. Sydney: Tactical Space Lab. 67–81.

Abram, S., Waltorp, K., Ortar, N. & Pink, S. (Eds) (2022) *Energy Futures*. Berlin: De Gruyter.

Abram S., Winthereik, B. R., Yarrow, T. & Sarkar, A. (Eds) (2019) *Electrifying Anthropology: Exploring Electrical Practices and Infrastructures*. London: Bloomsbury.

Adey, P. & Anderson, B. (2011) Event and Anticipation: UK Civil Contingencies and the Space – Times of Decision. *Environment and Planning A: Economy and Space*, 43 (12): 2878–2899. https://doi.org/10.1068/a43576.

Adey, P., Creswell, T., Yeonjae Lee, J., Nikolaeva, A., André Nóvoa, A. & Temenos., C. (2021) *Moving Towards Transition: Commoning Mobility for a Low-Carbon Future*. London: Bloomsbury.

Aeppel, T. (2021, August 2) The robot apocalypse is hard to find in America's small and mid-sized factories. *Reuters*. www.reuters.com/technology/robot-apocalypse-is-hard-find-americas-small-mid-sized-factories-2021-08-02/.

Akama, Y., Pink, S. & Sumartojo, S. (2018) *Uncertainty and Possibility*. London: Bloomsbury.

AlgorithmWatch (2019) Automating Society – Taking Stock of Automated Decision-Making in the EU. https://algorithmwatch.org/en/automating-society-2019/.

AlgorithmWatch (2020) Automated Decision-Making Systems in the COVID-19 Pandemic: A European Perspective. https://algorithmwatch.org/en/automating-society2020-covid19/.

Alimahomed-Wilson, J., Allison, J. & Reese, E. (2020) Introduction: Amazon Capitalism. In J. Alimahomed-Wilson & E. Reese (Eds) *The Cost of Free Shipping: Amazon in the Global Economy*. London: Pluto Press. pp. 1–18. https://doi.org/10.2307/j.ctv16zjhcj.7.

Altran [Capgemini] (2020) En-Route to Urban Air Mobility – on the fast track to viable and safe on-demand air services. Report. https://capgemini-engineering.com/as-content/uploads/sites/27/2020/03/en-route-to-urban-air-mobility.pdf.

Andersen, Z. J., Hoffmann, B., Morawska, L., Adams, M., Furman, E., Yorgancioglu, A., Greenbaum, D., Neira, M., Brunekreef, B., Forastiere, F., Rice, M. B., Wakenhut, F.,

Coleen, E., Boogaard, H., Gehring, U., Melén, E., Ward, B. & De Matteis, S. (2021) Air pollution and COVID-19: clearing the air and charting a post-pandemic course: a joint workshop report of ERS, ISEE, HEI and WHO. *European Respiratory Journal*, 58(2). https://doi.org/10.1183/13993003.01063-2021.

Andreassen, R., Nebeling Petersen, M., Harrison, K. et al. (Eds) (2017) *Mediated Intimacies: Connectivities, Relationalities and Proximities*. United Kingdom: Taylor & Francis.

Andrejevic, M. (2020) *Automated Media*. Oxford: Routledge.

Anybotics (n.d.) Meet ANYmal, your new inspector. www.anybotics.com/anymal-autonomous-legged-robot/.

Ash, J. (2018) *Phase Media*. London: Bloomsbury.

Association of Professional Futurists (n.d.) FAQ. www.apf.org/page/FAQ#5.

Austin, P. L. (2019, July 25) What Will Smart Homes Look Like 10 Years from Now? *Time*. https://time.com/5634791/smart-homes-future/.

Australia Human Rights Commission (2021) Human Rights and Technology. Final Report. Farthing, S., Howell, J., Lecchi, K., Paleologos, Z., Saintilan P. and Human Rights Commissioner, Santow E.https://tech.humanrights.gov.au/downloads.

Australian Government (2021, June) Australia's Artificial Intelligence Action Plan. www.industry.gov.au/data-and-publications/australias-artificial-intelligence-action-plan.

Autodesk (2020) Trust Matters: The high cost of low trust. Autodesk. https://construction.autodesk.com.au/resources/trust-matters-the-high-cost-of-low-trust/.

Awad, E., Dsouza, S., Kim., R. et al. (2018) The Moral Machine experiment. *Nature*, 563: 59–64. https://doi.org/10.1038/s41586-018-0637-6.

Bachelard, M. (2019, December 17) The day from hell: why the grid melts down in hot weather. *The Age*. www.theage.com.au/national/the-day-from-hell-why-the-grid-melts-down-in-hot-weather-20191216-p53khd.html.

Bainbridge, A. & Kent, L. (2020, December 15) Off-grid dream becomes reality as bushfire threat creates new era for power networks. *ABC News*. www.abc.net.au/news/2020-12-15/stand-alone-solar-systems-replacing-powerlines-after-bushfires/12905296.

Barrett, B. (2021, May 11) A Drone Tried to Disrupt the Power Grid. It Won't Be the Last. *Wired*. www.wired.com/story/drone-attack-power-substation-threat/?

Bayer Global (2021, April 13) *Interview: Chris Dancy, The Most Connected Man in the World - Part 2*. Video. YouTube. www.youtube.com/watch?v=VE_dq_FL0Xg.

Baym, N. K. (2013) Data not seen: The uses and shortcomings of social media metrics. *First Monday*, 18(10). https://doi.org/10.5210/fm.v18i10.4873.

BCS (2020, September 8) The public don't trust computer algorithms to make decisions about them, survey finds. The Chartered Institute for IT. www.bcs.org/articles-opinion-and-research/the-public-dont-trust-computer-algorithms-to-make-decisions-about-them-survey-finds.

Beckert, J. & Suckert, L. (2021) The future as a social fact. The analysis of perceptions of the future in sociology, *Poetics*, 84. https://doi.org/10.1016/j.poetic.2020.101499.

Benjamin, R. (2019) *Race After Technology*. Cambridge: Polity.

Bergquist, M. & Rolandsson, B. (2022) Exploring ADM in Clinical Decision-Making: Healthcare Experts Encountering Digital Automation. In S. Pink, M. Berg, D. Lupton & M. Ruckenstein (Eds) *Everyday Automation*. London: Routledge.

Berman, B. (2020, March 30) Vehicle cabin-air filters can combat coronavirus, but effort is problematic. *SAE International, News*. www.sae.org/news/2020/03/coronavirus-cabin-air-filtration.

Bertoncello, M., Martens, C., Möller, T. & Schneiderbauer, T. (2021, February 11) Unlocking the full life-cycle value from connected-car data. McKinsey & Co. www.

mckinsey.com/industries/automotive-and-assembly/our-insights/unlocking-the-full-life-cycle-value-from-connected-car-data.

BEUC (2020September) Artificial Intelligence: what consumers say – findings and policy recommendations of a multi-country survey on AI. The European Consumer Organisation. www.beuc.eu/publications/beuc-x-2020-078_artificial_intelligence_what_consumers_say_report.pdf.

Birhane, A. (2021) Algorithmic injustice: a relational ethics approach. *Perspective.* 2 (2). https://doi.org/10.1016/j.patter.2021.100205.

Birhane, A., Kalluri, P., Card, D., Agnew, W., Dotan, R., Bao, M. (n.d.) The Values Encoded in Machine Learning Research. Preprint under review. https://arxiv.org/pdf/2106.15590.pdf.

Bloch, E. (1995) *The Principle of Hope.* Cambridge, Mass: MIT Press.

Blumenthal, A. (2021, February 24) What Might Sheep and Driverless Cars Have in Common? Following the Herd. USC Viterbi, School of Engineering. https://viterbischool.usc.edu/news/2021/02/what-might-sheep-and-driverless-cars-have-in-common-following-the-herd/.

Boellstorff, T. (2012) The politics of similitude: Global sexuality activism, ethnography, and the Western subject. *Transcriptions* 2: 22–39.

Boffi, L. (2020) How to Turn Yourself into a Virtual Travel Companion in Someone Else's Car: Drawing Design Approaches from the Philosophy of Mind. In M. Di Nicolantonio, E. Rossi & T. Alexander (Eds) *Advances in Additive Manufacturing, Modeling Systems and 3D Prototyping. AHFE 2019. Advances in Intelligent Systems and Computing*, vol 975. Cham: Springer. https://doi.org/10.1007/978-3-030-20216-3_59.

Boffi, L., Wintersberger, P., Cesaretti, P., Mincolelli, G. & Riener, A. (2019) The first co-drive experience prototype. In *Proceedings of the 11th International Conference on Automotive User Interfaces and Interactive Vehicular Applications: Adjunct Proceedings* (AutomotiveUI '19). Association for Computing Machinery, New York, NY, 254–259. https://doi.org/10.1145/3349263.3351318.

Bourke, E. (2020, November 16) It's time to rethink indoor airflow to reduce the spread of COVID-19, say experts. *ABC News.* www.abc.net.au/news/2020-11-16/ventilation-indoor-airflow-could-be-important-against-covid-19/12881444.

Bourzac, K. (2020, September 25) COVID-19 lockdowns had strange effects on air pollution across the globe. *Chemical and Engineering News.* https://cendigitalmagazine.acs.org/2020/09/25/covid-19-lockdowns-had-strange-effects-on-air-pollution-across-the-globe-2/content.html?utm_email+=24EB42AE341B44C1745CE4615E.

boyd, d. & Crawford, K. (2012) Critical questions for Big Data. *Information, Communication & Society* 15 (5): 662–679. https://doi.org/10.1080/1369118X.2012.678878

Bryant, R. E. & Knight, D. (2019) *The Anthropology of the Future.* Cambridge: Cambridge University Press.

Burton, T. (2021, November 8) Ex-KPMG partner 'bullied, humiliated'. *Financial Review.* www.afr.com/politics/ex-kpmg-boss-bullied-humiliated-20211108-p596yx.

Buscher, V. (n.d.) Data in the natural and built environment. *ARUP.* www.arup.com/expertise/services/digital/data-in-the-built-environment.

Business Wire (2021, April 12) Blueair's HealthProtect™ Becomes First Air Purifier from Major Brand Tested to Remove Live SARS-CoV-2 Virus from Air. *Business Wire.* www.businesswire.com/news/home/20210412005621/en/%C2%A0Blueair%E2%80%99s-HealthProtect%E2%84%A2-Becomes-First-Air-Purifier-from-Major-Brand-Tested-to-Remove-Live-SARS-CoV-2-Virus-from-Air.

Cahour, B., Nguyen, C., Forzy, J-F. & Licoppe, C. (2012) *Using an electric car: a situated, instrumented and emotional activity.* In Proceedings of the 30th European Conference on

Cognitive Ergonomics (ECCE '12). ACM, New York, NY, 22–28. https://doi.org/10.1145/2448136.2448142.

Callon, M. (1987 [1999]) Society in the making: The study of technology as a tool for sociological analysis. In W.E. Bijker, T.P. Hughes & T. Pinch (Eds) *The Social Construction of Technological Systems*, 7th ed. Cambridge, MA: MIT Press, pp. 83–107.

Carey, M. (2018) *Mistrust: An Ethnographic Theory*. Chicago: University of Chicago Press.

Cellan-Jones, R. (2017, October 16) Artificial intelligence – hype, hope and fear. *BBC News*. www.bbc.com/news/technology-41634316.

Choy, T. (2011) *Ecologies of Comparison: An Ethnography of Endangerment in Hong Kong*. Durham and London: Duke University Press.

Clarey, C. (2020, August 3) Automated Line Calls Will Replace Human Judges at U.S. Open. *The New York Times*. www.nytimes.com/2020/08/03/sports/tennis/us-open-hawkeye-line-judges.html.

Coxworth, B. (2020, December 14) Underwater robot designed to keep tabs on fish farms. *New Atlas*. https://newatlas.com/marine/underwater-robot-cagereporter-fish-farms/.

Collington, R. & Mazzucato, M. (2021, September 20) Britain's public sector is paying the price for the government's consultancy habit. *The Guardian*. www.theguardian.com/commentis free/2021/sep/20/britain-public-sector-consultancy-habit-pandemic-private-services.

Collins, S. G. (2021) *All Tomorrow's Cultures*. New York: Berghahn.

Consultancy.uk (2021, August 23) Government selects McKinsey for future technology strategy work. www.consultancy.uk/news/28779/government-selects-mckinsey-for-future-technology-strategy-work.

Consulting.com (n.d.) The Complete Guide to Big 4 Consulting. www.consulting.com/big-4-consulting.

Cook, J. A. (2018) Hope, Utopia, and Everyday Life: Some Recent Developments. *Utopian Studies*, 29 (3), 380–397. https://doi.org/10.5325/utopianstudies.29.3.0380.

Cook, J. & Cuervo, H. (2019) Agency, futurity and representation: Conceptualising hope in recent sociological work. *The Sociological Review*, 67 (5):1102–1117. https://doi.org/10.1177/0038026119859177.

Corsin Jimenez, A. (2011) Trust in anthropology. *Anthropological Theory*, 11 (2): 177–196. https://doi.org/10.1177/1463499611407392.

Covington, D. (2021, October 11) Realise the value of your data. *KPMG*. https://home.kpmg/au/en/home/insights/2021/10/data-digital-transformation-mid-market-value-of-data.html.

Cowan, J. (2021, July 15) How Artificial Intelligence Is Fighting Wildfires. *New York Times*. www.nytimes.com/2021/07/15/us/wildfires-artificial-intelligence.html.

Crapanzano, V. (2003) *Imaginative Horizons*. Chicago: University of Chicago Press.

CSIRO (n.d.) About. www.csiro.au/en/About.

Cukier, K. N. & Mayer-Schoenberger, W. (2013) The rise of Big Data how it's changing the way we think about the world. *Foreign Affairs*. www.foreignaffairs.com/articles/2013-04-03/rise-big-data.

Curry, S. (2019, April 2) AI and ML: Greatest Hype or Hope? *Forbes*. www.forbes.com/sites/samcurry/2019/04/02/ai-and-ml-greatest-hype-or-hope/?sh=44b5be87382c.

Dahlgren, K., Pink, S., Strengers, Y., Nicholls, L. & Sadowski J. (2021) Personalization and the Smart Home: questioning techno-hedonist imaginaries. *Convergence*, 27 (5): 1155–1169. doi:10.1177/13548565211036801.

Dahlgren, K., Strengers, Y., Pink, S., Nicholls, N. & Sadowski, J. (2020) *Digital Energy Futures: Review of Industry Trends, Visions and Scenarios for the Home*. Emerging Technologies Research Lab (Monash University). Melbourne, Australia. www.monash.edu/__data/assets/pdf_file/0008/2242754/Digital-Energy-Futures-Report.pdf.

Dancy, C. (2016, January 21) Connected Home. *Chris Dancy*. www.chrisdancy.com/fa qblog/2016/1/21/connected-home.

Dányi, E., Spencer, M., Maguire, J., Knox, H. & Ballestero, A. (2021) Propositional politics. In J. Maguire, L. Watts & B. R. Winthereik (Eds) *Energy Worlds in Experiment*. Manchester: Mattering Press.

Data Feminism (2020) Introduction: Why Data Science Needs Feminism. *Data Feminism*. https://data-feminism.mitpress.mit.edu/pub/frfa9szd/release/6?from=10553&to=10774.

Davis, N. & Subic, A. (2018, May 18) Hope and fear surround emerging technologies, but all of us must contribute to stronger governance. *The Conversation*. https://theconversa tion.com/hope-and-fear-surround-emerging-technologies-but-all-of-us-must-contribute-to-stronger-governance-96122.

Deloitte (2021) Digital Consumer Trends 2021. Deloitte website. www2.deloitte.com/au/ en/pages/technology-media-and-telecommunications/articles/digitalconsumertrends.html.

Department for Education (2021) *Coronavirus (COVID-19): Guidance for Children's Social Care Services*. www.gov.uk/government/publications/coronavirus-covid-19- guidance-for-childrens-social-care-services/coronavirus-covid-19-guidance-for-localauthorities-on-childrens-social-care#virtual-visits-local-authorities (accessed 8 January 2021).

Department of Health (n.d.) *Epidemic Thunderstorm Asthma*. Victorian State Government. www.health.vic.gov.au/environmental-health/epidemic-thunderstorm-asthma.

DeNora, T. (2021) *Hope*. Basingstoke, UK: Palgrave Macmillan.

Diaz, A. (2021, March 18) Australia's air conditioning usage statistics 2020: The aircon is on, but nobody's home. *Finder*. www.finder.com.au/energy/aircon-statistics.

Digital Trends (n.d.) About Us. *Digital Trends*. www.digitaltrends.com/about/.

Di Ieva, A. (2019) AI-augmented multidisciplinary teams: hype or hope? *The Lancet*, 394 (10211): 16–22. https://doi.org/10.1016/S0140-6736(19)32626-1.

Dobson, A. S., Carah, N. & Robards, B. (2018) Digital intimate publics and social media: Towards theorising public lives on private platforms. In A.S. Dobson, B. Robards & N. Carah (Eds) *Digital Intimate Publics and Social Media*. Basingstoke, UK: Palgrave Macmillan, 3–27.

Douglas, M. (Ed.) (2004) [1970] *Witchcraft Confessions and Accusations*. Oxford: Routledge.

Douglas-Jones, R., Walford, A. & Seaver, N. (2021) Introduction: Towards an anthropology of data. *J R Anthropol Inst*, 27: 9–25. https://doi.org/10.1111/1467-9655.13477.

Dourish, P. & Gómez Cruz, E. (2018) Datafication and data fiction: Narrating data and narrating with data. *Big Data & Society*. https://doi.org/10.1177/2053951718784083.

Dow, A. (2021, May 2) 'Dramatic decrease in risk': Air purifiers placed in quarantine hotels. *The Age*. www.theage.com.au/politics/victoria/dramatic-decrease-in-risk-air-purifiers-pla ced-in-quarantine-hotels-20210501-p57o1c.html.

Duc, A. (2021, September 8) Panasonic to run nanoe X air quality solutions on GrabCar Medical cars. *Vietnam Investment Review*. https://vir.com.vn/panasonic-to-run-nanoe-x-a ir-quality-solutions-on-grabcar-medical-cars-87408.html.

Duque, M., Pink, S., Strengers, Y., Martin, R. & Nicholls, L. (2021) Automation, wellbeing and Digital Voice Assistants: Older people and Google devices. *Convergence*, 27 (5): 1189–1206. https://doi.org/10.1177/13548565211038537.

The Editors (2021, February 24) 10 Breakthrough Technologies 2021. *MIT Technology Review*. www.technologyreview.com/2021/02/24/1014369/10-breakthrough-technologies-2021/.

Edmonds, E. (2020, May 3) Self-Driving Cars Stuck in Neutral on the Road to Acceptance. *AAA Newsroom*. https://newsroom.aaa.com/2020/03/self-driving-cars-stuck-in-neutra l-on-the-road-to-acceptance/.

Ehrenkranz, M. (2020, October 2) New technology is helping fire-struck communities predict air quality better. *National Geographic*. www.nationalgeographic.com/science/a rticle/new-technology-helping-fire-struck-communities-predict-air-quality?

Elish, M. C. & boyd, d. (2018) Situating methods in the magic of Big Data and AI. *Communication Monographs*, 85 (1): 57–80, doi:10.1080/03637751.2017.1375130

Elliot, A. (2022) *Making Sense of AI: Our Algorithmic World*. United Kingdom: Wiley.

Elliot, H. (2020, April 23) Invisibility Cloaks and Air Purifiers: How Covid Will Change Cars. *Bloomberg News*. www.bloomberg.com/news/articles/2020-04-23/invisibility-cloaks-and-air-purifiers-how-covid-will-change-cars.

Esterwood, C. & Robert, L. P. (2021) Do You Still Trust Me? Human-Robot Trust Repair Strategies. *30th IEEE International Conference on Robot & Human Interactive Communication (RO-MAN)*: 183–188. https://doi.org/10.1109/RO-MAN50785.2021.9515365.

Etienne, H. (2021) The future of online trust (and why Deepfake is advancing it) *AI Ethics*. https://doi.org/10.1007/s43681-021-00072-1.

Eubanks, V. (2018) *Automating Inequality: How High-Tech Tools Profile, Police, and Punish the Poor*. New York: St. Martin's Press.

European Commission (2020, February 9) White Paper on Artificial Intelligence: A European approach to excellence and trust. Brussels. https://ec.europa.eu/info/sites/default/files/commission-white-paper-artificial-intelligence-feb2020_en.pdf.

European Commission (n.d.) Excellence and trust in artificial intelligence. https://ec.europa.eu/info/strategy/priorities-2019-2024/europe-fit-digital-age/excellence-trust-artificial-intelligence.

Ewing, J. (2021, July 14) How Germany Hopes to Get the Edge in Driverless Technology. *New York Times*. www.nytimes.com/2021/07/14/business/germany-autonomous-driving-new-law.html.

FBR (2021, October 15) Hadrian X® builds second house in Wellard (Video). FBR website. www.fbr.com.au/view/news-articles/20211015012848.

Ferguson, H. (2018) Making home visits: creativity and the embodied practices of home visiting in social work and child protection. *Qualitative Social Work*, 17 (1), 65–80. https://doi.org/10.1177/1473325016656751.

Ferguson, H., Kelly, L. & Pink, S. (2021) Social Work and Child Protection for a Post-pandemic World: The re-making of practice during COVID-19 and its renewal beyond it. *Journal of Social Work Practice*, https://doi.org/10.1080/02650533.2021.1922368.

Fleischer, T., Meyer-Soylu, S., Schippl, J. & Decker, M. (2019) Personal aerial transportation systems (PATS) – A potential solution for the urban mobility challenges? *Futures* 109: 50–62. https://doi.org/10.1016/j.futures.2019.03.006.

Floridi, L. (2019) Translating Principles into Practices of Digital Ethics: Five Risks of Being Unethical. *Philos. Technol.*, 32: 185–193. doi:10.1007/s13347-019-00354-x.

Forlano, L. (2019) Cars and Contemporary Communications | Stabilizing/Destabilizing the Driverless City: Speculative Futures and Autonomous Vehicles. *International Journal of Communication*, 13 (28). https://ijoc.org/index.php/ijoc/article/view/8844.

Forman, L. (2021, December 13) Tech Companies Bring Back the Human Touch: From online dating to social media, algorithms are getting more assistance from humans. *Wall Street Journal*. www.wsj.com/articles/tech-companies-bring-back-the-human-touch-11639396982.

Fors, V., Pink, S., Berg, M. & O'Dell, T. (2019) *Imagining Personal Data*. London: Bloomsbury.

Fowler, G. A. (2021, June 8) Amazon may be sharing your Internet connection with neighbors. Here's how to turn it off. *Washington Post*. www.washingtonpost.com/technology/2021/06/07/amazon-sidewalk-network/.

Frederiksen, M. (2014) Relational trust: Outline of a Bourdieusian theory of interpersonal trust. *Journal of Trust Research*, 4 (2), 167–192. https://doi.org/10.1080/21515581.2014.966829.

Gabrys, J. (2016, March 24) *Citizen Sensing: Recasting Digital Ontologies through Proliferating Practices*. Society for Cultural Anthropology Editors' Forum. Theorizing the Contemporary.

Digital Ontology series. https://culanth.org/fieldsights/citizen-sensing-recasting-digital-ontologies-through-proliferating-practices.

Gardner, A., Smith, A. L. & Steventon, A. (2021) Ethical funding for trustworthy AI: proposals to address the responsibilities of funders to ensure that projects adhere to trustworthy AI practice. *AI Ethics*. https://doi.org/10.1007/s43681-021-00069-w.

Gharbia, M., Chang-Richards, A., Lu, Y., Zhong, R. Y. & Li, H. (2020) Robotic technologies for on-site building construction: A systematic review. *Journal of Building Engineering*, 32 (101584). doi:10.1016/j.jobe.2020.101584.

Gillespie, N., Lockey, S. & Curtis, C. (2021) *Trust in Artificial Intelligence: A Five Country Study.* The University of Queensland and KPMG Australia. https://doi.org/10.14264/e34bfa3.

Gjøen, H. & Hård, M. (2002) Cultural Politics in Action: Developing User Scripts in Relation to the Electric Vehicle. *Science, Technology, & Human Values*, 27 (2): 262–281. doi:10.1177/016224390202700204.

Glon, R. (2021, March 20) 14 awesome flying taxis and cars currently in development. *Digital Trends*. www.digitaltrends.com/cars/all-the-flying-cars-and-taxis-currently-in-development/.

Goldenfein, J., Mulligan, D. K., Nissenbaum, H. & Ju, W. (2021) Through the Handoff Lens: Competing Visions of Autonomous Futures. *Berkeley Technology Law Journal*, 35 (3): 835–910. https://ssrn.com/abstract=3875889.

Graeber, D. (2013) It is value that brings universes into being. *HAU: Journal of Ethnographic Theory*, 3 (2) 219–243. https://doi.org/10.14318/hau3.2.012.

Graeber, D. (2018) *Bullshit Jobs: A Theory*. New York: Simon & Schuster.

Gregg, M. (2011) *Work's Intimacy*. Cambridge: Polity Press.

Gunawan, J., Choffnes, D., Hartzog, W. & Wilson, C. (2021) The COVID-19 Pandemic and the Technology Trust Gap. *51 Seton Hall Law Review*, 1505. https://ssrn.com/abstract=3874152.

Hage, G. (2016) Questions Concerning a Future-Politics. *History and Anthropology*, 27 (4): 465–467. https://doi.org/10.1080/02757206.2016.1206896.

Ham, B. (2021, May 17) Using machine learning to predict high-impact research. *MIT News*. https://news.mit.edu/2021/using-machine-learning-predict-high-impact-research-0517.

Hamilton, K & Ma, T. (2020, November 10) Electric Aviation Could Be Closer Than You Think. *Scientific American*. www.scientificamerican.com/article/electric-aviation-could-be-closer-than-you-think/.

Hao, K. (2021, May 6) AI consumes a lot of energy. Hackers could make it consume more. *MIT Technology Review*. www.technologyreview.com/2021/05/06/1024654/ai-energy-hack-adversarial-attack/.

Harle, J., Abdilla, A. & Newman A. (Eds) (2018) *Decolonising the Digital: Technology as Cultural Practice*. Sydney: Tactical Space Lab. http://ojs.decolonising.digital/index.php/decolonising_digital/issue/view/DecolonisingTheDigital.

Haug, M. (2020) Framing the Future through the Lens of Hope: Environmental Change, Diverse Hopes and the Challenge of Engagement. *Zeitschrift für Ethnologie – Journal of Social and Cultural Anthropology Berlin*, 145 (1): 71–91.

Hauge, B. (2013a) The air from outside: Getting to know the world through air practices. *Journal of Material Culture*, 18 (2):171–187. https://doi.org/10.1177/1359183513483908.

Hauge, B. (2013b) Fresh Air Practices in English and Scottish Homes. Natural Ventilation News. *Newsletter of the CIBSE Natural Ventilation Group*, 7, 4–9. https://backend.orbit.dtu.dk/ws/files/53238269/Natural_Ventilation_News.pdf.

Hawley, K. (2012) *Trust: A Very Short Introduction*. Oxford: Oxford University Press.

Hearn, P. (2021, March 4) Should you continue to buy air purifiers to protect you from the coronavirus? *Digital Trends*. www.digitaltrends.com/home/can-air-purifiers-protect-from-coronavirus/.

Henman, P. (2019) Of algorithms, Apps and advice: digital social policy and service delivery. *Journal of Asian Public Policy*, 12 (1): 71–89. https://doi.org/10.1080/17516234.2018. 1495885.

Hine, C. (2015) *Ethnography for the Internet: Embedded, Embodied and Everyday*. London: Bloomsbury.

Hirt, M. & Allen, S. (2021, September 14) 10 Smart Home Trends for 2021. *Forbes*. www. forbes.com/advisor/home-improvement/smart-home-tech-trends/.

Hjorth, L., Ohashi, K., Sinanan, J., Horst, H., Pink, S., Kato, F. & Zhou, B. (2020) *Digital Media Practices in Households: Kinship Through Data*. Amsterdam: Amsterdam University Press.

Hockenhull, M. & Cohn, M. L. (2021) Hot air and corporate sociotechnical imaginaries: Performing and translating digital futures in the Danish tech scene. *New Media & Society*, 23 (2), 302–321. https://doi.org/10.1177/1461444820929319.

Holger, D. & Chin, K. (2021, October 6) Google Rolls Out Emission-Curbing Tools for Nest Thermostat. *The Wall Street Journal*. www.wsj.com/articles/google-rolls-out-em ission-curbing-tools-for-nest-thermostat-11633503660.

House of Commons Business, Energy and Industrial Strategy Committee (2018) *Electric vehicles: Driving the Transition Fourteenth Report of Session 2017–19*. https://publications.pa rliament.uk/pa/cm201719/cmselect/cmbeis/383/383.pdf.

Høyer, K. G. (2008) The history of alternative fuels in transportation: The case of electric and hybrid cars. *Utilities Policy* 16: 63–71. http://dx.doi.org/10.1016/j.jup.2007.11.001.

Huber, C. & Sneader, K. (2021, June 21) The eight trends that will define 2021–and beyond. *McKinsey & Co*. www.mckinsey.com/business-functions/strategy-and-corpora te-finance/our-insights/the-eight-trends-that-will-define-2021-and-beyond.

Humanitech (2018) Harnessing the transformational power of technology for good. Huma- nitech, Australian Red Cross. www.redcross.org.au/globalassets/humanitech/pdf/Huma nitech-Position-Paper.pdf.

IBM (n.d.) Building Trust in AI. www.ibm.com/watson/advantage-reports/future-of-artifi cial-intelligence/building-trust-in-ai.html.

Iliadis, A. & Russo, F. (2016, December) Critical data studies: An introduction. *Big Data & Society*. doi:10.1177/2053951716674238.

Ingold, T. (2021) *Imagining for Real: Essays on Creation, Attention and Correspondence*. Oxford: Routledge.

Ingold, T. & Hallam, E. (2007) Creativity and Cultural Improvisation: An Introduction. In E. Hallam & T. Ingold (Eds) *Creativity and Cultural Improvisation*. Oxford: Berg, 1–24.

Iyer, N., Chair, C. & Achieng, G. (2010) Afro Feminist Data Futures. *Pollicy*. https:// archive.pollicy.org/wp-content/uploads/2021/03/Afrofeminist-Data-Futures-Report- ENGLISH.pdf.

Jackson, S. (2019) Repair as Transition: Time, Materiality, and Hope. In I. Strebel, A. Bovet & P. Sormani (Eds) *Repair Work Ethnographies: Revisiting Breakdown, Relocating Materiality*. Basingstoke, UK: Palgrave Macmillan.

JafariNaimi, N. (2018) Our Bodies in the Trolley's Path, or Why Self-driving Cars Must *Not* Be Programmed to Kill. *Science, Technology, & Human Values*, 43 (2): 302–323. doi:10.1177/0162243917718942.

Jaguar Land Rover (2021, March 16) Jaguar Land Rover's future air purification technology proven to inhibit viruses and bacteria by up to 97 percent. *Jaguar Landrover Newsroom*. https:// media.jaguarlandrover.com/news/2021/03/jaguar-land-rovers-future-air-purification- technology-proven-inhibit-viruses-and-0.

Jamal, U. (2021, June 16) Robotic ship sets off to retrace the Mayflower's journey. *AP News*. https://apnews.com/article/europe-robotics-science-technology-business-16e2544aec 715f4f5cd3de7ef4792c80.

Jansen, S. (2016) For a Relational, Historical Ethnography of Hope: Indeterminacy and Determination in the Bosnian and Herzegovinian Meantime. *History and Anthropology*, 27 (4): 447–464. https://doi.org/10.1080/02757206.2016.1201481.

Jasanoff, S. (2015a) Future Imperfect: Science, Technology, and the Imaginations of Modernity. In S. Jasanoff & S-H. Kim (Eds) *Dreamscapes of Modernity: Sociotechnical Imaginaries and the Fabrication of Power.* Chicago: University of Chicago Press, 1–33.

Jasanoff, S. (2015b) Imagined and Invented Worlds. In S. Jasanoff & S-H. Kim (Eds) *Dreamscapes of Modernity: Sociotechnical Imaginaries and the Fabrication of Power.* Chicago: University of Chicago Press, 321–342.

Jasanoff, S. (2021) The Dangerous Appeal of Tech. *MIT Technology Review* 124 (4): 16–17. www.technologyreview.com/2021/06/30/1026329/dangerous-technology-driven-future-technological-determinism/.

Jiang, S., Li, Y., Lu, Q. et al. (2021) Policy assessments for the carbon emission flows and sustainability of Bitcoin blockchain operation in China. *Nat Commun*, 12: 1938. https://doi.org/10.1038/s41467-021-22256-3.

JLL (2020, November 17) Global workforce expectations are shifting due to COVID-19. JLL. www.us.jll.com/en/trends-and-insights/research/global-workforce-expectations-shifting-due-to-covid-19.

Joby Aviation (2021, June 2) Joby Aviation Announces Infrastructure Partnership with Largest Mobility Hub Operator in North America. www.jobyaviation.com/news/joby-aviation-announces-infrastructure-partnership/.

Johnson, C. (2020) Is demand side response a woman's work? Domestic labour and electricity shifting in low income homes in the United Kingdom. *Energy Research & Social Science*, 68. https://doi.org/10.1016/j.erss.2020.101558.

Jones, E. & Safak, C. (2020, August 8) Can algorithms ever make the grade? *Ada Lovelace Institute.* www.adalovelaceinstitute.org/blog/can-algorithms-ever-make-the-grade/.

JPL (2021, July 1) NASA's Self-Driving Perseverance Mars Rover 'Takes the Wheel'. Nasa Jet Propulsion Laboratory, California Institute of Technology. www.jpl.nasa.gov/news/nasas-self-driving-perseverance-mars-rover-takes-the-wheel.

Kapteyn, M. G., Pretorius, J. V. R. & Willcox, K. E. (2021) A probabilistic graphical model foundation for enabling predictive digital twins at scale. *Nat Comput Sci*, 1: 337–347. https://doi.org/10.1038/s43588-021-00069-0.

Kenner, A. (2018) *Breathtaking: Asthma Care in a Time of Climate Change.* Minneapolis, MN: University of Minnesota Press.

Ketter, W. (2019) How We Can Embrace the Electrical Vehicle Transition by Adopting Smart Charging. *World Economic Forum.* www.weforum.org/agenda/2019/05/how-charging-for-electricity-on-a-sliding-scale-could-power-the-electric-vehicle-transition/.

Kitchin, R. (2021) *The Data Revolution: A Critical Analysis of Big Data, Open Data and Data Infrastructures.* 2nd ed. London: Sage.

Kleist, N. & Jansen, S. (2016) Introduction: Hope over Time—Crisis, Immobility and Future-Making. *History and Anthropology*, 27 (4): 373–392. https://doi.org/10.1080/02757206.2016.1207636.

Knox, H. (2021a) Climate change and the politicisation of the mundane. In J. Maguire, L. Watts & B.R. Winthereik (Eds) *Energy Worlds in Experiment.* Manchester: Mattering Press.

Knox, H. (2021b) Hacking anthropology. *J R Anthropol Inst*, 27: 108–126. https://doi.org/10.1111/1467-9655.13483.

Konrad, K. & Böhle, K. (2019) Socio-technical futures and the governance of innovation processes: An introduction to the special issue. *Futures*, 109: 101–107. https://doi.org/10.1016/j.futures.2019.03.003.

Korosec, K. (2015, August 20) The most hyped emerging technology of 2015. *Fortune*. https://fortune.com/2015/08/20/self-driving-car-hype/.

KPMG (2020) Trust in Artificial Intelligence: Australian Insights 2020. https://home.kpmg/au/en/home/insights/2020/10/artificial-intelligence-trust-ai.html.

Krebs, S. (2021) Maintaining the Mobility of Motor Cars: The Case of (West) Germany, 1918–1980. In S. Krebs & H. Weber (Eds) *The Persistence of Technology Histories of Repair, Reuse and Disposal*. Bielefeld: Transcript Verlag.

Lanzeni, D. (2016) Smart global futures: Designing affordable materialities for a better life. In S. Pink, E. Ardevol & D. Lanzeni (Eds) *Digital Materialities*. London: Bloomsbury.

Lanzeni, D. & Pink, S. (2021) Digital material value: Designing emerging technologies. *New Media & Society*, 23 (4): 766–779. https://doi.org/10.1177/1461444820954193.

Lehtiniemi, T. & Ruckenstein, M. (2019) The social imaginaries of data activism. *Big Data & Society*. https://doi.org/10.1177/2053951718821146.

Leprince-Ringuet, D. (2021, March 20) Technology will create millions of jobs. The problem will be to find workers to fill them. *ZDNet*. www.zdnet.com/article/technology-will-create-millions-of-jobs-the-problem-will-be-to-find-workers-to-fill-them/.

Lewis, J. D. & Weigert, A. (1985) Trust as a Social Reality. *Social Forces*, 63 (4): 967–985. https://doi.org/10.2307/2578601.

Li, P. P. (2012) When trust matters the most: The imperatives for contextualising trust research. *Journal of Trust Research*, 2 (2): 101–106. https://doi.org/10.1080/21515581.2012.708494.

Lindgren, T., Fors, V., Pink, S. & Osz, K. (2020) Anticipatory Experience in Everyday Autonomous Driving. *Personal and Ubiquitous Computing*, 24: 747–762. https://doi.org/10.1007/s00779-020-01410-6.

Lindgren, T., Pink, S. & Fors, V. (2021) Foresighting Autonomous Driving: anethnographic approach. *Technological Forecasting and Social Change*, 173. doi:10.1016/j.techfore.2021.121105.

Lockey, S., Gillespie, N. & Curtis, C. (2020) *Trust in Artificial Intelligence: Australian Insights*. The University of Queensland and KPMG Australia. https:///doi.org/10.14264/b32f129.

Lohr, S. (2021, June 24) The Internet Eats Up Less Energy Than You Might Think. *The New York Times*. www.nytimes.com/2021/06/24/technology/computer-energy-use-study.html.

Lomborg, S. (2022) Everyday AI at Work: Self-tracking and Automated Communication for Smart Work. In S. Pink, M. Berg, D. Lupton & M. Ruckenstein (Eds) *Everyday Automation*. London: Routledge.

Loukissas, Y. A. (2019) *All Data Are Local: Thinking Critically in a Data-Driven Society*. Cambridge, MA: MIT Press.

Luhmann, N. (1979) *Trust and Power*. Cambridge: Polity Press.

Lupton, D. (2016) *The Quantified Self: A Sociology of Self-Tracking*. Cambridge: Polity.

Lupton, D. & Watson, A. (2022) Research-Creations for Speculating about Digitised Automation: Bringing Creative Writing Prompts and Vital Materialism into the Sociology of Futures. In *Qualitative Inquiry*.

MacDonald, L. & Durkee, M. (2020, December 1) Public Trust and Transparency. UK Government Centre for Data Ethics and Innovation. https://cdei.blog.gov.uk/2020/12/01/public-trust-and-transparency/.

Magali P., Jemelin, C. & Louvet, N. (2011) Driving an electric vehicle. A sociological analysis on pioneer users. *Energy Efficiency*, 4: 511–522. https://doi.org/10.1007/s12053-011-9123-9.

Mager, A. & Katzenbach, C. (2001) Future imaginaries in the making and governing of digital technology: Multiple, contested, commodified. *New Media & Society*, 23(2): 223–236. doi:10.1177/1461444820929321.

Maguire, J., Watts, L. & Winthereik, B. R. (Eds) (2021) *Energy Worlds in Experiment*. Manchester: Mattering Press.

Mahmud, L. (2021) Feminism in the House of Anthropology. *Annual Review of Anthropology* 50 (1): 345–361. www.annualreviews.org/doi/abs/10.1146/annurev-anthro-101819-110218.

Malo, J. (2019, December 15) The inner Melbourne suburbs at growing risk of coastal flooding linked to climate change. www.domain.com.au/news/the-inner-melbourne-su burbs-at-growing-risk-of-coastal-flooding-linked-to-climate-change-917783/.

Marhold, K. (2021) Of Buses, Batteries and Breakdowns: The Quest to Build a Reliable Electric Vehicle in the 1970s. In S. Krebs & H. Weber (Eds) *The Persistence of Technology Histories of Repair, Reuse and Disposal*. Bielefeld: Transcript Verlag.

Markham, A. (2013) Undermining 'data': A critical examination of a core term in scientific inquiry. *First Monday* 18 (10). http://firstmonday.org/ojs/index.php/fm/article/view/4868.

Markham, A. (2021) The limits of the imaginary: Challenges to intervening in future speculations of memory, data, and algorithms. *New Media & Society*, 23 (2): 382–405. https://doi.org/10.1177/1461444820929322.

Marr, B. (2021, December 7) The 7 Biggest Consumer Technology Trends In 2022. *Forbes.* www.forbes.com/sites/bernardmarr/2021/12/07/the-7-biggest-consumer-technology-trends-in-2022/?sh=f8d8a4d4ea29.

Marr, B. (2021, September 27) The 5 Biggest Technology Trends in 2022. www.forbes.com/sites/bernardmarr/2021/09/27/the-5-biggest-technology-trends-in-2022/?sh=479f3a6d2414.

Matheny, M., Thadaney Israni, S., Ahmed, M. & Whicher D. (Eds) (2019) *Artificial Intelligence in Health Care: The Hope, the Hype, the Promise, the Peril*. NAM Special Publication. Washington, DC: National Academy of Medicine. https://nam.edu/artificial-intelligence-special-publication/.

Mattingly, C. & Throop, J. (2018) The Anthropology of Ethics and Morality. *Annual Review of Anthropology*, 47 (1): 475–492. www.annualreviews.org/doi/abs/10.1146/annurev-anthro-102317-050129.

McCracken, G. (2020) Mapping the future, how to, when to, why to. https://mapping-the-future.com/.

McGee, P. (2021, July 19) Robotaxis: have Google and Amazon backed the wrong technology? *Financial Times*. www.ft.com/content/46ff4fe4-0ae6-4f68-902c-3fd14d294d72.

McKinsey & Co. (n.d. a) The Top Trends in Tech. www.mckinsey.com/business-functions/mckinsey-digital/our-insights/the-top-trends-in-tech.

McKinsey & Co. (n.d. b) There's No Place Like [a connected] Home. McKinsey & Co. www.mckinsey.com/spcontent/connected_homes/index.html.

McKinsey & Co. (2019, December 1) Voices on Infrastructure: The impact and opportunities of automation in construction. McKinsey & Co. www.mckinsey.com/business-functions/operations/our-insights/the-impact-and-opportunities-of-automation-in-construction.

McKinsey & Co. (2021, February 24) Prediction: The future of CX. *McKinsey Quarterly*. www.mckinsey.com/business-functions/marketing-and-sales/our-insights/prediction-the-future-of-cx.

McKinsey & Co. (2021, September 7) Why the Automotive Future Is Electric. McKinsey & Co. www.mckinsey.com/industries/automotive-and-assembly/our-insights/why-the-automotive-future-is-electric.

Medlen, P. (2021, October 17) WA motoring lobby says 'range anxiety' is to blame for slow take-up of electric vehicles. *ABC News*. www.abc.net.au/news/2021-10-17/range-anxiety-hinders-electric-vehicle-take-up-in-wa/100527038.

Melenbrink, N., Werfel, J. & Menges, A. (2020) On-site autonomous construction robots: Towards unsupervised building. *Automation in Construction*, 119, 103312. https://doi.org/10.1016/j.autcon.2020.103312.

Michael, M. (2016) Speculative Design and Digital Materialities: Idiocy, Threat and Compromise. In E. Ardevol, S. Pink & D. Lanzeni (Eds) *Digital Materialities: Design and Anthropology*. London: Bloomsbury: 99–113.

Milne, G. (2020) *Smoke and Mirrors: How Hype Obscures the Future and How to See Past It*. London: Little Brown.

Miyazaki, H. (2004) *The Method of Hope: Anthropology, Philosophy and Fijan Knowledge*. Stanford, CA: Stanford University Press.

Miyazaki, H. (2006) Economy of Dreams: Hope in Global Capitalism and Its Critiques. *Cultural Anthropology*, 21 (2): 147–172. www.jstor.org/stable/3651601.

Moore, H. L. (2004) Global anxieties: concept-metaphors and pre-theoretical commitments in anthropology. *Anthropological Theory* 4 (1): 71–88.

Morawska, L., Zhu, T., Liu, N., Amouei T., Mehdi, D. F., Andrade, M., Barratt, B., Broomandi, P., Buonanno, G., CarlosB., Ceron, L., Chen, J., Cheng, Y., Evans, G., Gavidia, M., Guo, H., Hanigan, I., Hu, M., Jeong, C. H., Kelly, F., Gallardo, L., Kumar, P., Lyu, X., Mullins, B. J., Nordstrøm, C., Pereira, G., Querol, X., Yezid Rojas Roa, N., Russell, A., Thompson, H., Wang, H., Wang, L., Wang, T., Wierzbicka, A., Xue, T. & Ye, C. (2021) The state of science on severe air pollution episodes: Quantitative and qualitative analysis. *Environment International*, 156. https://doi.org/10.1016/j.envint.2021.106732.

Morgan, B. (2020, March 5) 50 Leading Female Futurists. *Forbes*. www.forbes.com/sites/blakemorgan/2020/03/05/50-leading-female-futurists/?sh=6fc41d778c90.

Moroşanu, R. (2016) *An Ethnography of Household Energy Demand in the UK*. Basingstoke, UK: Palgrave Macmillan.

Morozov, E. (2013) *To Save Everything, Click Here: Technology, Solutionism, and the Urge to Fix Problems that Don't Exist*. London: Penguin Books.

Mühlfried, F. (2019) *Mistrust: A Global Perspective*. Basingstoke, UK: Palgrave Macmillan.

Nafus, D. (2014) Stuck data, dead data, and disloyal data: The stops and starts in making numbers into social practices. *Distinktion: Scandinavian Journal of Social Theory*, 15: 208–222. https://doi.org/10.1080/1600910X.2014.920266.

Nayeri, F. (2021, April 7) Is 'Femtech' the Next Big Thing in Health Care? *New York Times*. www.nytimes.com/2021/04/07/health/femtech-women-health-care.html.

Nicholls, L., Strengers, Y, Dahlgren, K., Pink, S. & Martin, R. (2021) *Digital Energy Futures: Demand Management Opportunities*. Melbourne: Emerging Technologies Research Lab (Monash University). www.monash.edu/__data/assets/pdf_file/0011/2765387/DEF-Demand-Management-Opportunities-Report.pdf.

Noortman, R. R. (2021) Data Design Futures: Who Is Responsible? In R-H. Liang, A. Chiumento, M. Zuniga, P. Pawełczak, M. Funk & Y. Chuang (Eds), *Proceedings of the 1st CHIIoT Workshop on Computer Human Interaction in IoT Applications* (pp. 1–5).

Old Ways New (n.d.) The Tracker Data Project. Old Ways, New website. https://oldwaysnew.com/research-dev#spatial-awareness.

O'Neill, O. (2017) Accountable Institutions, Trustworthy Cultures. *Hague J Rule Law* 9: 401–412. https://doi.org/10.1007/s40803-017-0055-0.

O'Neill, O. (2018) Linking Trust to Trustworthiness. *International Journal of Philosophical Studies*, 26 (2): 293–300. https://doi.org/10.1080/09672559.2018.1454637.

Özden-Schilling, C. (2015) Economy Electric. *Cultural Anthropology*, 30 (4): 578–588. https://doi.org/10.14506/ca30.4.06.

Özden-Schilling, C. (2021) *The Current Economy: Electricity Markets and Techno-Economics*. Stanford, CA: Stanford University Press.

Paleja, A. (2021, November 22) World's First Autonomous Electric Container Ship Completed Its First Trip. *Interesting Engineering*. https://interestingengineering.com/worlds-first-autonomous-electric-container-ship-completed-its-first-trip.

Panasonic Malaysia (2021, January 13) *Inhibits Novel Coronavirus (COVID-19) with Portable nanoe^{TM} X Generator up to 99.99%**. Video. YouTube. www.youtube.com/watch?v=sjYp ujStdAk.

Parrot, A., Umbenhauer, B. & Arshaw, L. (2020, January 15) Digital twins. Bridging the physical and digital. *Deloitte Insights*. www2.deloitte.com/us/en/insights/focus/tech-trends/ 2020/digital-twin-applications-bridging-the-physical-and-digital.html.

Pink, S. (1997) *Women and Bullfighting*. Oxford: Berg.

Pink, S. (2004) *Home Truths*. Oxford: Berg.

Pink, S. (2007) Walking with Video. *Visual Studies*, 22 (3): 240–252. https://doi.org/10. 1080/14725860701657142.

Pink, S. (2008a) Re-thinking Contemporary Activism: from community to emplaced sociality. *Ethnos*, 73 (2): 163–188. https://doi.org/10.1080/00141840802180355.

Pink, S. (2008b) An urban tour: The sensory sociality of ethnographic place-making. *Ethnography*, 9 (2): 175–196. https://doi.org/10.1177/1466138108089467.

Pink, S. (2012) *Situating Everyday Life*. London: Sage.

Pink, S. (2017) Ethics in a changing world: between theory and practice. In S. Pink, V. Fors & T. O'Dell (Eds) *Theoretical Scholarship and Applied Practice*. Oxford: Berghahn.

Pink, S. (2019) Afterword. Electricity as Inspiration: towards indeterminate interventions. In S. Abram, B. R. Winthereik, T. Yarrow & A. Sarkar (Eds) *Electrifying Anthropology: Exploring Electrical Practices and Infrastructures*. London: Bloomsbury.

Pink, S. (2021a) *Doing Visual Ethnography*. 4th ed. London: Sage.

Pink, S. (2021b) Digital Futures Anthropology. In H. Geismer & H. Knox (Eds). *Digital Anthropology*. London: Bloomsbury.

Pink, S. (2021c) Sensuous Futures: re-thinking the concept of trust in design anthropology. *Senses & Society*, 6 (2): 193–202. https://doi.org/10.1080/17458927.2020.1858655.

Pink, S. (2022a) Trust in Automation. In S. Pink, D. Lupton, M. Berg & M. Ruckenstein (Eds) *Everyday Automation*. London: Routledge.

Pink, S. (2022b) Design Anthropological Filmmaking for Automated Futures. *Qualitative Inquiry*.

Pink, S., Akama, Y. & Fergusson, A. (2017) Researching Future as an Alterity of the Present. In J. Salazar, S. Pink, A. Irving & J. Sjoberg (Eds) *Anthropologies and Futures*. Oxford: Bloomsbury.

Pink, S., Berg, M., Lupton, D. & Ruckenstein, M. (Eds) (2022) *Everyday Automation*. Oxford: Routledge.

Pink, S., Dahlgren, K., Strengers, Y. & Nicholls, L. (2022) Anticipatory Infrastructures, Emerging Technologies and Visions of Energy Futures. In J. ValkonenV. Kinnunen, H. Huilaja & T. Loikkanen (Eds) *Infrastructural Being: A Naturecultural Approach*. Basingstoke, UK: Palgrave Macmillan.

Pink, S., Ferguson, H. & Kelly, L. (2021) Digital social work: Conceptualising a hybrid anticipatory practice. *Qualitative Social Work*. doi:10.1177/14733250211003647.

Pink, S., Fors, V. & Glöss, M. (2018) The contingent futures of the mobile present: beyond automation as innovation. *Mobilities*. 13 (5): 615–631. https://doi.org/10.1080/17450101. 2018.1436672.

Pink, S., Fors, V., Lanzeni, D., Duque, M., Sumartojo, S. & Strengers, Y. (2022) *Design Ethnography*. Oxford: Routledge.

Pink, S., Gomes, A., Zilse, R., Lucena, R., Pinto, J., Porto, A., Caminha, C., de Siqueira, G. M. & Duarte de Oliveira, M. (2018) Automated and Connected?: Smartphones and Automobility through the Global South. *Applied Mobilities* 6 (1): 54–70, https://doi.org/ 10.1080/23800127.2018.1505263.

Pink, S., Lacey, J., Harvey, L., Sumartojo, S., Duque, M. & Moore, S. (2019) Recycling traffic noise: transforming sonic automobilities for revalue and well being. *Mobilities*, 14 (2): 233–249, doi:10.1080/17450101.2018.1548882.

Pink, S. & Lanzeni, D. (2018) Future Anthropology Ethics and Datafication: Temporality and Responsibility in Research. *Social Media + Society*. https://doi.org/10.1177/2056305118768298.

Pink, S., Lanzeni, D. & Horst, H. (2018) Data anxieties: Finding trust in everyday digital mess. *Big Data & Society*. https://doi.org/10.1177/2053951718756685.

Pink, S. & Leder Mackley, K. (2016) Moving, Making and Atmosphere: routines of home as sites for mundane improvisation. *Mobilities* 11 (2): 171–187. https://doi.org/10.1080/17450101.2014.957066.

Pink, S., Leder Mackley, K., Moroşanu, R., Mitchell, V. & Bhamra, T. (2017) *Making Homes: Ethnographies and Designs*. Oxford: Bloomsbury.

Pink, S. & Lewis, T. (2014) Making Resilience: Everyday Affect and Global Affiliation in Australian Slow Cities. *Cultural Geographies*, 21 (4): 695–710. https://doi.org/10.1177/1474474014520761.

Pink, S., Lingard, H. & Harley, J. (2016) Digital Pedagogy for Safety: the construction site as a collaborative learning environment. *Video Journal of Education and Pedagogy*, 1 (1): 1–15. https://doi.org/10.1186/s40990-016-0007-y.

Pink, S., Lingard, H. & Harley, J. (2017) Refiguring Creativity in Virtual Work: The Digital-Material Construction Site New Technology. *Work and Employment*, 32 (1): 12–27. https://doi.org/10.1111/ntwe.12075.

Pink, S., Lucena, R. Pinto, J., Porto, A., Caminha, C., de Siqueira, G. M., Duarte de Oliveira, M., Gomes, A. & Zilse, R. (2019) Location and Awareness: emerging technologies, knowing and mobility in the Global South. In R. Wilken, G. Goggin & H. Horst (Eds) *Location Technologies in International Context*. London: Routledge.

Pink, S., Morgan, J. & Dainty, A. (2014) Safety in movement: Mobile workers, mobile media. *Mobile Media & Communication*, 2 (3): 335–351. https://doi.org/10.1177/2050157914537486.

Pink, S., Ortar, N., Waltorp, K. & Abram, S. (2022) *Energy Futures*. Berlin: De Gruyter.

Pink, S., Osz, K., Fors, V. & Lanzeni, D. (2021) Simulating and Trusting in Automated Futures: Anthropology and the Wizard of Oz. In M. Kazubowski-Houston & M. Auslander (Eds) *In Search of Lost Futures: Pushing the Boundaries of Ethnography into the Imagined and the Unimaginable*. Basingstoke, UK: Palgrave Macmillan.

Pink, S., Osz, K., Raats, K., Lindgren, T. & Fors, V. (2020) Design Anthropology for Emerging Technologies: trust and sharing in Autonomous Driving futures. *Design Studies*, 69. https://doi.org/10.1016/j.destud.2020.04.002.

Pink, S. & Postill, J. (2019) Imagining Mundane Futures. *Anthropology in Action*, 26 (2): 31–41. doi:10.3167/aia.2019.260204.

Pink, S., Raats, K., Lindgren T., Osz, K. & Fors, V. (2022) An Interventional Design Anthropology of Emerging Technologies. In M. Hojer Bruun, A. Wahlberg, D.B. Kristensen, R. Douglas-Jones, C. Hasse, K. Høyer, and B. R. Winthereik (Eds). *The Handbook for the Anthropology of Technology*. Basingstoke, UK: Palgrave Macmillan.

Pink, S., Ruckenstein, M., Berg, M. & Lupton, D. (2022) Introduction: Everyday Automation: setting a research agenda. In S. Pink, M. Berg, D. Lupton & M. Ruckenstein (Eds) *Everyday Automation*. London: Routledge.

Pink S., Ruckenstein, M., Willim, R. & Duque, M. (2018) Broken data: Conceptualising data in an emerging world. *Big Data & Society*. doi:10.1177/2053951717753228.

Pink, S. & Salazar, J. F. (2017) Anthropologies and Futures: setting the agenda. In J. Salazar, S. Pink, A. Irving & J. Sjoberg (eds) *Anthropologies and Futures*. Oxford: Bloomsbury.

Pink, S., Salazar, J. F. & Duque Hurtado, M. (2019) Everyday Mundane Repair: the material entanglements of improvisation and innovation. *Tapuya: Latin American Science, Technology and Society*, 2 (1): 458–477. doi:10.1080/25729861.2019.1636619124.

Pink, S. & Seale, K. (2017) Imagining and Making Alternative Futures: Slow Cities as sites for anticipation and trust. In M. Castells et al., *Alternative Economies*. Cambridge: Polity Press.

Pink, S., Tutt, D., Dainty, A. & Gibb, A. (2010) Ethnographic methodologies for construction research: Knowing, practice and interventions. *Building Research and Information*, 38 (6): 647–659. doi:10.1080/09613218.2010.512193.

Pink, S., Vallentine, B., Duque, M., Fridman, I., Lanzeni, D., Lundberg, R. & Sumartojo, S. (2022) *City Sensing Data Futures*. Prepared by the Emerging Technologies Lab, Monash University, for the City of Melbourne. Melbourne, Australia.

Power Compare (n.d.) Search results for Bitcoin. Power Compare website. https://power compare.co.uk/?s=bitcoin.

Premier of Victoria (2021, September 22) *Following the Three Vs for a Safe Return to School.* Premier of Victoria, The Hon. Daniel Andrews. www.premier.vic.gov.au/following-three-vs-safe-return-school.

Purtil, J. (2021, January 24) Heatwaves may mean Sydney is too hot for people to live in 'within decades'. *ABC Science News*. www.abc.net.au/news/science/2021-01-24/heatwaves-syd ney-uninhabitable-climate-change-urban-planning/12993580?utm_campaign=abc_news_ web&utm_content=link&utm_medium=content_shared&utm_source=abc_news_web.

PwC (2021) PwC's Responsible AI. AI you can trust. www.pwc.com/gx/en/issues/data-and-analytics/artificial-intelligence/what-is-responsible-ai.html.

PwC (n.d. a) PwC website. www.pwc.com/.

PwC (n.d. b) The New Equation. Our strategy. Helping clients build trust with their stakeholders and deliver sustained outcomes. PwC website. www.pwc.com/gx/en/the-ne w-equation/the-new-equation-strategy.html.

PwC (n.d. c) Connected Home 2.0. PwC website. www.pwc.co.uk/industries/power-utilities/insights/connected-home.html.

Raats, K., Fors, V. & Pink, S. (2020) Trusting Autonomous Vehicles: an interdisciplinary approach. *Transportation Research Interdisciplinary Perspectives*. 7 (100201). https://doi.org/ 10.1016/j.trip.2020.100201.

Reichman, K. (2021, July 6) Volocopter Receives Prerequisite Approval from EASA to Begin eVTOL Aircraft Production. *Aviation Today*. www.aviationtoday.com/2021/07/ 06/volocopter-receives-prerequisite-from-easa-to-begin-producing-it-evtol-aircraft/.

Richardson, R. (2021) Defining and Demystifying Automated Decision Systems (March 24). *Maryland Law Review*. https://ssrn.com/abstract=3811708.

Riedel, R. (2021, November 19 a) Rideshares in the sky by 2024: Joby Aviation bets big on air taxis. Bonny Simi interviewed by Robin Riedel. McKinsey & Co. www.mckinsey. com/industries/aerospace-and-defense/our-insights/rideshares-in-the-sky-by-2024-joby-a viation-bets-big-on-air-taxis.

Riedel, R. (2021, November 19 b) Speeding up everyday travel: Lilium prepares for takeoff. Daniel Wiegand interviewed by Robin Riedel. McKinsey & Co. www.mckinsey.com/ industries/aerospace-and-defense/our-insights/speeding-up-everyday-travel-lilium-prepares-for-takeoff?

Roitman, J. (2013) *Anti-crisis*. Durham & London: Duke University Press.

Rottinghaus, A. R. (2021) Smart Homes and the New White Futurism. *Journal of Futures Studies*, 25 (4): 45–56. https://jfsdigital.org/articles-and-essays/vol-25-no-4-june-2021/ smart-homes-and-the-new-white-futurism/.

Row, Y-K., Kim, C. M. & Nam, T-J. (2016) DooBoo: Pet-Like Interactive Dashboard towards Emotional Electric Vehicle. In *Proceedings of the 2016 CHI Conference Extended Abstracts on Human Factors in Computing Systems (CHI EA '16)*. New York, NY: Association for Computing Machinery: 2673–2680. doi:10.1145/2851581.2892460.

Russouw, N. (Host) (n.d.) Let's talk robotics with Mark Pivac. [Audio podcast episode]. Exaptec. www.exaptec.com.au/podcast/2021/6/1/lets-talk-robotics-with-mark-pivac.

Ryghaug, M. & Toftaker, M. (2016) Creating transitions to electric road transport in Norway: The role of user imaginaries. *Energy Research & Social Science*, 17: 119–126. https://doi.org/10.1016/j.erss.2016.04.017.

Sainato, M. (2020, February 5) I'm not a robot': Amazon workers condemn unsafe, grueling conditions at warehouse. *The Guardian.* www.theguardian.com/technology/2020/feb/05/amazon-workers-protest-unsafe-grueling-conditions-warehouse.

Sadowski, J. (2020) *Too Smart: How Digital Capitalism is Extracting Data, Controlling Our Lives, and Taking Over the World.* Cambridge, MA: The MIT Press.

SAE (2021, May 3) SAE Levels of Driving Automation™ Refined for Clarity and International Audience. SAE blog. www.sae.org/blog/sae-j3016-update.

Saif, I. & Ammanath, B. (2020, March 25) 'Trustworthy AI' is a framework to help manage unique risk. *MIT Technology Review.* www.technologyreview.com/2020/03/25/950291/trustworthy-ai-is-a-framework-to-help-manage-unique-risk/.

Salazar, J. F. (2017) Speculative Fabulation: Researching worlds to come in Antarctica. In J. Salazar, S. Pink, A. Irving & J. Sjoberg (Eds) *Future Anthropologies.* Oxford: Bloomsbury.

Salazar, J. F., Pink, S., Irving, A. & Sjoberg, J. (Eds) (2017) *Anthropologies and Futures: Techniques for researching an uncertain world.* Oxford: Bloomsbury.

Samimian-Darash, L. & Rabinow, P. (Eds.) (2015) *Modes of Uncertainty: Anthropological Cases.* Chicago: University of Chicago Press.

Scharff, V. (1991) *Taking the Wheel: Women and the Coming of the Motor Age.* Albuquerque: University of New Mexico Press.

Schatzki, T. R. (2010) *The Timespace of Human Activity: On Performance, Society, and History as Indeterminate Teleological Events.* Plymouth: Lexington Books.

Seaver, N. (2021) Everything lies in a space: cultural data and spatial reality. *J R Anthropol Inst*, 27: 43–61. https://doi.org/10.1111/1467-9655.13479.

Sheller, M. (2021) *Advanced Introduction to Mobilities.* Cheltenham, UK: Edward Elgar Publishing.

Shin, D. (2021) The effects of explainability and causability on perception, trust, and acceptance: Implications for explainable AI. *International Journal of Human-Computer Studies*, 146 (102551). https://doi.org/10.1016/j.ijhcs.2020.102551.

Shone, G. & Humairah, L. (2021, December 9) Will we be hailing taxis from the sky by 2025? www.euronews.com/next/2021/11/10/will-we-be-hailing-taxis-from-the-sky-by-2025.

Shore, C. & Wright, S. (2015) Audit Culture Revisited: Rankings, Ratings, and the Reassembling of Society. *Current Anthropology* 56 (3): 421–444. https://doi.org/10.1086/681534.

Shore, C. & Wright, S. (2018) How the Big 4 Got Big: Audit Culture and the Metamorphosis of International Accountancy Firms. *Critique of Anthropology* 38 (3): 303–324. https://doi.org/10.1177/0308275X18775815.

Shove, E. (2010) Beyond the ABC: Climate Change Policy and Theories of Social Change. *Environment and Planning A: Economy and Space*, 42 (6): 1273–1285. https://doi.org/10.1068/a42282.

Sinanan, J. & Hjorth, L. (2018) Careful families and care as 'kinwork': An intergenerational study of families and digital media use in Melbourne. In B. Neves & C. Casimiro (Eds) *Connecting Families? Information & Communication Technologies in a Life Course Perspective.* Bristol: Policy Press.

Sjoberg, J. (2017) Ethno science fiction: Projective improvisations of future scenarios and environmental threat in the everyday life of British youth. In J. Salazar, S. Pink, A. Irving & J. Sjoberg (Eds) *Future Anthropologies.* Oxford: Bloomsbury.

Sliwinski, A. (2016) The Value of Promising Spaces: Hope and Everyday Utopia in a Salvadoran Town. *History and Anthropology*, 27 (4): 430–446, https://doi.org/10.1080/02757206.2016.1207638.

Smart Citizen (n.d.) Smart Citizen website. https://smartcitizen.me/.

Smith, A., Fressoli, M., Galdos Frisancho, M. & Moreira, A. (2020) *Post-automation: Report from an International Workshop*. University of Sussex Business School, UK. https://sro.sussex.ac.uk/id/eprint/90735/.

Smith, C. (2021, December 13) 8 Venture Capital and Technology Trends to Watch in 2022. *Forbes*. www.forbes.com/sites/chrissmith1/2021/12/13/8-venture-capital-and-technology-trends-to-watch-in-2022/?sh=58afcc6c7c38.

Smith, J. W. (2021, November 9) The imperative of imagination is the future of Insights. *Kantar*. www.kantar.com/inspiration/org/the-imperative-of-imagination-is-the-future-of-insights?

Smith, R. C. & Otto, T. (2016) Cultures of the Future: Emergence and Intervention in Design Anthropology. In R.C. Smith, K.T. Vangkilde, M. G. Kjærsgaard, T. Otto, J. Halse & T. Binder (Eds) *Design Anthropological Futures*. London: Bloomsbury Academic. 19–36.

Sneath, D., Holbraad M. & Pedersen, M. A. (2009) Technologies of the Imagination: An Introduction. *Ethnos: Journal of Anthropology*, 74 (1): 5–30.

Sousa Santos, A. M, (2021) Violence, Rumor, and Elusive Trust in Mocímboa da Praia, Mozambique. *Social Analysis: The International Journal of Anthropology*, 65 (3): 1–23. https://doi.org/10.3167/sa.2021.6503OF3.

Sparkes, M. (2021, December 15) AI writes better stories when it works backwards from an ending. *New Scientist*. www.newscientist.com/article/2301120-ai-writes-better-stories-when-it-works-backwards-from-an-ending/.

Spencer, S. W. (2021, September) Humanitarian AI. The hype, the hope and the future. *Humanitarian Practice Network*. Network Paper 85. https://odihpn.org/wp-content/uploads/2021/11/HPN-Network-Paper_AI_web_181121.pdf.

Spiegelhalter, D. (2020) Should We Trust Algorithms? *Harvard Data Science Review*, 2 (1). https://doi.org/10.1162/99608f92.cb91a35a.

Stenquist, P. (2020, November 19) An Angel on the Shoulder of Your Teenage Driver (or at Least a Snitch). *New York Times*. www.nytimes.com/2020/11/19/business/teen-driver-monitoring-systems.html.

Stilgoe, J. (2019) Self-driving cars will take a while to get right. *Nat Mach Intell* 1, 202–203. https://doi.org/10.1038/s42256-019-0046-z.

Stilgoe, J. (2020) *Who's Driving Innovation? New Technologies and the Collaborative State*. Basingstoke, UK: Palgrave Macmillan.

Stilgoe, J. (2021) How can we know a self-driving car is safe? *Ethics Inf Technol.*, 23: 635–647. https://doi.org/10.1007/s10676-021-09602-1.

Stilgoe, J. & Cohen T. (2021) Rejecting acceptance: learning from public dialogue on self-driving vehicles. *Science and Public Policy*, 48 (6): 849–859. https://doi.org/10.1093/scipol/scab060.

Strathern, M. (Ed.) (2000) *Audit Cultures: Anthropological Studies in Accountability, Ethics and the Academy*. London: Routledge.

Strengers, Y. (2013) *Smart Energy Technologies in Everyday Life Smart Utopia?* Basingstoke, UK: Palgrave Macmillan.

Strengers, Y., Dahlgren, K., Nicholls, L., Pink, S., Martin, R. (2021) *Digital Energy Futures: Future Home Life*. Melbourne: Emerging Technologies Research Lab (Monash University). www.monash.edu/__data/assets/pdf_file/0011/2617157/DEF-Future-Home-Life-Full-Report.pdf.

Strengers, Y., Dahlgren, K., Pink, S., Sadowski, J. & Nicholls, L. (2022) Digital Technology and Energy Imaginaries of Future Home Life: Comic-strip Scenarios as a Method to Disrupt Energy Industry Futures. *Energy Research and Social Science*, 84 (102366).

Strengers, Y., Duque, M., Mortimer, M., Pink, S., Eugene, A., Martin, R., Nicholls, L., Horan, B. & Thomson, S. (2021) *Smart Homes for Seniors: Intelligent Home Solutions for Independent Living*, Final research evaluation report, McLean Care, Monash University and Deakin University, Melbourne, Australia. https://intelligenthomesolutions.com.au/wp-content/uploads/2021/02/Final-Report.pdf.

Strengers, Y. & Kennedy, J. (2020) *The Smart Wife: Why Alexa, Google Home and Other Smart Home Devices Need a Feminist Reboot*. 1st ed. Cambridge, MA: The MIT Press.

Strengers, Y., Kennedy, J. Arcari, P. Nicholls, L. & Gregg, M. (2019) Protection, Productivity and Pleasure in the Smart Home: Emerging Expectations and Gendered Insights from Australian Early Adopters. In *2019 CHI Conference on Human Factors in Computing Systems Proceedings* (CHI 2019), Glasgow, Scotland, UK. ACM, New York, NY, USA. Paper 645, 13 pages. https://doi.org/10.1145/3290605.3300875.

Strengers, Y., Pink, S. & Nicholls, L. (2019) Smart energy futures and social practice imaginaries: forecasting scenarios for pet care in Australian homes. *Energy Research and Social Science*, 48: 108–115.

Svensson, J. (2022) Coffee with the Algorithm: Imaginaries, Maintenance and Care in the Everyday Life of a News-ranking Algorithm. In S. Pink, M. Berg, D. Lupton & M. Ruckenstein (Eds) *Everyday Automation*. London: Routledge.

Taylor, A. (2021) Future-proof: bunkered data centres and the selling of ultra-secure cloud storage. *J R Anthropol Inst*, 27: 76–94. https://doi.org/10.1111/1467-9655.13481.

Technical University of Munich (2021, December 10) *European Forest Condition Monitor. Real-time, Interactive Monitoring of Forest Health*. Technical University of Munich, Sustainability Research News. www.tum.de/en/about-tum/news/press-releases/details/37071.

Tesla (n.d.) Results for HEPA. https://shop.tesla.com/search?searchTerm=HEPA.

The Tesla Team (2016, May 2) *Putting the Tesla HEPA Filter and Bioweapon Defense Mode to the Test*. Tesla blog. www.tesla.com/blog/putting-tesla-hepa-filter-and-bioweapon-defense-mode-to-the-test.

Thames TV (2018, September 13) *Retro Electric Car | Enfield E8000 | The Future of the Electric Cars | Drive in | 1977*. [Video]. YouTube. www.youtube.com/watch?v=qfHx0FsZXKQ.

Tolmie, P., Crabtree, A. & Rodden, T. (2007) Making the home network at home: digital housekeeping. In L. Bannon, I. Wagner, C. Gutwin, R. Harper & K. Schmidt (Eds) *ECSCW 2007: Proceedings of the 10th European Conference on Computer-Supported Cooperative Work*. Limerick, Ireland, 24–28 September. Paris: Springer.

Trafton, A. (2020, August 31) Robot takes contact-free measurements of patients' vital signs. *MIT News*. https://news.mit.edu/2020/spot-robot-vital-signs-0831.

UK Government (2021, September 22) National AI Strategy. www.gov.uk/government/publications/national-ai-strategy.

UKRI (2020, November 4) New Trustworthy Autonomous Systems projects launched. *UK Research and Innovation*. www.ukri.org/news/new-trustworthy-autonomous-systems-projects-launched/.

United States Government (n.d.) Advancing Trustworthy AI. www.ai.gov/strategic-pillars/advancing-trustworthy-ai/.

University of Glasgow (2021, September 6) Stretchy robot worms could inch their way into new tech applications. *University of Glasgow, University News*. www.gla.ac.uk/news/headline_809459_en.html.

Van, T. (n.d.) Panasonic cooperates with grab to apply its Nanoe X technology in 2,000 Grabcar vehicles in Vietnam. *ESSI.* https://ess.com.vn/2000-grabcar-vehicles-to-be-e quipped-with-panasonic-nanoe-x-air-quality-solutions/.

Wainwright, M. (2017) Sensing the Airs: The Cultural Context for Breathing and Breath-lessness in Uruguay. *Medical Anthropology*, 36 (4): 332–347. https://doi.org/10.1080/01459740.2017.1287180.

Wakefield, J. (2021, October 14) Neighbour wins privacy row over smart doorbell and cameras. *BBC News.* www.bbc.com/news/technology-58911296.

Waltz, E. (2021, February 2) AI Predicts Asymptomatic Carriers of COVID-19. *IEEE Spectrum.* https://spectrum.ieee.org/ai-predicts-asymptomatic-carriers-of-covid19.

White, A. & Bloomberg (2020, July 17) Siri and Alexa are at the center of the European Union's probe into the 'Internet of things'. *Fortune.* https://fortune.com/2020/07/16/siri-alexa-voice-assistants-european-union-antitrust-inquiry/.

WHO (2021, March 1) *Roadmap to Improve and Ensure Good Indoor Ventilation in the Context of COVID-19.* Geneva: World Health Organization. Licence: CC BY-NC-SA 3.0 IGO. www.who.int/publications/i/item/9789240021280.

Williams, S. (2021, September 9) How our energy efficient homes are a breeding ground for COVID-19. *Domain.* www.domain.com.au/news/how-our-energy-efficient-homes-are-a-breeding-ground-for-covid-19-1086246/.

Willim, R. (2016) *Broken Data: Broken World.* Video. https://vimeo.com/robertwillim.

Wooton, H. (2021, November 16) McKinsey advising on net zero modelling limits trans-parency: Labor. *Financial Review.* www.afr.com/companies/professional-services/mckinsey-advising-on-net-zero-modelling-to-limits-transparency-labor-20211115-p5994b.

Wyatt, S. (2021) Metaphors in critical Internet and digital media studies. *New Media & Society*, 23 (2): 406–416. https://doi.org/10.1177/1461444820929324.

Yen, H. & Krisher, T. (2021, November 10) Congress mandates new car technology to stop drunken driving. *AP News.* https://apnews.com/article/coronavirus-pandemic-joe-biden-technology-business-health-068ee87392b0cca1444053b854a514dd.

Young, C. (2021, May 3) 3D Printed 'Artificial Leaves' Could Provide Sustainable Energy on Mars. *Interesting Engineering.* https://interestingengineering.com/3d-printing-microalgae-for-sustainable-energy-on-mars.

Zewe, A. (2021, December 9) Machine-learning system flags remedies that might do more harm than good. *MIT News Office.* https://news.mit.edu/2021/machine-learning-treatments-1209.

Zhang, P. (2020, March 13) Geely announces 'Healthy Car' project plan. *CnTechPost.* https://cntechpost.com/2020/03/13/geely-announces-healthy-car-project-plan/.

Films

Morgans, P. (Director) (2022) *Social Work and Child Protection in the COVID-19 Pandemic.* www.youtube.com/watch?v=hl8z1nZq95s&t=2s.

Pink, S. (Director) (2021) *Smart Homes for Seniors.* Documentary film. 33mins. Emerging Technologies Research Lab, Monash University, Australia.

Pink, S. (Director) (2022) *Digital Energy Futures.* Documentary film. Emerging Technologies Research Lab, Monash University, Australia.

Pink, S. & Astari, N. (Directors) (2015) *Laundry Lives.* Documentary Film. 40 mins. www.la udnrylives.com.

INDEX

Printed in the United States
by Baker & Taylor Publisher Services